The Many Faces of Jesus Christ

About the Author

Volker Küster, born in 1962, is a lecturer in Comparative Religion, Missiology and Ecumenics at the University of Heidelberg. He is presently a visiting scholar at the Theological University in Kampen, the Netherlands. His fields of study include intercultural theology and hermeneutics, the theology of religions, inter-religious dialogue and comparative religion. He is the author of *Theologie im Kontext. Zugleich ein Versuch über die Minjung-Theologie* (1995); *Jesus und das Volk im Markusevangelium. Ein Beitrag zum interkulturellen Gespräch in der Exegese* (1996), and of numerous articles in theological journals and lexicons.

The 'Academy for Intercultural Studies', founded in 1996 by DaimlerChrysler AG, is a network of German universities that was founded to develop models for continuing education. The Academy fosters intercultural dialogue and tries to increase the intercultural competence of German and foreign scientists and leading figures in economy, administration, media, education and politics. Volker Küster was awarded the Academy's 1999–2001 prize for his 'outstanding contributions to the theory and praxis of intercultural dialogue'.

The Many Faces of Jesus Christ

Intercultural Christology

Volker Küster

ORBIS BOOKS

Maryknoll, New York 10545

The Catholic Foreign Mission Society of America (Maryknoll) recruits and
trains people for overseas missionary service. Through Orbis Books, Maryknoll
aims to foster the international dialogue that is essential to mission. The books
published, however, reflect the opinions of their authors and are not meant to
represent the official position of the Society.

To obtain more information about Maryknoll and Orbis Books, please visit our
website at www.maryknoll.org.

Originally published as *Die vielen Gesichter Jesu Christi: Christologie
interkulturell* by Volker Küster, in 1999 by Neukirchener Verlag, Neukirchen-
Vlyun.

Copyright © Neukirchener Verlag 1999

English translation copyright © John Bowden 2001

First published in 2001 in Great Britain by
SCM Press
9–17 St Albans Place
London NI ONX

First published in 2001 in the United States by
Orbis Books
PO Box 308
Maryknoll, NY 10545–0308

Manufactured in Great Britain.

Library of Congress Cataloging-in-Publication Data

Küster, Volker, 1962–
    [Vielen Gesichter Jesu Christi. English]
    The many faces of Jesus Christ : intercultural Christology / Volker Küster.
    p.cm.
    Includes bibliographical references and index.
    ISBN 1–57075–354–7 (pbk.)
        1. Jesus Christ—Person and offices. 2. Christianity and culture—
    Developing countries.
    I. Title.

BT205.K8413 2001
232'.09—dc21   01–046498

Second printing June 2004

Contents

List of Illustrations and Charts

Illustrations

Tables

Acknowledgments of Illustrations

Edilberto Merida, Crucifixion: sculpture of clay and wood
with the kind permission of the Maryknoll Fathers and
Brothers, Maryknoll, New York.

Francois Goddart, African crucifix: cement sculpture
with the kind permission of Vivant Univers, Photos-Service,
Namur, Belgium.

Nyoman Darsane, Creation of sun and moon: batik
with the kind permission of the artist.

Soloman Raj, Refugees from East Pakistan: woodcut
with the kind permission of the artist.

Foreword

Robert J. Schreiter

If any single area of theology is especially poised to raise questions about the nature and practice of inculturation, it is surely christology. The fact of the Incarnation itself places us already on a series of boundaries: between the divine and the human, between the particular and the universal, between eternity and time. The questions raised for culture span the entire range of christological discourse, from what significance Jesus' having been born in a specific time and place might have, to the cultural and linguistic differences that plagued the christological controversies of the fourth and fifth centuries.

Thus, christology is an excellent place to begin to see what the attempts at theology in different cultures might mean for the general practice of theology, and especially for traditional themes in theology, such as christology, grace or eschatology. One need not necessarily embrace the position that all theology begins in christology; it is sufficient to see it as a privileged point of entry into the larger enterprise.

Heretofore, work on christology from an intercultural perspective has largely centred on phenomenologies of the current contributions to christology from throughout the world church. These books have been helpful in bringing to awareness how Jesus Christ is being presented and being confessed among Christians in very different circumstances. Most of them stop short of any cross-cultural analysis of what these many faces of Christ so presented might mean for how christology has been understood heretofore, or for facing the challenges to traditional formulations of christology with which the churches are now confronted. For example, one thinks of the need to reassess the criteria by which a confession of Christ in context is made: what are the boundaries of legitimacy as to how Christ is presented? Or what is perhaps the most burning question in christology today: how are Christian claims about the significance of the Christ event to be situated among the other religions of the world? The answers to these questions cannot be arrived at solely by pondering the history of christology (although such historical reflection remains necessary). One must try to grasp what is being said about Christ by Christians today.

The great merit of Volker Küster's book is that, while he does take us through the phenomenological review of representative christologies from around the world, he also engages them critically. He does this both through a framework for understanding Christ and culture, but also in terms of ongoing questions which have to be asked once again, such as where the starting point of christology should be situated, the relationship of christology to soteriology, and how one articulates christology in light of trinitarian belief. In so doing, he opens the way for what might be termed a cross-cultural systematic theology, wherein the full range of Christian belief in all its interconnections might be viewed from the horizon of the many cultures of the world church. To be sure, such a proposal so to view the whole of theology is a project which still lies in the future. There is still much to be done in laying the groundwork for this. Even an exhaustive review of current christologies in the world church is not yet possible. But what Küster does here is to open an important path into contemporary christology which takes us beyond a kind of theological tourism, marvelling at all the exotic understandings of Jesus today, into engagement with basic christological issues. By his critical assessment of these authors, and situating their contributions within larger discussions, he shows that they are being taken seriously as equal players on the theological field. And by bringing us back time and again to the perennial issues, he offers signposts into the larger, more complex future.

Along with these important contributions, Küster provides yet another in his epilogue. He rightly notes that many of the christological studies he has examined in the book draw their biblical base largely from the Synoptic Gospels. This is true, and the

reasons for this are several. One certainly has been the importance of narrative in many of these theologies, and the power of
the Gospel narratives addressing contexts today. Another is the
need to sketch out somewhat different readings of Jesus than
christological traditions have largely supplied. Yet, as Küster
points out, a full christological picture has to take into account
the importance of the figure of Paul as well. He provides the out-
line of a way that these christologies might be able to embark
upon this. This enlarges the scope of the contextual christologies
he examines, and at the same time calls for another look at how
traditional christological discourse in the world church, relying
heavily as it has on the Johannine and Pauline literatures, might
in turn incorporate more fully the synoptic witness.

It will no doubt be some time before a full cross-cultural christology can be worked out. A great deal of work has to be done
on many fronts: both gathering and assessing current reflection
on christology, and rereading the biblical and subsequent theological tradition. Volker Küster has given us an important beginning with this book, and points the way to the tasks still ahead of
us. His book serves as an excellent introduction to important
new developments in christology as it is being reshaped by the
experience of the world church.

Introduction

Relatively unnoticed by the discussion of systematic theology in Germany, since the end of the 1960s and the beginning of the 1970s a large number of christological sketches have been presented in the countries of Africa, Asia and Latin America by individual theologians or theological movements. Only in the rarest instances have there been whole books on christology; usually there are only short articles or individual chapters in larger publications. They belong to a theological genre which, depending on preference, is called *Third World Theology* after its origin, or *contextual theology* after the method on which it is based. The attempt to approach these theologies through the traditional headings in dogma does not do justice to their claim, and generally speaking is not very promising. However, that does not apply to christology. Probably more than any other theme it is suitable both as a hermeneutical key to understanding them and also as a point of comparison between the different sketches. Moreover, at the end of the day it is the christology that decides whether or not for the person concerned, faith in Jesus Christ finds a home in its context or not.[1]

The selection of christologies presented here is meant to be representative, but makes no claim to completeness. I have been concerned not so much to describe the work of particular theologians from the perspective of christology as to enquire about recurring links between themes and the comparability of the sketches investigated. My sources are exclusively male, roughly between sixty and eighty years of age; some of them have already died. They belong to the first generation of contextual theologians. I am aware that there is still a good deal of confusion in this division into generations. My criterion of selection was for those concerned to have been theologically active over a lengthy period and for their works to be available in Western languages, preferably English and German. At the same time that produced a gallery of the grand old men of contextual theologies. Their theological careers began after the end of the Second World War in the wake of secular emancipation movements, in a phase of the decolonialization and reordering of the world. To keep in the discussion during these revolutionary times they had to redefine their standpoint as Christian intellectuals and develop a pluriform, contextual-Christian identity. Here they often moved in the sphere of cultural renaissances and became involved in a dispute with other social elites over the interpretation of their own history. From the Catholic side the Second Vatican Council (Vatican II) was a further stimulus towards new theological developments.

The reason for the not inconsiderable difference in the ages of my protagonists is the epoch-making divide of the Second World War. This meant that some theologians were late in coming on the scene. But some joined the theological revolution only at an advanced age. So there is a shift in generations upon us now, but its consequences cannot yet be foreseen.

Initially Third World theology was purely a matter for men. In this respect it was just the same as the Western theology which in other respects it liked to attack. A turning point is marked here by the Ghanaian theologian Mercy Amba Oduyoye's term 'the irruption within the irruption'[2] proclaimed on the occasion of the First General Assembly of the Ecumenical Association of Third World Theologians (EATWOT)[3] in New Delhi, India, in 1981. The Final Statement of the dialogue meeting between EATWOT and Western theologians in Geneva in 1983 concluded:

> Neither Third World men nor First World women can determine the Third World women's agenda. Third World women maintain that sexism must not be addressed in isolation, but within the context of the total struggle for liberation in their countries.[4]

Today women theologians from the Third World have long been making their own contributions. Even if the age-range here extends from forty to sixty, I generally assign the women to the second generation of contextual theologians. Common to Third World women theologians is their description of the situation of women as 'oppressed of the oppressed'. On the basis of their gender women are oppressed not only in the socio-economic and political structures but also by cultural and religious factors. Therefore the Third World women theologians are often somewhat critical of inculturation.

A separate volume has long been needed to do justice to the broad spectrum of these theologies of women from the Third World, which works out both their relationship to the theologies of their male colleagues of the first generation and also to Western feminist theologies.[5] However, in the light of recent publications, I quickly dropped my original plan to add to this book a chapter about the christology of women from the Third World.

From the perspective of systematic theology the discussion of contextual theologies belongs under the rubric 'gospel and culture'. Here gospel traditionally means both the preaching of Jesus and also the community's preaching about Jesus Christ. The definition of the term culture is far more complicated.[6] I follow closely Clifford Geertz,[7] who understands culture as a complex fabric of meaning and system of symbols created by men and women, which we must interpret like a text:

> The concept of culture I espouse . . . is essentially a semiotic one. Believing, with Max Weber, that man is an animal suspended in webs of significance he himself has spun, I take culture to be those webs, and the analysis of it to be therefore not an experimental science in search of law but an interpretative one in search of meaning.[8]

The definition of the relationship between culture and religion poses a further problem. Geertz interprets religion as a *cultural system*:[9]

> . . . a *religion* is: (1) a system of symbols which acts to (2) establish powerful, pervasive, and long-lasting moods and motivations in men by (3) formulating conceptions of a general order of existence and (4) clothing these conceptions

with such an aura of factuality that (5) the moods and motivations seem uniquely realistic.[10]

Thus according to Geertz the same premises apply to the concept of religion as to the more comprehensive concept of culture. Unlike Geertz, however, I interpret the 'self-spun web of significance' which he claims religion to be as the expression of an *experience of resonance*.[11] Religiosity is a basic human constant. Biography, *the* basic human text, is always already open to transcendence. The same goes for the worlds of meaning of literary texts and whole cultures, which I regard as *con*texts. Religion appears at this interface with the transcendent. It is at the same time a human way of coping with contingency and the resonance of the transcendent. Unlike Geertz, as an academic theologian I deliberately adopt a 'religious perspective'.[12]

When I speak of religion I always mean the empirical religions. There is no such thing as 'religion' in the abstract. Culture and religion are dialectically related and reciprocally interpenetrate each other. Every culture is shaped by the religions which occur in it. Conversely, every religion which enters another culture takes something of its old culture with it, whereas at the same time a reciprocal effect on the new culture develops.

In our case this means for the relationship between gospel and culture that the gospel is accessible only in a culturally mediated form. Mission in the sense of the gospel crossing the boundaries of culture is therefore, always also a cultural contact. In the typology of cultural contact proposed by Urs Bitterli[13] – *first contact, collision, relationship* – the christological attempts which are presented in what follows would be classed as cultural relationship. Western theological tradition and African, Asian and Latin American cultures and religions enter into a deep reciprocal relationship. The theological processes which take place here are still largely open.

Whereas in my study of South Korean Minjung theology I worked with empirical field research and interviews,[14] this time I have taken the classical approach and worked purely through texts. Each context is introduced only in so far as it depicts itself in texts. The contexts discussed must be seen as constructions of reality.

The present volume is divided into three parts, the longest of which, the middle one, is further subdivided into four chapters. The sections, which are numbered sequentially, all form closed units in themselves. In the first part I mark out my field in terms of method and systematic theology. My initial hypothesis is that in the contextual theologies the biblical stories and the Christian traditions (text) on the one hand and the local human experiences (context) on the other are related dialectically in a hermeneutical circle and are, as Ernst Lange puts it, *pledged* to one another.[15] In this process the biblical stories evoke those *generative* themes of the text (Paulo Freire) which become relevant in the context with the generative themes prevalent in the concrete situation. Thus the generative themes which govern the text and the particular context are interwoven in a way analogous to the stories which are their vehicles.

In the second part I spell this out by means of contextual christologies from Africa, Asia and Latin America. The framework of the external arrangement of this part goes by geographical and typological factors (Chapters A–D). In accordance with the themes which predominantly determine them, in the case of contextual theologies I distinguish between a socio-economic, and political or a cultural-religious type. The liberation theologies which are to be assigned to the first type have more the character of theological movements; it is only subsequently that individual theologians emerge. By contrast, the theologies of inculturation or dialogue with a cultural and religious orientation are more markedly the intellectual constructions of individuals. Whereas under the term inculturation theology I sum up the whole spectrum of the debate about the cultural and religious dimension of the context, I designate as dialogue theologies a special species of this type. Even if dialogue theologians are firmly intent on conversation with another religious tradition, at the same time they also contribute indirectly to an inculturation of the gospel in a particular context.

For my account I have almost always sought an approach through parallel theological biographies in which each time two theologians from the context concerned are put side by side and the commonalities and divergences in their christological positions are brought out. Underlying this is the conviction that alongside the cultural-religious, socio-economic and political, ecological as well as gender factors, the biographies of the theologians concerned also governs the contextuality of their theology. The individual sections can be read separately as self-contained studies. However, brought together they demonstrate an inner framework which is structured by the christological themes evoked each time in the different contexts. Part Three then cross-cuts between the two frameworks in a systematics of contextual christologies.

Something of a framework to my investigation is given in the prologue and the epilogue by two biblical-theological narrations, which reconstruct the life and work of Jesus and Paul against the background of their cultural environment. Whereas the liberation theologians have made the life of Jesus the constitutive element of christology, so far the theology of Paul has been almost completely left out. Wrongly, to my mind, the relevance of his doctrine of justification – where, in Paul, it already stands against the background of the cultural conflicts in his context – has not yet been sounded out for discussion of Christian identity in the pluralism of cultures and religions.

I. CONTEXTUAL CHRISTOLOGY IN INTERCULTURAL PERSPECTIVE

Prologue: Jesus and Culture

The person of Jesus stands at the beginning of any christology – that is the creed of the liberation theologians. In what follows I shall attempt a narrative reconstruction of the life of Jesus, adopting the insights of socio-historical exegesis. This trend in research particularly takes into account the context of the biblical texts and thus in the sphere of Western academic theology stands closest to the contextual theologies.

As the son of a Jewish mother Jesus[1] was a Jew by birth. We know little about his childhood and youth apart from legendary material. However, his later public teaching shows that he was brought up in the Jewish faith. The Gospels focus on the time of his public activity: one or two, at most three years[2] at the end of a short life. There has been much dispute over their value as sources. They are testimonies of faith, not eye-witness reports; nevertheless something of the man Jesus can still be recognized behind them.

There is a dispute as to whether Jesus was born in Bethlehem (Matt. 2.1–8; Luke 2.1–21; cf. John 7.40–43), but his name is closely associated with Nazareth in Galilee (Mark 1.9; Luke 1.26; Matt. 2.23; Mark 6.1–6 par.; John 1.45f.). Here he grew up in a large family (Mark 3.31–35 par.; 6.3 par.) as the son of a craftsman (Matt. 13.55), a carpenter or joiner (*tekton*). As was then the custom, Jesus learned his father's profession (Mark 6.3). Whether and how long he worked at it we do not know, but as a rule from an early stage children had to contribute towards supporting the family. During his public activity, at any rate, he no longer earned his own living, unlike Paul later.

Jesus will have spoken Aramaic; we cannot rule out the possibility that he had some knowledge of Greek.[3] Certainly Palestine was on the periphery of the Roman empire, but the

colonial rulers made their presence felt there, and for oppor-
tunistic reasons the local upper class had already embraced the
culture of Hellenism.[4] Only about four miles from Nazareth lay
Sepphoris, destroyed by the Romans in the course of a punitive
action in connection with the unrest after the death of Herod I
(4 BC).[5] Herod Antipas (king from 4 BC to AD 39), the ruler of
the region in which Jesus was active, pressed on with rebuilding
it to make it the capital of his tetrarchy. Perhaps Joseph and his
son worked for a while at this great building site. Later, while
Jesus was going round the north shore of Lake Gennesaret
preaching, Tiberias, founded by Herod Antipas around AD 18
and elevated to become the new capital of Galilee in AD 26, was
constantly in view. Jesus will also have gone along the Via Maris,
the most important trade route of Palestine, which linked Egypt
with the region of the Euphrates;[6] a connecting link branched off
to Sepphoris. Jesus' wanderings took him near to Hellenistic
cities: Tyre and Sidon (Mark 7.31; Matt. 15.21), Caesarea
Philippi (Mark 8.27; Matt. 16.13) and the Decapolis (Mark
5.20; 7.31) are mentioned. But the difference in wealth and
education between the small Hellenistic upper class and the bulk
of the rural population of Galilee was immense.[7] As the child of
ordinary people, Jesus had only limited opportunities of education. But he has a charismatic gift, knows the scriptures and can
expound them. Moreover he draws on the wisdom of the people.
His parables reflect the world of simple people: farmers, fishermen and craftsman. However, he also knows about large estates,
financial dealings and speculations (Mark 12.1–12 par.; Matt.
18.21–35; 20.1–16; 25.14–30 par.; Luke 12.16–21; Luke
16.1–9).

The beginning of Jesus' public activity is closely bound up with
the person of John the Baptist (Mark 1.1–8; Matt. 3.1–12; Luke
3.1–20; Mark 6.14–29 par.; John 1.19–34, 35f.; 3.22–36).[8]
However, what influence John had on his preaching remains
obscure. The Jesus tradition rates John highly. Time and again it
has been conjectured that Jesus and some of his disciples were
originally followers of John the Baptist. But despite the fragmentary nature of the tradition it is still clear that he had something
to say which went beyond the eschatological penitential preaching of the Baptist.

Jesus proclaimed the kingly rule of God. The poor and the oppressed,[9] the toll collectors, sinners and prostitutes, the sick and weak, women[10] and children[11] get a special place in the kingdom of God. His miracles, the healings of the sick and the feedings, are signs that the kingly rule of God is already anticipated in his presence.[12] This tension between the 'now already' and the 'not yet', as later dogmatic theology is fond of putting it, is indissoluble. Jesus calls on the rich and powerful to repent (Mark 10.17–31 par.; Luke 6.24f.; 12.13–21). Certainly he is not the head of a political resistance movement,[13] but his public appearances must have been felt to be eminently political. He probably had no illusions about the rulers 'who lord it over their people' (Mark 10.42).[14] He called Herod Antipas a fox (Luke 13.32) and a reed shaken by the wind (Matt. 11.7),[15] and explicitly warned his disciples against him. However, unlike the Zealots, the Jesus movement was peaceful in orientation. For example, no one need be opposed to paying taxes to the emperor (Matt. 12.13–17).

Jesus understood the host of his followers as a counter-society in which one was to serve another (Mark 10.42–45). Fishermen (Mark 1.16–20) and a toll collector (Mark 2.13–17 par.) were among his disciples. None of them was rich; they may have had just enough to live on. At any rate, when they followed his call they did not leave much behind. Probably at an early stage women belonged to his fellowship, though the group of twelve comprised only men. Others who joined had been socially uprooted at a previous time. The evangelist Mark speaks of the *ochlos*, the mass of people around Jesus, who came together where he taught, some of whom probably also followed him.[16]

Travelling round in Galilee and the adjacent regions, Jesus healed the sick and taught in the synagogues, in houses or simply in the open air. Even where he left Galilean territory he predominantly moved in a Jewish environment. He avoided going directly into the Hellenistic cities (Mark 1.45). The Torah is the basis of his teaching. Even if he blunted norms where they were too oppressive for ordinary people (*kleine leute*), he never abolished them (Matt. 5.17). No men or women are to be further discriminated against in religion by the laws of cleanness if their wretched social situation compels them, say, to practise a profession thought of as unclean (Mark 7.1–23). To show mercy to the poor, the sick and the hungry does not clash with the sabbath commandment (Mark 2.23–3.6). His disciples do not fast, since for them with his presence a time of joy has dawned (Mark 2.18f.). He tightens up other commandments, like the marriage law (Mark 10.1–12); probably also because of the libertinistic customs of the upper class, which according to the account in the Gospels led to an escalation in the conflict between John the Baptist and Herod (Mark 6.17–19). Jesus can sum up the law and the prophets in the twofold commandment to love (Mark 12.28–34 par.).[17] Anyone who observes this has already done well.

Jesus is the founder of a renewal movement within Judaism.[18] Alongside those prophetic movements which gathered around, say, John the Baptist and Jesus there were the Essenes, the Pharisees, the Sadducees and the Zealots.[19] The New Testament depicts an intrinsically pluralistic Judaism. There was never such a thing as the 'Jews' in opposition to Jesus, as they are stylized over some stretches of the Gospels by the evangelists, because of their experience of the painful process of detachment from their Jewish mother religion.[20] Jesus' sphere of activity was the Jewish people. He did not envisage an organized mission to the Gentiles. The abrupt statement 'Go nowhere among the Gentiles and do not enter any city of the Samaritans' (Matt. 10.5b) is perhaps still a reflection of this. Nevertheless, in frontier territory now and then he will have encountered members of other groups of people. The story of the Syro-Phoenician woman is told as an example (Mark 7.24–30 par.).[21] To begin with, Jesus rejects her request for help with reference to the privilege of Israel, but then he allows himself to be convinced by her faith. With the centurion of Capernaum (Matt. 8.5–13)[22] he is less hesitant, perhaps because they were virtually 'neighbours', or because the elders of the synagogue asked him. But he does not enter the centurion's house. In Luke Jesus shows a certain interest in the Samaritans (Luke 9.51–56; 10.25–37; 17.11–19). That could be something like bringing home the heretics.

Provisionally perhaps we might say that anyone among the Gentiles who showed faith was not rejected in principle. However, according to the Jewish view the Gentiles are added only at the eschaton (Isa. 2.2–5). Jesus will also have seen it like that; at any rate, that was the view of some of his followers who, soon after his death, and still expecting an imminent end, began to persuade Gentiles with this very argument (Mark 13.10).[23]

Jesus knew that he had been sent to the Jews. He did not think of a blanket proclamation, but every man and woman of his people was to have the possibility of hearing about him. That is why he travelled around, healed and taught. Jesus sent out his disciples to do the same thing (Mark 6.7–13 par.). After news of him had resounded throughout the land of Galilee, he went up to Jerusalem, where his reputation had preceded him. He must have been aware that he was going into danger. Already in Galilee there had been repeated conflicts with the local upper class and the religious authorities. Jesus was aware of the violent fate of the prophets.[24] He will have been afraid, and at an early stage this was stylized in the Gethsemane episode (Mark 14.32–42). Now he penetrated the centre of Jewish religion and taught in the temple. His saying about the temple (Mark 14.58; cf. John 23.19–21) is focussed on institutionalized religion and its representatives, but at the same time it puts in question the status of Jerusalem as a holy city. The symbolic cleansing of the temple (Mark 11.15–17 par.; John 2.13–16) must have been felt as a direct blow against the pilgrim tourism from which wide circles in Jerusalem will have profited. This is still reflected in the twofold basis for the charge against Jesus 'both in the hearing before the Sanhedrin (Mark 14.57–64) and also in the crucifixion scene (Mark 15.29–32)'.[25] Whereas the temple aristocracy accuse Jesus because of his claim to be Messiah, some who remain anonymous denounce him because of his polemic against the temple.

The evangelist John certainly hits on part of the truth when he reports that the Jewish authorities wanted to avoid intervention by the Romans (John 11.47–50; 18.14). But they probably first felt that their own positions had been attacked and therefore reflected on how they could do away with Jesus. To accuse him before Pilate as a Jewish rebel who was making claims to rule was a skilful move. The Romans were generally not squeamish in dealing with trouble-makers. The description of Pilate's hesitation may be more a gesture of servility by the evangelists towards the Romans (Matt. 27.11–24; John 18.28–40). Moreover Jesus was not stoned as a religious deviant but died on the cross of the Roman colonial power. The people had turned from him, the disciples had fled, and even Peter had betrayed him. Anyone who showed sympathy had to expect reprisals. In some circumstances such a person could himself be nailed to the cross. Nevertheless the women stood afar off (Mark 15.40f.).

On the morning of the third day, when the women came to anoint him, the tomb was empty. The same day there were appearances of Jesus to the women (Mark 16.9f.; Matt. 28.9f.; John 20.11–18) who had followed him and to the disciples (Mark 16.12–14 par; John 20.19–21.22). Belief in his resurrection is grounded in this.[26] His followers met again and handed on the good news.

The news about him and his message – probably the gospel comprised both at an early stage – demanded to be handed on. At a very early stage the good news extended beyond the Jewish sphere. As it crossed cultural boundaries the question arose how the relationship between the gospel and culture was to be defined, initially focussed on the problem of the relationship between Jews and Gentiles.[27] This can be demonstrated in exemplary form by the life and mission of Paul.[28] However, theoretical reflection on the processes which took place here developed only at a much later stage. Some modern approaches to theory will be presented in the further course of this first part.

§ 1 Christology and Culture

1. Christ and culture

With his book *Christ and Culture*[1] the American theologian and social ethicist H. Richard Niebuhr has presented a typology of the possibilities of defining the relationship between Christianity and culture which has been taken up again only in more recent discussion. The range of types extends from the exclusivism of radical Christians who see *Christ against culture* to the inclusive perspective of cultural Christians, for whom *Christ is the fulfiller of culture* (the Christ of culture). Between these two extreme positions Niebuhr mentions three mediating answers which, starting from the experience that Christ and culture cannot either stand side by side in isolation or go into each other, relate the two entities. These different attempts at mediation are put forward by the church of the centre. Whereas the dualists see *Christ and culture in contradiction with each other* (Christ and culture in paradox), a contradiction which has continually to be balanced in specific situations, the synthesists locate *Christ above culture*, in which he is never wholly taken up. Dualism and synthesis are therefore modifications of the extremes of exclusivism and inclusivism, which are not practicable. Niebuhr himself favours the third type, the conversionists, for whom *Christ is the transformer of culture*. The three mediating types constructed by Niebuhr each emphasize a premise which basically is also shared by the other two.

- Christ and the (particular) culture equally require loyalty from their followers or adherents (dualists).
- Christ is never completely taken up in a culture (synthesists).
- Christ is an authority critical of culture (conversionists).

Table 1: Christ and culture (Niebuhr)

Radical Christians		Church Christians mediating answers		Cultural Christians
Exclusivists	Dualists	Conversionists	Synthesists	Accommodationists
Christ against culture	Christ and culture in paradox	Christ the transformer of culture	Christ above culture	Christ the fulfiller of culture
I John, Tertullian, Tolstoy	Paul, Luther, Kierkegaard	Augustine, Calvin	Justin, Clement, Thomas Aquinas	Christian Gnosticism, Abelard, Culture Protestantism

In his preface Niebuhr pays his respects to Ernst Troeltsch, whose typology of 'the sociological development of Christian thought'[2] he merely claims to modify.[3] Troeltsch characterizes as the two opposing social forms of Christianity the *church*, which on the basis of its self-understanding as a mediator of salvation 'can adjust itself to the world' and thus is accessible to broad levels of the population, and the *sect*, whose adherents are governed by expectations of the end-time and in small groups 'live apart from the world'. Alongside these Troeltsch sets *mysticism*, whose representatives transform the Christian religion 'into a purely personal and inward experience'. Troeltsch's types of the definition of the relationship between religion and the world are in a way related concentrically, with mysticism as a form of internalized religion in the centre and the church as the community turned towards the world in the outermost ring; between them is the sect as a group turned away from the world. By contrast Niebuhr's typology has a polar structure, with a clear emphasis on Christ or the gospel.

When Niebuhr speaks of culture he has Western culture in view. This is evident not least from the way in which he sometimes uses civilization as a synonym. By contrast, in missiological discussion on the theme, the perspective broadens to the pluralism of cultures and religions worldwide. As a result the relationship between the basic co-ordinates of culture becomes more complex in two respects:

(1) Cultural pluralism: Only in contact with alien cultures is an awareness heightened that the gospel is only accessible to us at all in a culturally mediated form. Therefore contact between cultures always contains the opportunity of correcting cultural narrowness in the interpretation of the gospel.

(2) Religious pluralism: At the same time in this cultural contact Christianity also encounters alien religions. Without wanting to get into a discussion of a *theology of religions*, one can maintain that its two antagonistic basic options *exclusivism* and *inclusivism*[4] are quite compatible with Niebuhr's typology. The *extra ecclesiam nulla salus*[5] which for a long time has been advocated towards the other religions associates the exclusivists among the theologians of religion with Niebuhr's radical Christians. Representatives of the inclusivist position who think that they can discover in other religions the saving effectiveness of the *logos spermatikos*[6] or accept their adherents into salvation history as *anonymous Christians*[7] in the end represent a theology which sees the expectations of salvation in the other religions fulfilled in Christianity. They share this thought-pattern with Niebuhr's culture Christians or accommodationists.

I already explained at the beginning how far I understand religion as a cultural system. So if I speak of gospel and culture, I also mean the religious dimension of the particular culture. As distinct from Troeltsch's concentric and Niebuhr's polarizing typology, I myself tend towards a dialectical perspective on the relationship between gospel and culture as this is already indicated in the mediating answers of the latter. I shall go on to spell this out in more detail under the heading of *contextual theology*.

2. Gospel and culture[8]

One of my premises was that mission is always also cultural contact. However, the centuries-old tradition of Christianity in the West has made awareness of the way in which the gospel crossed cultural boundaries on its way from Palestine into present-day Europe fade.[9] Niebuhr's three mediating answers are variants of a basic type, which sees Christ or the gospel and culture in a relationship of tension. Impracticable though a radical exclusivism and the inclusivism of the culture Christians may seem, as tendencies they are also present in the mediating models as the two basic options of Christian soteriology.[10] The universal promise of salvation in Jesus Christ takes all human beings into the history of God with his creation (inclusivism). At the same time other ways of salvation are excluded as a result (exclusivism).

It proves quite possible to transfer Niebuhr's typology to intercultural discourse. A current version of exclusivism is the polemic of the British Lesslie Newbigin, who is pessimistic about culture. Those whom Niebuhr calls accommodationists are akin to the missiological model of accommodation not only in name but also conceptually. We will also encounter inclusivist approaches here and there at a later stage, on our journey through the christological sketches of the Third World theologians.[11] However, depending on their basic structure, the theologies of inculturation or contextual theologies are dialectical differentiations of the notion of mediation.

Exclusivism

Lesslie Newbigin (1909–1998) was himself a missionary in India for more than thirty years (with interruptions).[12] When he came home, at an advanced age he produced a whole series of publications which accuse Western culture of having forgotten the gospel.[13]

Although he never concealed his theological proximity to evangelical positions, Newbigin was always also a committed ecumenist. He is to be put on the traditional church unity wing within the ecumenical movement, which still revolves above all around the Faith and Order Commission. Newbigin played an important part in the church union of South India (1947). Following that, the office of Bishop of Madurai and Ramnad was conferred on him (1947–1959). Released by his church for the office of General Secretary of the International Missionary Council (1959–1961), Newbigin was then the architect of the integration of this body into the WCC. As the first director of the newly-founded Division for World Mission and Evangelism, at the same time he held office as Deputy General Secretary of the WCC (1961–1965). After a further period as bishop of the Church of South India in Madras (1965–1974) he taught missiology at the Selly Oak Colleges in Birmingham (1974–1979). Newbigin also continued to be active in the church. In 1978 he was elected Moderator of the General Assembly of the United Reformed Church (URC). From 1980 to 1988 he then took over a congregation in a key area of Birmingham which without his involvement would have been closed by the local leadership of the URC.[14]

Newbigin diagnoses a 'disappearance of hope' (1)[15] in the culture of the West. He makes the Enlightenment, which has long come up against its limits, the root of all evil. The crisis scenario sketched by Newbigin, painted in simple black and white, has apocalyptic features (36). Western culture is 'approaching death' (3), it 'has no future and . . . life therefore has no meaning' (25). Newbigin repeatedly goes back to Augustine and his age as an analogy to this turning point in time. 'A uniquely brilliant culture was coming to the end of its life' (63). For Newbigin, Augustine's dictum '*Credo ut intelligam,* I believe in order that I may understand' (24), is significant for 'the shift through which the classical world-view was replaced by that of the Bible and then – fifteen centuries later – the development was reversed again [in the Enlightenment]'.[16] Now, it may be concluded, we face another revision, which replaces the Enlightenment and restores the biblical paradigm. Newbigin subsumes capitalism and Marxism under 'our culture'; as antagonistic streams of Enlightenment tradition (3), these have both equally forced Christianity back into the private realm. The scientific world-view forms the generally recognized 'fiduciary framework', (29f.); here facts are put above values and doubt above dogma. The nation state became the guarantor of an individual striving for happiness (15). As a result the God of the Bible was robbed of his function of providing and guaranteeing norms. Church and theology have internalized this paradigm and limited themselves to the private sphere. Here Newbigin calls for a radical change. He proclaims the gospel as *public truth,*[17] though he cannot give a plausible account of what he associates with this concept. At the same time he has before his eyes Islam as a hidden model, which he makes into a hostile image: 'today it is the only global ideology which can challenge the prevailing ideology and offer a coherent alternative'.[18]

> Our Muslim fellow-citizens are not afraid of proclaiming the faith of Islam as truth – as public truth, to which ultimately all must submit.[19]

Despite all assertions that he is not talking about a reconstitution of the *corpus Christianum*, Newbigin wants to replace the Enlightenment paradigm with the gospel as a framework of reference. The plea for the restoration of dogma brings with it obsolete claims to absoluteness. Talk of 'Committed Pluralism'[20] does not take pluralism seriously.[21] It is correct that church and theology have a public responsibility and must become able to take part in the discourse again. However, in a pluralistic society this is possible only in the awareness that one has to compete with other frameworks of meaning. On a superficial examination Newbigin also seems to concede this. However, on closer inspection, as the reverse of exclusivism one can see an inclusivism which does not scorn whatever in the legacy of the Enlightenment is compatible with its own position, but in other respects envisages a culture tailored to its own desires. The gospel is itself to have an effect in creating culture. This does away with Niebuhr's polarization. This 'Christ against Western culture' attitude, brought to a head, sees in Christ at the same time the fulfiller of a purged culture which would certainly find it difficult to deny its Western lineage.[22]

Accommodation

Accommodation, the assimilation of the proclamation of the gospel to a particular culture, was practised long before the term existed. The problem to which the accommodation model seeks to respond goes back to the beginnings of Christian faith. The successive expansion of Christianity westwards into the Greek, Roman and Germanic spheres, in the south to Egypt, North Africa and Ethiopia, and in the east as far as India and China,[23] involved the crossing of cultural boundaries. With the world mission which began in the wake of colonialism and imperialism in modern times, the gospel then came up against the global pluralism of cultures and religions. The efforts at assimilation which can be observed here are guided by the notion that the content and cultural form of the gospel are to be clearly separated. Just as the kernel of a nut is brought to light when the shell is removed, so too the gospel can be extracted from its cultural covering. The metaphors of clothing and vegetation which are likewise customary in this context suggest that the gospel is given a new cultural garb or is transplanted into a new cultural breeding-ground. The rites or accommodation controversy is usually cited as the example of the problem of accommodation.[24] It was sparked off by the missionary activity of the Jesuits in Asia. In China Matteo Ricci (1552–1610) had allowed the veneration of Confucius and ancestors, as civil practices, for Christians as well. He himself dressed like a Confucian scholar. He attempted to gain a footing in China through a double strategy, communicating Western science while at the same time adopting Eastern customs. His accreditation at the Chinese imperial court bears witness to the success of this strategy. In his work *The True Doctrine of God*[25] Ricci seeks to demonstrate that Confucianism reaches its perfect form only in Christian faith. The book found its way into the canon of Chinese classics.

Roberto de Nobili (1577–1656), who belonged to the same order as Ricci, carried on a mission among the Brahman caste in India. Dressed as a Brahman, he claimed that with the gospel he was bringing back to India the fifth Veda[26] which, it was believed, had been lost. In accordance with the mission strategy of their order, with their preaching of the gospel both sought to establish links with the upper class. They learned the vernacular and studied the respective cultures and religions. Basically they represented a theology which presents the gospel as the fulfilment of the particular culture. The dispute which was sparked off over them was governed by very different factors. The Dominicans and Franciscans who had made their way to China condemned the rites, again in accordance with the mission strategy of their orders, according to the practice among the people, and thereupon rejected them as superstition. In addition to this rivalry between the orders there were also national differences between the missionaries of Spanish and Portuguese origin, and church-political rivalries between patronage and propaganda.

Theoretical reflection began with the foundation of mission studies at the beginning of the twentieth century. Here the term accommodation came to be used above all in the Catholic sphere. Thomas Ohm (1892–1962) then differentiated the accommodation model, giving it three stages: *accommodation, assimilation, transformation*. For him accommodation denotes the assimilation of the preaching of the church to a particular culture; assimilation the adoption of elements from this culture; and transformation their theological reshaping.[27]

The term *indigenization* came to be used in the Protestant discussion in the 1950s, though it has proved to be somewhat vague. It origins lie in the 'three-self' formula put forward by Rufus Anderson (1796–1880) and Henry Venn (1796–1873) for the independence of the churches – *self-governing, self-supporting, self-propogating* – and above all for the discussion on 'church and people' which was significant for German Protestant missiology.[28] Shoki Coe[29] criticized the static concept of culture and the orientation of this concept on the past which goes with it.

The *translation models* developed in evangelical circles are a modern variant of the accommodation model. Referring to the difference between a literal translation and a paraphrase, Charles Kraft speaks of 'formal correspondence' and 'dynamic equivalence'.[30]

The criticism of the accommodation model can be summed up in three key words – *static, hierarchical* and *ecclesiocentric*.

• Accommodation is based on a static notion of gospel and culture and the relationship between the two. No change in the two entities or reciprocal influence is part of the calculation.

• The event of accommodation has a hierarchical structure; there is a clear downward slope between the 'subject of mission' and 'the object of mission'.

• The church alone is the subject of accommodation.

Nevertheless the accommodation model represents clear progress by comparison with the exclusivism of *extra ecclesiam nulla salus*. The alien culture and religion of the mission object is no longer generally rejected, but at any rate is investigated and put to use for the preaching of the gospel. However, this instrumentalization of culture to provide a new 'package' for the gospel is countered by cultural change and the specific dynamic of the gospel and the reciprocal processes which result. The step from the accommodation model to the inculturation model is inherent in the matter itself.

Inculturation

Vatican II also marks a turning point in Catholic theology in respect of the question of defining the relationship between gospel and culture.

• The reform of the liturgy[31] follows the premise 'that the Christian people should be able to understand it [the liturgy] and take part in it fully, actively and as a community' (Art. 21). Permission for use of the vernacular is fundamental here (Art. 36). 'Adaptation to the temperament and traditions of peoples' (Arts 37–40) is explicitly provided for. The church 'respects and fosters the qualities and talents of the various races and nations. Anything in these people's way of life which is not indissolubly bound up with superstition and error she studies with sympathy, and, if possible, preserves intact' (Art. 37). Special mention is made of initiation (Art. 65) and music (Art. 119). Assimilation should also take place in respect of 'sacred art, sacred furnishing and vestments' (Art. 128). The authority to decide always lies with the hierarchy, the local conferences of bishops and Rome.

• Because of the high value placed on the local church, local culture similarly comes more markedly into view.

• The democratization of the concept of culture in the Pastoral Constitution[32] signals an awakening awareness of the dynamic of cultural processes.

Even if the Council texts themselves still speak of 'assimilation', they have prepared the way for a new departure in theology (of mission), which is later confirmed with the neologism '*inculturation*'. The proximity to the technical terms 'enculturation' or 'acculturation' from cultural anthropology on the one hand and to the theological concept of 'incarnation' on the other has encouraged the conjecture that here a fusion of these con-

ceptions has taken place. But in the process the distinct connotation of the individual terms is often all too easily levelled out.
• Enculturation is a variant of the more frequent term socialization in cultural anthropology. What is meant is a person growing into his or her own culture, in childhood as conditioning, and later also in a critical controversy with tradition.
• By comparison, acculturation denotes the contact between two cultures and the reciprocal effects which emerge here.
• The synonymous use of inculturation and incarnation is to be ruled out *a priori* as inadequate because of the different subjects which are involved here. But analogizing language in the sense of a basic theological structure is also at least problematical. It suggests that the gospel is available without a cultural shell and can time and again be reincarnated or inculturated (the kernel-husk model).[33] Here first of all reference to a kenotic understanding of the incarnation is helpful.[34]

However, if the gospel is accessible to us only in a culturally mediated form, mission is always also acculturation. If the local church is seen as the subject of mission, mission can at the same time be described as a process of enculturation in a particular culture. So inculturation oscillates between the two concepts of cultural anthropology. By comparison with accommodation, inculturation denotes a dynamic, reciprocal process. However, it largely remains ecclesiocentric. In more recent official documents the meaning of the term inculturation is again reduced to the concept of accommodation.[35]

Contextual theology

It is arguable how far the theologies of inculturation, dialogue and liberation formulated in Third World countries in the wake of Vatican II can be summed up under the term inculturation, within the framework of a broader concept of culture derived from the Pastoral Constitution of the Council, *Gaudium et Spes* (Art. 53).[36] However, I think that *contextual theology* is the term with the greatest capacity for integration.

The concept of contextualization is a parallel development in WCC circles to the Catholic debate on inculturation. It has its *Sitz im Leben* in the reform of theological education. The

Theological Education Fund[37] has elevated contextualization to a theological programme in its Third Mandate. On this basis I have developed a theory of contextual theology.[38] In accordance with their thematic orientation I distinguish between a cultural-religious and a socio-economic and political type of contextual theology. The model of inculturation and its prior forms of accommodation, indigenization and translation models can be subsumed under the cultural-religious type. The liberation theologies with their predecessors development theology and new political theology form the second socio-economic and political strand of tradition. The ecological and gender questions have recently been added.

The consultation process engaged in by the Ecumenical Association of Third World Theologians (EATWOT) is already a success story, because here the two great streams of tradition have been fused and there has been a cross-fertilization. The future visibility of the contextual theologies will markedly depend on whether their representatives succeed in being continually involved in the many dimensions of their particular context.

Table 2: Contextual theology

Cultural-religious type	Socio-economic and political type
Accommodation/ indigenization/ translation models	Development theology/new political theology
Inculturation theologies	Liberation theologies

Contextual theologies: the cultural-religious, socio-economic, political, ecological and gender dimensions[39]

As well as the typologizing by thematic perspectives which is only briefly sketched out here (Table 2), I have developed a modified model of the hermeneutical circle for understanding the in-depth structures of the contextual theologies. Already in Martin Heidegger and Hans-Georg Gadamer the hermeneutical circle is not understood as a closed circle of argument but as a model of how the process of understanding takes place.[40] However, whereas in Heidegger and Gadamer the art of understand-

ing stands in the centre, for me hermeneutics is at the same time
the production of meaning, which brings about a growth of
meaning in the text.

Here by theology I understand not only academic or even
systematic theology in the narrower sense, but any form of critical reflection on faith. To want to measure contextual theologies
by the criterion of Western academic theology will not do justice
to them, since these are the theologies from which they seek
emancipation.[41] That has led to an epistemological break. The
founding manifesto of EATWOT remarks here:

> To be faithful to the gospel and our peoples we must think
> about the realities of our own situation and interpret the word
> of God in relation to these realities. We reject as inadequate a
> merely academic theology which is separate from action. We
> are ready to make a radical break in epistemology which
> makes commitment the first act of theology and enters into a
> critical reflection or the real praxis of reality of the Third
> World.[42]

Contextual theologies keep arising anew in the hermeneutical
circle (Illus.1) between text and context. They are open systems
with no claim to permanence or universal validity. They constantly react to the facts of the moment, and remain necessarily
fragmentary. Each of these interpretations of the text is fixing the
meaning at one point but does not exhaust the reservoir of meaning of the text. At the same time any interpretation represents an
increase of meaning in the text which is preserved in *tradition*.

The criteria must be arrived at in the hermeneutical process
itself. The perspective of the context puts the question of relevance to contextual theology, asking how far it succeeds in
announcing the relevance of the gospel in each situation (*criterion of relevance*). The concern for the poor and oppressed in the
liberation theologies and the support for an acceptance of people
in their particular cultural identity by the inculturation theologies are two such criteria of relevance which are accessible intersubjectively. These generative themes[43] relevant for the contexts
concerned are at the same time capable of being linked to two
generative themes of the text: Jesus' concern for the poor and
oppressed of his time and Paul's doctrine of justification by faith

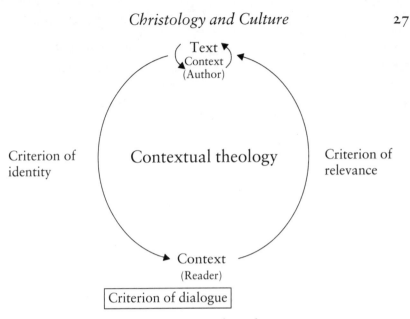

Illustration 1: The hermeneutical circle

alone in the context of the differences between Jewish Christians and Gentile Christians. Accordingly there are two questions about the context in the hermeneutical process. Alongside the context of interpretation the circumstances in which the text originates are also relevant. At the same time contextual theology must be examined from the perspective of the text in terms of its congruence with the gospel (*criterion of identity*). This hermeneutical circle between text and context is constantly followed. As we have seen, the criteria of relevance and identity are dialectically related to each other.

At a first glance, one might assume here a vicious circle (circulus vitiosus). But the circular movement described does not run between two static entities. In particular in Third World countries the context constantly changes, on the basis of cultural change and social upheavals. Here the *con*-texts are themselves also texts, constructions of reality which are created by individual theologians or whole communities of interpretation. Cultural renaissances and mythological or theological reconstructions of history are the result. They often lead to hermeneutical disputes between the different interest groups within a context over the interpretation of their own culture and history. Theology must time and again adopt a new attitude to these variants. At the same time the text appears in a new light in the changed situation and sets free new meanings. Therefore in relation to the text I shall speak of a *relational constant*. But if the hermeneutical circle between a *variable* (context) and a relational constant (text) is progressing, then it is not a vicious circle but a *circulus progredieus*.

The premises derived from Niebuhr's three mediating answers[44] also apply to the model of contextualization. However, the polar or linear notion which puts Christ in relation to culture in a particular way is dissolved by a dialectical or circular thinking. As opposed to Niebuhr's optimism that culture in its totality can be transformed by the message of Christ, the starting point for the contextualization model is that while something new arises in the hermeneutical process between gospel and culture, it is within the framework of reference of the particular culture. It follows from our first premise, the twofold loyalty or Christian-contextual bi-identity, that the two other premises for the hermeneutical process necessarily also apply the other way round.

• Culture is never completely taken up in the contextual interpretation of the gospel. As the hermeneutical circle is followed time and again, there is constantly a new constellation simply on the basis of the cultural change.

• Culture is a critical authority in the dispute over interpretations of the gospel. It opens up new perspectives on the text breaking up seemingly established readings.

Christianity today is a global narrative and interpretative community.[45] From this our third criterion follows: any contextual theology must be open to discussion in the ecumenical forum (*criterion of dialogue*).[46]

In what follows, christology will to some degree serve me as a probe to detect the commonalities, divergences and opportunities for ecumenical learning in the connections between themes in contextual theologies.[47] While the thematic typology provides the outer framework of the division, and within the course of the account an inner framework will crystallize out which takes on stronger contours from the perspective of the text. Before we set out, however, let me first explain my systematic theological premises.

§2 Christology in Context – Intercultural Christology

As a Christian theologian I am writing about a religious tradition in which I myself stand and to which I feel bound. I said at the beginning that I am adopting a 'religious perspective'. However, no hermeneutical privilege derives from this. On the contrary, academic honesty demands that I make my critical reflection on faith intersubjectively accessible. Having in the first part marked out the field of themes in which I am moving, I shall now deal with the theological framework. I intend to do that by three theses: about the field with which christology is concerned, the structure of christological discourse, and inter-cultural discourse about the different christological concepts.

(1) Christology is talk of the life, death and resurrection of Jesus Christ.

Like all stories, the biblical stories of the Old and New Testament are meant to be retold. They point beyond themselves. However, to meet with interest from their particular hearers, they must develop their relevance to the situation of those who hear them. Narrating is a reciprocal process between the narrator, who in our case, however, retreats behind the biblical stories (text); the narrator's history; and the narrator's hearers, who are each to a high degree shaped by their specific contexts. In this constellation we can already see the beginnings of the basic structure of the hermeneutical circle between text and context.

Christological discourse is a hermeneutical event. The life, death and resurrection of Jesus are to some degree the iconographic corner-points from which christology can be retold time and again. The span of the story of Jesus runs from the description of his life – annunciation to Mary, birth in the manger, flight to Egypt, presentation in the temple, Jesus' public activity in Galilee, journey to Jerusalem and entry into the city – through his death on the cross on Golgotha to the resurrection. Depending on which of the three corner-points the story is developed from, a different central *perspective* opens up on Jesus Christ. These options are typically represented by the three great confessions: incarnational theology in the Catholic confession; the theology of the cross in the Protestant confession; and resurrection theology in the Orthodox confession.

• In Catholicism, following tradition, the incarnational christology of the early church has long been maintained. Belief in the incarnation of God in Jesus Christ has made Mary, the mother of God, with the child Jesus the symbol of Catholic piety. From the central perspective of the incarnation the death of Jesus on the cross appears as the consequence of his career. The resurrection then follows with some necessity for the notion of the incarnation, which was extended back from the birth into pre-existence. Moreover, in the modern discussion about a christology 'from below', from the Catholic side time and again there has been emphasis on the continuity with the Chalcedonian christology 'from above'. This is a new interpretation of it 'under the presuppositions of modern thought'.[1]

• The incarnation is in no way negated in the Reformation. In his sermons Luther could speak quite vividly of the humanity of Jesus.[2] But there was a clear shift in perspective. In his Heidelberg Disputation of 1518[3] Luther polemically attacks the piety of the law and righteousness by works. The sinner is justified by grace alone. However, that means neither that the end of the law has come nor that the believer is not obligated to act rightly, but rather radically opposes a link between human action and divine salvation. In stating 'that God is to be found only in suffering and cross' (supporting argument for Thesis XXI), Luther makes the cross of Jesus Christ the hermeneutical key to knowledge of God. Only 'the theology of the cross names things by their right name' (Thesis XXI). This *theologia crucis* portrays Jesus as the *Christus patiens*. The painting of the cross on Matthias Grünewald's Isenheim Altar, dated 1515, is a congenial parallel to Luther's theology of the cross.[4] Here the programme runs from the annunciation to Mary through the birth to the resurrection, though the pedrella with the mourning always remains visible. The crucifixion to some degree adjusts the central theological perspective, which is memorialized in the pedrella. However, just as the body covered with sores has found its counterpart in the depiction of the risen Christ on the right panel of the recto side, so too Luther holds cross and resurrection together. 'So it is not sufficient nor useful for anyone to know God in his glory and majesty if he does not know him at the same time in the humility and shame of the cross' (supporting argument for Thesis XX).

• The approach of Orthodox christology leads through the liturgy and icons. The celebration of Easter night is an introduction to the central perspective of the resurrection. The Risen Christ is portrayed as the Pantocrator, the ruler of the worlds. Orthodox theology is a *theologia gloriae*,[5] which venerates the Risen Christ as the *Christus victor*. In the iconic depictions Christ is victor even on the cross. Finally, the high value attached to the Panhagia[6] also echoes the incarnation.

This sketchy comparison of the three great strands of tradition in Christian faith by way of christology already shows that it is an intrinsically plural, open system. This pluralism is grounded in the fact that specific men and women must time and again bear new testimony to their belief in the triune God. The biblical writings themselves are already an account of experiences which people have had with God. After it came into being over a lengthy period in different contexts, was collected and time and again also reworked by redactors, the originally mostly oral tradition finally took literary form. In respect of christology that means that in the letters of Paul, the Synoptic Gospels and the Gospel of John we already have at least five distinct christologies.

I see Christian faith as a broad stream of tradition which takes its starting point from the history of God with Israel and the renewal and simultaneous universalization of the old covenant in the person of Jesus Christ. This picture is to be understood completely in space and time and thus historically. The tradition is orientated towards the eschaton and ultimately to some degree flows towards God and into God. Sometimes side streams branch off and can issue in a syncretism or peter out in a heresy, but can also often after a certain time flow back into the main stream and broaden its bed. In their complexity and difference from one another, the three main currents of Orthodoxy, Catholicism and Protestantism already make it clear that there can be a unity only in diversity. However, this internal pluralism should be experienced as wealth and not as a threat to the identity within each confession. Of course there is a danger that, to continue the metaphor, the broad stream issues in an ocean of arbitrariness. Here the narrative and interpretative community's capacity to integrate is needed, which Christianity has done from the beginning.

(2) The biblical stories about Jesus Christ, the narratives of believers, men and women, on the one hand, and the themes which determine them on the other, are the two complementary forms shaping the text. They come to interact with the stories of men and women and the generative themes of the con-text which govern them. As a result a dense fabric of stories and themes takes shape.

The biblical stories, narrated as they were in a particular context, call for interpretation. In order to be able to develop their relevance for the particular situation there is a need for a mediation of the identity of Christian faith which is expressed in them. The stories evoke the themes which must be discussed again in this context. The dogmatic clarifications of the early church can be regarded as typical. In the foreground stood the question of the *vere homo, vere deus*. In the trinitarian dispute the argument was primarily about the divinity, and then in the christological dispute primarily about the humanity. The discussion was governed by the soteriological question. The meanings established in the context of Hellenistic and Roman culture have long been an ingredient of the tradition. However, their normativity must time and again be renegotiated in the inter-cultural dialogue.

The attempt to drive a wedge between the stories and the themes which govern them is *a priori* doomed to failure. Anyone who wanted to hand down only the themes and let the stories get forgotten would rob believers of their home. Moreover the themes would soon have lost their power of expression, for the stories are their vehicles.[7]

In his philosophy of stories, Wilhelm Schapp[8] has characterized stories as paradoxically having a beginning and at the same time not having a beginning (88) and thus (unintentionally) has already attested that they have an openness to transcendence. For him, the definition of being human is to be enmeshed in histories (123). Although Schapp repeatedly resorts to examples from the theological sphere, we do not find in him the dialectical element of the reciprocal relationship between the biblical stories (text) and everyday stories (context). Whereas people are always already enmeshed in stories and continue to be so, at the same time they interpret these stories by *miteinander versprechen* (*pledging* them to one another, Ernst Lange). They interpret their own stories through the biblical stories and vice versa. Here the stories evoke the themes by which they are governed. So my starting point is not a canon in the canon from which everything can be derived; rather, in analogy to the network of stories in which we are entangled, I assume a whole web of *generative themes* which time and again are rearranged.

I have taken over the term 'generative themes' from Paulo Freire's *Pedagogy of the Oppressed*.[9] Freire has developed his pedagogical scheme on the basis of his experiences with literacy programmes and adult education in Brazil. Here he and his colleagues dealt with the 'problem of adult education as a question how one learns to read and at the same time develops consciousness'.[10] They wanted to get away from what Freire calls 'the "banking" concept of education, in which the scope of action allowed to the students extends only as far as receiving, filing, and storing the deposits',[11] and in the direction of a 'problem-posing' 'dialogical' education, 'a pedagogy which must be forged *with* not *for*, the oppressed (whether individuals or peoples) in the incessant struggle to regain their humanity'.[12] There are no longer teachers and students, as in a traditional school, but only teacher-students and student-teachers, who work together in cultural circles. To prepare the ground for this method, Freire's teams at first practised participatory observation in the particular spheres that they entered. Together with representatives of the population they investigated the generative words and themes of the local community. These are generative because the relevant words or themes when linked together make it possible to disclose the whole linguistic or thematic universe of a community.[13] For Freire, the criteria for the selection of generative words are (1) their wealth of phonemes, (2) their phonemic difficulty, and (3) their pragmatics, 'i.e. the greatest possible embedding of the word in a given social, cultural and political reality'.[14] As examples he cites, among other things, 'slum', 'rain', 'plough', 'land' and 'food'.[15] If the generative words primarily serve in learning word-formation and associating word and writing, the generative themes disclose the overall context of a culture. In the context of Brazil such generative themes were 'poverty', 'oppression' and 'freedom'. In discovering their own identity through their capacity for language, people at the same time learn to distinguish between nature and culture. In respect of this 'anthropological concept of culture' Freire speaks of a *hinged theme*[16] which makes it possible to bring together generative themes. Although his language is steeped in theology to a high degree, Freire omits religion as a potential hinge theme. Granted, he calls for a prophetic church and sympathizes with liberation theology, which in turn received important impulses from him, but he leaves it at that. Freire's concept remains defective because he omits the religious dimension.[17]

The people whom Freire wants to make literate are at the same time believing Christians. The base communities are a place of *conscientization*. Their thematic universe is interwoven with the universe of Christian themes. Gospel and culture are dialectically related. The generative themes of Christian faith and Brazilian culture, the biblical stories and the stories of the people, interpenetrate, expound one another and are recognizable in one another.

I commented that the stories evoke the generative themes which constitute the identity of Christian faith. We shall go on to play that out by means of the generative theme 'christology'. Christology for its part collects together a whole series of generative themes. In life, death and resurrection I have already mentioned three. However, the text can unfold its relevance only if these themes are linked with the generative themes of a particular context. Just as stories expound one another, so too the generative themes are to be interlocked. In this connection I speak of the *linking of themes*. Different *types* can be distinguished in this linking of themes, for example our socio-economic and political or cultural-religious type of contextual theologies, which thematically we have defined so far merely from the side of the context. In the course of our investigation they must also be contoured from the side of the text. Finally I call the concrete formulations of these types *models*.

(3) The pluralism of contextual christologies needs an intercultural theology which lays down the rules of dialogue and weaves together the different discourses.

Wherever a strand of tradition claims absoluteness for itself, there are collisions of interests. In earliest centuries conflicts within Christianity were often resolved with violence. The civil war in Northern Ireland with its religious overtones is an outcome of this baneful tradition. But it must also remain a constant thorn in our flesh that Christians today still mutually deny faith or refuse to participate in the eucharist instead of accepting one another in their difference, allowing themselves to be enriched by it and together celebrating their faith.

Christian faith lives from the multiplicity of strands of traditions which preserve its richness, open up different perspectives on the truth and, ideally, mutually correct one another. In trast to the darker time of the wars of religion, today there is something like an ecumenical culture of dialogue. Not everyone speaks with everyone else, and the institutional resistance is certainly still considerable, but so far even in an ecumenically lean time the discussions have not yet been broken off. The same can be said of the reception of the contextual theologies. These theologies are the street urchins of Western academic theologies, but the option for the poor[18] and the question of pluriform cultural-Christian identities remain prevalent in our discussions, even if only as a stumbling block. At any rate they cannot just be suppressed.

In this case, reality is far ahead of theoretical awareness and reflection. As a global narrative and interpretative community, Christianity needs an inter-cultural theology which operates between the different contextual forms of Christian faith. It reflects on the theological processes which take place in cultural contacts, reveals foundational connections and formulates rules for dialogue.[19] Intercultural theology is a pluralistic concept. But alongside these components of fundamental theology, intercultural theology also works in forming tradition, by preserving different contextual sketches and bringing them into dialogue with one another. My theory of contextual theology and the christological reflections in this volume are meant to be elements of such an intercultural theology.

EATWOT was a pioneer in posing the question of commonalities, divergences and cross-fertilization – in respect of the latter term I prefer to speak of opportunities for ecumenical learning. This question will accompany us as a leitmotif on our journey through the different contextual christologies and at the end provide the heuristic framework for the summary.

II. CHRISTOLOGY IN A DIVERSITY OF CONTEXTS

A. '. . . to proclaim the gospel to the poor.' Christology in the Context of Poverty and Oppression in Latin America

Crucifixion: sculpture of clay and wood
(Edilberto Merida, Peru)

Christ is hanging on a crudely made wooden cross. He has the physiognomy of an Indio. However, his beard and hairstyle are still reminiscent of traditional iconography. The oversized crude hands and feet belong to a campesino who goes barefoot, worn down by hard work in the fields. The sculpture is formed of clay, from the earth which he has worked in the sweat of his brow. On his head the crown of thorns sits heavily, and a cloth is slung round his loins. Blood flows from his open side. His eyes are closed in agony. The wide-open mouth with the thick lips seems to be uttering a choked cry. God is present in the midst of suffering.

§3 Historical Reconstruction: Christological Discourse at the Time of the Conquista

Even if God came earlier than the missionary,[1] the first images of Christ only reached present-day Latin America from 1492 on with the Conquistadores and the priests who accompanied them. Besides depictions of the Christ child with Mary, above all two themes became influential: the tortured body, Christ dying or as a dead man, and Christ as ruler, the Risen One in his glory.

1. The Spanish Christ[2]

For centuries the Spanish Christians had offered tough resistance to the Moorish conquerors of the Iberian peninsula. Their agony is reflected in impressive likenesses of the suffering and dying Christ.

> This Christ, who is as immortal as death, does not rise. Why not? He awaits nothing but death. From his half-open mouth, which is as black as the indecipherable mystery, he flows towards the nothingness that he never reaches . . . This corpse of Christ, which as such does not think, which is free of the pain of thinking and hindrance, the soul overburdened with mourning, asked the Father to spare it the cup of suffering. And how should the thought pain it if it is merely moist, dead flesh encrusted with blood, with black shed blood . . . This Spanish Christ who has never lived, black as the cloak of the earth, lies there flat, outstretched, without a soul and without

hope, eyes closed, his face directed towards heaven, which is sparing with rain and scorches the bread . . .[3]

The first crossing of the Atlantic by Columbus in 1492 had been immediately preceded by the reconquest of Granada. The Catholic rulers Ferdinand II of Aragon and Isabella of Castile granted him the equipment for his journey in the euphoria of this victory. The Reconquista was to be followed by the Conquista. Columbus himself was inspired by religious mysticism. He proudly bore his name, in which in a strange coincidence the ambivalence of the project becomes clear: Christophorus, the 'bearer of Christ', Columbus (Spanish *Colón*), the 'new settler'.[4] Spanish messianism aimed at conquest and conversion, in that order. Correspondingly Christ is depicted as a heavenly monarch.

The two images are to some degree two sides of the one coin of colonialist propaganda. The dying or dead Christ is an offer of identification in suffering, without arousing hope – the resurrection is distant. Even today, in the popular Catholicism of Latin America, Good Friday is the greatest day of celebration.[5] The other side, Christ the ruler, is embodied in the Spanish king and the colonial rulers, to whom the Indios are to bend the knee in veneration. In both cases the christology degenerates into an instrument of oppression. At an early stage resistance against it grew.

2. The Indios as the poor of Jesus Christ

Today Bartolomé de Las Casas (1484–1566)[6] has become a symbol of the resistance to the genocide of the Conquista. The liberation theologians, above all Gustavo Gutiérrez from Peru (born 1928), have long since declared him their ancestor in a large-scale hermeneutical construct of history.[7]

The young Bartolomé saw the first Indians as early as 1493 in Seville, his birthplace. Christopher Columbus, having returned from his first 'voyage of discovery', led them in procession on his solemn entry into the city. Bartolomé's uncle and father joined Columbus on his second voyage (1493). The father brought his son an Indio boy back as page (1499). However, on the orders of

Isabella, this unauthorized gift by Columbus to his men who had served him had to be returned and all Indio slaves sent back to their homeland. But almost eighteen months passed before the Indio boy was returned (1501). Then in 1502 Las Casas himself travelled into the New World. He made a living as a gold prospector and landowner (*encomendero*). In 1506 he returned to Spain, was ordained priest in Rome in 1507, and the same year sailed back to Espanõla.

Las Casas was initially part of the colonial system, even if at an early stage he was opposed to its practices in dealing with the Indios. Through him the content of the 1511 Advent sermon of the Dominican Antonio de Montesino has been handed down. The Dominicans had worked out this sermon together. Las Casas quoted the following section word for word:

> You are all in mortal sin, and in it you live and die because of the cruelty and tyranny which you practise against these innocent people. Say, with what right and what justice do you hold these Indios in such cruel and fearful servitude? With what authority have you waged such abhorrent wars against these people, who were gentle and peaceful in their lands and of whom you destroyed countless with death and unprecedented devastations? Why do you keep them so oppressed and tormented, without giving them food and looking after them when they are sick, so that they die of the excessive work which you impose on them? Or to put it more precisely: Why do you kill them, simply to dig and gain gold day by day? What are you doing to teach them to recognize God, their creator, to be baptized, to come to mass, to observe feast days and Sundays? Are these not human beings? Do they not have a rational soul? Are you not obliged to love them as yourselves? Do you not understand that? Do you not feel that? How can you fall into such a deep sleep of insensitivity? Be sure that in the state in which you are you can no more save yourselves than the Moors and Turks who have no faith in Jesus Christ and do not even desire him![8]

A discourse of law and sin develops, in which theological and legal arguments are closely interwoven. The Dominicans accuse the Conquistadores of being in mortal sin because in their greed for gold they exploit the Indios and kill them. Anyone who does not convert and change his behaviour will be refused absolution. At the same time they admonish the Spaniards about their duty to proclaim the gospel to the Indios. The Spanish king, alerted by the Conquistadores, insists on his rights, which he derives from the papal bull *Inter cetera*. Las Casas will later argue that precisely on the basis of this document the king is obliged to evangelize and care for his subjects. The Provincial of the Dominican Order in turn, invited by the king to regulate his Frailes, now accuses them of sin and admonishes them to do their real duty, to convert the unbelievers, and not to hinder their mission by becoming involved in the political situation. The interweaving of theological and legalistic arguments runs through the whole discussion about the way in which the Conquista is being carried out.

Las Casas seems to have been deeply impressed by the sermon. However, it is arguable whether he heard it himself. But the influence of the Dominicans (he finally joined in 1522), shaped his change of awareness. He met Pedro de Cordóba, his later 'spiritual director', as early as 1510; Pedro had come to Espanõla as superior with a first group of Dominicans. In 1512 an unknown Dominican father refused Las Casas absolution because he had not yet freed his Indio slaves. That same year, as an army chaplain, Las Casas took part in the conquest of Cuba and in Caonao was witness to a massacre among the Indios. He was tormented with deep doubts. He dates his conversion to the Indios, the poor of Jesus Christ, to the year 1514. In the meantime, himself an *encomendero* on Cuba, he had to give a Pentecost sermon to the Spaniards settled there. His meditation on Sirach 34 is a classic instance of a contextual exegesis of the Bible. The key biblical passage runs:

> If one sacrifices from what has been wrongfully obtained, the offering is blemished; the gifts of the lawless are not acceptable. The Most High is not pleased with the offerings of the ungodly; and he is not propitiated for sins by a multitude of sacrifices. Like one who kills a son before his father's eyes is the man who offers a sacrifice from the property of the poor.

The bread of the needy is the life of the poor; whoever deprives them of it is a man of blood. To take away a neighbour's living is to murder him, to deprive an employee of his wages is to shed blood. (Sirach 34.18–22)

Las Casas rediscovers in the Indios the poor of whom the Bible speaks again and again. His experience and the biblical text expound each other. This insight radicalizes him.

After careful reconsideration, Las Casas frees his own Indios, even if he has to fear that outside the protection which he has granted them they will be enslaved and murdered by others. However, in the end this step seems to him to be indispensable, in order to break with the colonial system. Only in this way can he attain the freedom to fight it. The discovery that the Indios are the poor of the gospel was theologically only the first step. It was not far from that to the insight that the suffering Christ is himself present in the poor. With this very argument he justifies to one of his supporters the peaceful colonization of Venezuela carried out by Las Casas (1520/21), the profit of which was to go to the king:

The clergyman who knew of this astonishment said: Senõr, if you saw how they lay hands on our Lord Jesus Christ, shame and insult him, would you not ask with great persistence and with all your might for him to be given to you, so that you could revere him, serve him, give him presents and do for him all that you must do as a true Christian? He answered: Yes, certainly. And if they did not want to give him generously but sold him, would you not buy him? Beyond doubt, he said, I would buy him. Then the clergyman added: In this way too, senõr, I have acted. For I allowed Jesus Christ, our God, in the West Indies, to be insulted, struck and crucified, not once but a thousand times, by the fact that the Spaniards oppress and destroy these people and take away from them room for repentance and penance by prematurely robbing them of their lives. And so they die without faith and without sacraments. I have very often begged and prayed the king's council to support them and remove the hindrances to their redemption which are there, because the Spaniards keep in prison those who are already allotted and also those who are not yet allotted. They will not allow Spaniards to go to a particular place on the continent where the religious, servants of God, have begun to preach the gospel, and where the Spaniards on this broad land hinder them with their violent acts and bad example and blaspheme the name of Christ. They have told me: That is not possible, for it would mean that the Frailes hold the land in possession without the king having use of it. Then I saw how they wanted me to buy the gospel and consequently Christ by flogging him, striking him on the back and crucifying him. I decided to buy him by offering the king many possessions, incomes and transitory riches in the way of which your grace will have heard.[9]

Las Casas' Venezuela adventure ended in fiasco. Despite such setbacks, until his death at an advanced age Las Casas remains an advocate of the poor and oppressed Indios. As a theologian he argues with the Bible, as a lawyer also with natural law. Politically, time and again he was able to get a hearing for himself at court as a spokesman for the Indios.

§4 Christopraxis in the Discipleship of Jesus

Leonardo Boff (Brazil) and Jon Sobrino (El Salvador)

The appearance of Gustavo Gutiérrez's *Theology of Liberation* in 1972[1] marks a *kairos* in the more recent history of Latin American theology. With it, Gutiérrez, who is regarded by many as the founder and grand old man of this theological trend,[2] presented a first systematic basis. He proclaims a *prophetic* theology 'based on the gospel and the experiences of men and women who have committed themselves to the process of liberation in the oppressed and exploited land of Latin America'.[3] Gutiérrez had presented his thoughts for the first time a month before the beginning of the Second General Assembly of the Latin American Conferences of Bishops in Medellin in 1968;[4] he was one of its theological advisors. Pursuing their aim to carry forward the implementation of the reform potential of the resolutions of Vatican II in the Latin American context, the delegates prepared the way for a new ecclesiological and theological departure towards a 'church of the poor'.[5] Moreover, the analysis of the Latin American situation and the role of the church takes up a great deal of space in Gutiérrez. Theologically, a tremendous theological optimism can be traced, which makes him speak of the creation of a new person.[6] In good Pauline terms what is meant is the new person in Christ.

1. Towards a liberating christology

Set alongside Gutiérrez's *Theology of Liberation*, Leonardo Boff's work *Jesus Christ Liberator*,[7] published in the same year, looks more like a stolid textbook.[8] Its genesis from a series of articles based on his teaching in Petrópolis[9] cannot wholly be denied, and much serves simply to communicate knowledge. However, in the foreword to the English edition the author emphasizes that the message of liberation has been understood,[10] though because of the political situation his freedom to publish was severely limited. Boff, too, makes the claim to be writing against the background of his Latin American context,[11] but does not want to make any analysis himself. His interest is more in the direction of systematic theology. The same is true of Jon Sobrino's[12] work *Christology at the Crossroads*[13] published four years later. Nevertheless, in terms of their influence both these books can be regarded as the standard works of Latin American liberation christology.[14]

Leonardo Boff,[15] a Brazilian of Italian descent, was born in Concórdia/Santa Catarina in 1938, the oldest son of a teacher. The family situation was modest, but the father, himself brought up by the Jesuits, made it possible for all his children, including the girls, to have a university education. Of his ten brothers and sisters, Leonardo's younger brother Clodovis (born 1944) likewise achieved a certain prominence as a liberation theologian.[16] Brought up in the strictness and piety of Italian popular Catholicism, at the age of eleven Leonardo entered the minor seminary of the Franciscans. He studied philosophy and theology in Curitiba and Petrópolis, with among others Bonaventura Kloppenburg, later one of his severest critics, and Paulo Evaristo Arns, who as cardinal of Sao Paulo then became a promoter of liberation theology, as well as Constantino Koser, from 1967 to 1979 Minister General of the Franciscan Order. Soon after being ordained priest in 1964, Boff went to Munich for further study (1965–70); there he heard lectures by Leo Scheffczyk, Heinrich Fries, Karl Rahner, the exegete Otto Kuss and also Wolfhart Pannenberg. In 1970 he presented his dissertation on 'The Church as Sacrament against the Background of Experience of the World'.[17] That same year Boff was called to the chair of systematic theology at the Franciscan college of philosophy and theology in Petrópolis as successor of B. Kloppenberg. Alongside his own extensive literary production he acted as a lively editor in the publishing house Vozes, owned by the order, among other things for the famous *Revista Eclesiastica Brasileira* and the Portuguese edition of *Concilium*. Boff says that he was moulded by his time as a priest in a slum in Petrópolis and by his contact with the base communities in the diocese of Acre-Parus in the Amazon rain forest.[18] After massive clashes with the Congregation of Faith over liberation theology,[19] in 1992 Boff left the order and now works as a freelance writer. A chair in ethics and spirituality was established for him at the state university of Rio de Janeiro.[20]

Boff's contemporary Jon Sobrino[21] was born in Spain in 1938. He entered the Jesuit order in 1956 at the age of eighteen, and since 1957 he has belonged to its Central American province. In 1963 he gained a licentiate in philosophy and the humanities, and in 1965 also a diploma in engineering, both in the University of St Louis. He concluded his study of theology at the Jesuit College of St Georgen in Frankfurt in 1975 with a doctoral thesis on 'The Significance of Cross and Resurrection in the Theologies of Jürgen Moltmann and Wolfhart Pannenberg'.[22] He had been ordained priest already in 1969. Sobrino teaches philosophy and theology at the Central American University of José Siméon Canas in San Salvador, El Salvador.

The two early works that we shall now look at more closely[23] still clearly draw on their authors' doctoral work. They discuss intensively German-language theology and exegesis – especially also Protestant works. Over wide areas they run parallel in structure and content.

Boff begins with a survey of historical-critical research into Jesus (B, 1–31) and of the hermeneutical discussion (B, 32–48). His five characteristics of a future Latin American christology mentioned in this context (B, 43–47) are the most-quoted passages of the whole work and so should also be mentioned here: (1) the primacy of the anthropological element over the ecclesiastical; (2) the primacy of the utopian element over the factual; (3) the primacy of the critical element over the dogmatic; (4) the primacy of the social element over the personal; (5) the primacy of orthopraxis over orthodoxy.

However, these five primacies characterize liberation theology as a framework of reference in general rather than liberation christology in particular. They do not satisfactorily characterize the overall conception of the book. In various articles Boff spelt out the criticism of the church hierarchy already becoming evident here. However, they caused a furore only when they were brought together and published in *Church, Charisma and Power*.[24] In the framework of his christology, criticism of the institution remains secondary. The hermeneutical approach and the starting point with the historical Jesus are the really distinctive features.

Sobrino already acknowledges both on the first pages of his book (S, 1–16). By means of the christologies of Rahner, Pannenberg and Moltmann he illustrates the three different approaches by way of incarnation, resurrection or cross (S, 17–40). He likewise ends his introduction by putting Latin-American christology in the overall context of liberation theology (S, 33–37).

In Boff and Sobrino the life, death and resurrection of Jesus Christ equally form the framework for the construction of the first part. For them the proclamation of the kingdom of God stands at the centre of the activity of Jesus (B, 52f.; S, 41). Sobrino seeks access through the faith of Jesus (S, 79–145) and prayer (S, 146–78). Boff portrays Jesus as the liberator in a comprehensive sense (B, 63–79). In both, at the centre of Part Two stands the distinction between the historical Jesus and the kerygmatic Christ and the dogmas of the early church (B, 178–205). In Boff there then follow some remarks on the cosmic christology which he puts forward (B, 206–63). Sobrino sums up his reflections on historical christology once again in a series of theses (S, 346–95). An appendix deals with the Christ of the Ignatian Exercises (S, 396–424). Sobrino has written a foreword to the English edition of his book (S, xv-xxvi), Boff an epilogue to his (B, 264–295).

The structure of the argument correlates with the largely parallel construction. So it makes sense to sum up their central christological statements in four theses. The network of christological themes developed in them is varied in all liberation theologies,[25] even if it is rarely presented in such a concentrated way.

(1) Liberating christology is hermeneutical christology.

The confession of the hermeneutical circle as the basic structure of any theological reflection is the common property of Latin American liberation theology and thus also stands at the beginning of the christologies of Boff (B, 5, 39) and Sobrino.[26] The biblical writings already offer a pluralism of christological concepts (B, 5–7, 12; S, 5). These are the post-Easter testimonies of faith (B, 2; S, 273), each of which arose in a specific situation (B, 5–7; S, 13). Even if the dogmas of the early church notably reduce this potential of differentiation in order to bring to bear the universality of the message of Christ, it is equally true that they too are interpretations in a particular situation (B, 182; S, 318).

Like all theological discourse, christology is contextually conditioned. Each generation must reformulate its christology in accordance with the changing context (B, 1; S, 347). Boff and Sobrino claim to be doing this in the situation of poverty and oppression in Latin America in the 1970s. They proclaim Jesus Christ as the liberator. Sobrino refers to the hermeneutical privilege of a certain possibility of being able to correlate the conditions at the time of Jesus with those of Latin America in his day (S, 12). Boff can only do this in the epilogue to the English edition, under the pressure of circumstances (B, 279). However, there are some cautious indications in the five primacies already mentioned (B, 43, 46f.). But contextuality is not only a methodological premise; rather, it is inherent in the christological process itself. Talk of Jesus Christ presses for reformulation, specifically in order to demonstrate time and again his universal validity (B, 12; S, 341, 348).

(2) Liberating christology is relational christology

This relationality of Jesus Christ (B, 195; S, 50, 60) can be demonstrated at three points.

• The relationality of the historical Jesus and the kerygmatic Christ.
It is the declared aim of Boff and Sobrino to overcome the

distinction between the historical Jesus and the kerygmatic Christ (B, 19; S, 275, 305). They bring back the historical Jesus into christology (S, 79). The life, death and resurrection of Jesus Christ are equally the subject of christological discourse. This then prevents too narrow a soteriology (B,10; S, 8). In order to justify their starting point with the historical Jesus, both authors are concerned to demonstrate an implicit christology in the preaching and activity of Jesus (B, 12, 52; S, 48, 68), which already anticipates the explicit post-Easter christology. The historical Jesus and the kerygmatic Christ are to be related to one another (B, 19), moreover christological statements are only possible at all in the light of the historical Jesus (S, 305). Any christological scheme must therefore, be measured by the story of Jesus (B, 28; S, 129, 291).

• The relationality of Jesus, the Son, and God, the Father.
Jesus' relation to God, as it can be demonstrated in his preaching, his faith and prayer, and in his activity, is a demonstration of implicit christology (B, 17; S, 60, 105). Jesus preaches neither himself nor a remote God, but the kingdom of God (B, 37, 52; S, 41), the dawn of which he promises and already anticipates in his activity (B, 54, 142; S, 47f., 68). The eschatological proviso is preserved (B, 55; S, 63). Jesus believes in a God present in history (S, 44), whose action has manifested itself in an exemplary way in the Exodus event. Salvation history and history of the world are one. Jesus' life, preaching and activity – and then also his death and resurrection, only from a post-Easter perspective – make God himself manifest in Jesus' relation to the Father.

• The relationality of God, Father, Son and human beings.
If on the one hand God has revealed himself in Jesus Christ, so at the same time on the other he is the image of the perfect human being (B, 197, 204f.). At the same time the poor and the oppressed in whom Jesus Christ is present become the image of the 'otherness' of God (S, 368). Christological statements are always at the same time statements about God and human beings.

Relationality is a hermeneutical category. In order to be able to express the *vere homo et vere deus* (B, 194) and to keep it in balance (B, 183), christological discourse must always relate the historical Jesus to the kerygmatic Christ, God the Father and Son, and believers to one another.

(3) Liberating christology is incarnational christology.[27]

The triad of the life, death and resurrection of Jesus Christ already forms the span of the incarnation. At this point Boff and Sobrino are shaped by Catholic tradition (B, 155, 188; S, 124). Jesus' death on the cross is in line with his incarnation among ordinary people and his whole career. The overcoming of death in the resurrection gives the presence in suffering an eschatological dimension. The resurrection is an impulse for the hope of liberation; however, often this has only an implicit effect, mediated through the span of the incarnation. Here there is clearly thought from the perspective of the kenosis into suffering.

Despite the weak pneumatology, both ultimately have a trinitarian approach (B, 253f., 259).[28] However, whereas Boff shows undisguised sympathy for cosmological speculations, Sobrino, following Moltmann, puts the crucified God at the centre of his reflections. Boff thinks in the light of the cosmos and in terms of the cosmos. Christ is the mediator of creation and the reconciler of all. By contrast Sobrino reflects more markedly on what the happens within the Trinity. For both, the Spirit is the medium of communication both *ad intra* (B, 253) and *ad extra*.

(4) Liberating christology is a christology of discipleship.

Just as Jesus not only articulates his faith by preaching the kingdom of God but also makes it visible in his activity, so too his followers must convert (B, 64; S, 57) and follow in his footsteps in faith and works (B, 231, 245; S, 50). It is not the imitation of Christ in the sense of merely copying him (S, 132); but a life in discipleship which makes the message of the dawn of the kingdom of God in Jesus Christ relevant in the particular situation (B, 220; S, 12), and active work for the kingdom of God are required here (S, 50). Christology can only be formulated at all in the discipleship of Jesus (S, 108, 275).

The interdependence of these four characteristics of liberating christology is clear. Relationality is the driving force in the hermeneutical circle. If God manifests himself in Jesus Christ, but believers get to know him rightly only as disciples of Jesus, these are hermeneutical processes which are indebted to the relationality of God the Father, the Son, and the believers.

2. The Christ present in the poor

It is the abiding merit of Boff and Sobrino, by adopting the christologies of incarnation and discipleship from the tradition and reshaping them hermeneutically and relationally, to have put liberation theology on a solid christological basis. However, their early writings only suggest what was soon to become the distinctive feature of liberation theology: the rediscovery of the presence of Christ in the poor. From a post-Easter perspective the one who has come to preach the gospel to the poor is himself present – as the Risen One – in the poor of this world (Matt. 25). What Bartolomé de Las Casas proclaimed for the Indios at the time of the Conquista now becomes the good news for the poor of the whole sub-continent. Here liberation theology provides its own answer to the question of theodicy. The kenosis of Jesus Christ, his presence in suffering, offers the poor, *contrary to the facts* [29] of the conditions in which they live, a restitution of their dignity before God. Through this, christology performs the function of providing identity. In the promise that Jesus Christ is with them, the poor regain their self-respect. Ignacio Ellacuria,[30] who was murdered by the death squads in San Salvador in 1989, goes one step further when he speaks of a 'historic soteriology' (580). The crucified people is not only the 'continuation in history of the life and death of Jesus' (590) but in it also the 'extension of Jesus' redemptive work' (592). However, he does not explain the second point further (603). It is above all this active aspect which has led to vigorous opposition to liberation theology. Still, talk of the crucified people can refer to the tradition of the Suffering Servant songs. A new martyrology develops which embraces not only the murdered priests and ordinary believers who gave their lives as disciples of Jesus, but also those unknown victims of oppression who according to Jon Sobrino have suffered a *material martyrdom*.[31]

The adoption of the generative theme of the presence of Jesus Christ in the suffering of the poor and oppressed in liberation theology is to some extent a modern version of Luther's basic hermeneutical principle 'that God is to be found only in suffering and cross'.[32] The liberation theologians 'call things by their right names'.[33] However, unlike Luther, they develop a *corporate theologia crucis*. This reference to community is constitutive of liberation theologies, whose African and Asian versions we shall look at more closely at the end of this way through the christological sketches of the Third World. But first we shall turn to the christologies which have been developed in the context of the cultures and religions of Africa and Asia.

B. 'But you, who do you Africans say that I am?' Christology in the Context of African Tribal Cultures and Religions

African crucifix; cement sculpture (François Goddart, Zaire)

The mask hangs on a Latin cross with a double border and an inlay of white mosaic stones. These also fill the space which is formed in the semicircular halo of the mask between the border and the five triangles arranged in the form of a star which structure it. The crown of thorns is stylized ornamentally as a sign of dignity. The halo is matched formally by the tiers formed by locks of hair which adorn the lower half of the mask. The splendour of the locks stands in some contrast to the short hairstyle of the head. The artist has shaped the surface of the face in a remarkable way with a coarse grain. By contrast the real physiognomy, like the whole mask, is precisely symmetrical. The half-open eyes mark the horizontal axis, and the nose the vertical axis. The bridge of the nose becomes the two thick eyebrows, the lines of which are drawn out through the cheeks to the corner of the mouth. The result is a heart-shaped ornament, the top of which is formed by the lower side of the lips, in the shape of a lozenge. On the forehead the mask has three cowrie shells, symbols of fertility. One of the central functions of masks in traditional Africa is the representation of ancestors or spirits which assume a presence in them. By analogy the Christ mask represents the Christus praesens. *This crucifix is not a representation of suffering. It is the Lord on the cross, the* Christus victor, *the primal source of life.*

§5 Models of African Christology

Whereas John S. Mbiti (born 1931), one of the Protestant founding fathers of African theology,[1] had to note in an early article
(1967)[2] that 'there are no African ideas about christology' (72),
according to the estimation of his Catholic counterpart Charles
Nyamiti (born 1931), a bare quarter of a century later (1989),[3]
the situation had fundamentally changed: 'There is no doubt that
christology is the subject which has been most developed in
today's African theology.'[4] Mbiti mentions 'four pillars' for
theological work in Africa. If we assign (1) 'the Bible' and (2) 'the
theology of the earlier churches' to the *text* and (3) 'the traditional African heritage and (4) the living experience of the church
in Africa' to the *context,* our scheme of text and context appears.
Mbiti works on his theme by asking two questions: (1) What
christological statements of the New Testament do the Africans
prefer? and (2) Where can points of contact with the African
world of ideas be found? On the basis of the researches of Harold
W. Turner on sermons of the 'church of the Lord' (Aladura),[5]
one of the independent African churches,[6] Mbiti comes to the
conclusion that Africans are particularly taken with those New
Testament traditions which portray Jesus as the *Christus victor.*
'By contrast, there is no interest in the death of Christ and
sacrifice as such' (75). However, Mbiti's argument has not gone
unchallenged.[7] According to him the African world of ideas lacks
the dimension of the future. Christology closes this gap.

> In the traditional notions there is a great vacuum in respect of
> the future, and Jesus fills it by being understood first and fore-
> most as victor over the powers which from time immemorial
> have dominated African life. (76)

The second part of the argument that Jesus Christ finds veneration as victor over the powers of evil seems essentially more plausible, given the different conceptions of time. Mbiti himself has repeatedly put forward the thesis that the African Christians tend towards a soteriology orientated on this world which leaves little room for notions like sin and atoning death.[8]

On the question of points of contact Mbiti already points the way through honorific titles (79), a procedure which is to assert itself as a leitmotif in further development. The essential analogies are: the position of the chief (81); rites of passage and initiation (77f.); kinship, which includes the dead (78, 83); and healing (83). The models of African christology are developed later from these particular elements. For his survey article Charles Nyamiti can already refer back to a wealth of material; he structures this on the framework of *inculturation theology* and *liberation theology*[9] with which we are familiar. In this chapter we shall turn to the inculturation theologies.[10]

1. Jesus Christ, the chief

The title of chief has its New Testament equivalent in the way in which Jesus is addressed as Lord (*kyrios*). In his account, F. Kabasélé (born 1948)[11] orientates himself on the Luba[12] Missal of the diocese of Mbuji-Mayi. Following the liturgical reform of Vatican II,[13] a missal has been created which is not a translation from the Latin; rather it has been 'rewritten, with one eye on the texts of the day, and another on the culture of those who pray' (103). The term chief is extremely diverse. The colonial rulers were already called *mukalengé*, chief, in the general sense, but so too were the missionaries and later the representatives of the indigenous clergy. Titles like *ntita* for chiefs who have the right to initiate and invest other chiefs and *luaba* for those claiming to be chiefs are different; they imply an elevation of those so designated and remain reserved to few. The *power* held by the chief is the central category. Bantu[14] Christians attest that for them 'Christ is Chief, and that his person is in perfect conformity with the very essence of Bantu power' (112). 'The prerogatives of a Bantu chief are seen to have been fully realized by Jesus Christ' (105). Kabasélé makes five points in connection with this.

• *Jesus Christ is the chief because he is a hero.*
Jesus has put a stop to the evil powers and defied Satan. He has thus shown that he can protect and defend his community. The Luba Missal describes this with a whole series of warlike metaphors. Christ is '*Cimankinda* of the countless arrows' (106) and 'the one who never trifles with his hatchet, the one whose hatchet never fails to strike home' (*mukokodi-wa-ku-muele*, 106).

• *Jesus Christ is the chief because he is the son and emissary of the chief.*[15]
Among the Luba it is 'ancestral terminology' (108) to address God with the title chief (*Mulopo*).[16]

> That Christ is the Son of God, the Bantus have learned only through Christian revelation. But that God is the Chief of the universe, the ultimate recourse, they know by their ancestral faith. The theological discourse of the Bantu religions asserts this from beginning to end. (108)

Christ is called Mulopo, because he has revealed himself as son of the chief, but also because he is his emissary who traditionally likewise bore this title.

• *Jesus Christ is the chief because he is strong.*
The Bantu chief is placed 'at the intersection of the earthly and the Beyond, a sphere called by the Bantu the region of the 'strong' (bakolé) (109). He is the mediator to the ancestors and God and has therefore to be initiated. Through him life flows into the community which he is supposed to foster and to protect. His strength is the 'participation in being' (109).

• *Jesus Christ is the chief because he is generous and wise.*
The chief is concerned for the interest of the community. He constantly gives his counsel in accord with the will of the ancestors, and this at the same time guarantees him their support.

> To a Muntu, Christ appears as Wisdom itself, from the fact that he follows the will of the 'Father', doing nothing that he does not see the Father do (John 5.19). (111)

Only the one who proves worthy of the Father has an opportunity to decide the election of chief for himself.

• *Jesus Christ is the chief because he is the reconciling mediator.*
'Disunion among the people is the most pernicious of evils'
(112). Here the chief must intervene so as not to break the flow
of life.

The dignity of Jesus as chief finds its visible expression in the
liturgical use of traditional attributes of a chief, such as a leopard
skin, elephant tusks or spears.

2. Jesus Christ, the master of initiation

The approach chosen by Anselme Titianma Sanon (born 1937),
bishop of the diocese of Bobo-Dioulasso in Burkina-Faso, for his
description of Jesus as master of initiation is suggestive and
related to experience.[17] Like the office of chief, that of the master
of initiation is also threatened by cultural upheavals. But Sanon
sees initiation essentially from a pedagogical perspective,[18] as a
school of life which is always life in community. 'The initiation
comes from the ancestors.'[19] Like the chief, the master of initiation must also be initiated into his role as mediator. The master
must himself have taken the way of initiation. From depictions of
the life of Jesus Sanon can demonstrate that Jesus was initiated
into his Jewish tribal community.[20] But this initiation is completed with cross and resurrection.[21] 'In Jerusalem and nowhere
else is the place of the supreme initiation.'[22] The form of address
to Jesus as master of initiation takes on at least four dimensions
in Sanon:

• *Jesus Christ is the master of initiation because he himself
has undergone the phases of initiation in an exemplary way
(analogical dimension).*
The process of initiation can purely formally be an analogy to the
death and resurrection of Jesus Christ.

> Death, burial and resurrection are well-known phases in any
> process of initiation. This is the trial of separation and detach-
> ment, of being buried somewhere in the forest, in a cage or in
> the desert, and the return to a new life, to a new form of social
> and religious life.[23]

- *Jesus Christ is the master of initiation because he has completed his initiation vicariously for us (soteriological dimension).*

Christ's oblation, his total gift by the sacrifice on the cross, is the act of initiation for himself definitively, and it is valid with regard to all human beings. It is the visibly foundational act of the Redemption.[24]

- *Jesus Christ is the master of initiation because he leads us in the initiation as our elder brother (pedagogical dimension).*

In matrilineal tribal societies the oldest brother has a prominent role.[25] He carries out the ancestor rites or leads the group of those to be initiated. In the case of Jesus the pedagogy of initiation becomes an exercise in discipleship[26] and the mystery of the kingdom of God.

In this context, discipleship of Christ is initiation into the community of believers, the church. Christology and ecclesiology are closely linked.[27] To Sanon the catechumenate and baptism seem to be striking parallels. The Vatican II reform of the liturgy which has already been mentioned here provides the possibility of being active in shaping it. Moreover Sanon extends the perspective from christology to Christian rites of initiation generally.[28] The question of the participation of Christians in village initiation is also discussed in this context.

- *Jesus Christ is the master of initiation because he uses the language of the symbol and at the same time evokes a symbolic christology (aesthetic dimension).*

However, for Sanon, christology also has an aesthetic dimension: 'Jesus is our master of initiation because after the manner of the experienced masters of initiation he has shown us the supreme values in the form of symbols.'[29] But at the same time Sanon wants to make African symbolism transparent to christology: 'To see the face of Christ, to recognize his African face, is to find an African name for him.'[30]

3. Jesus Christ, the ancestor[31]

We have seen that chief and master of initiation are both also mediators to the ancestors and that authority accrues to them through this contact with the divine sphere. At the same time, because of this existence in the borderland between the divine and the human world, both must be initiated. It is obvious that the ancestors as *'source of life* and *obligatory route* to the Supreme Being' (116) themselves provide a title for Jesus Christ.[32]

> Not just anyone accedes to the rank of an Ancestor. It is not enough to die; one must have 'lived well', that is, have led a virtuous life. (118)

Alongside (1) model ethical behaviour, as further criteria Kabaselé mentions (2) descendants, for life must be perpetuated, and (3) a natural, good death. 'The role of mediation of life between God and human beings is played only by those who have fulfilled [these conditions]' (118).

Kabaselé explains the possibility of transferring the title of ancestor to Christ by means of four aspects:

• *Jesus Christ is the ancestor because he mediates life.*
Just as in the traditional notion of ancestors, so too Jesus mediates in fullness the life given by God. Life is always life in community, it is 'a life at once biological and spiritual' (120). The current of life flows from God through Jesus into his community which Jesus encourages and preserves by his presence.

• *Jesus Christ is the ancestor because he is present among the living.*
In Africa, communion with the ancestors extends beyond death. The ancestors are actively drawn into community life and take part in it themselves. But Jesus Christ has also promised such presence beyond death to his followers.

• *Jesus Christ, the ancestor, is at the same time the eldest.*
In Bantu terms the ancestors are at the same time the eldest, the ones who 'are closer to the sources and foundations. They came first' (121). As we already saw in the case of the title of chief, this title too was originally a divine predicate. 'Christ, God's only Son, likewise receives the attribute of "Eldest"' (121). At the same time he becomes our elder brother,[33] to whom we are to pay respect and who is our mediator to the Father.

It is the eldest brother who makes an offering to the Ancestors and to the Supreme Being on behalf of all the rest. (122)

• *Jesus Christ is the ancestor because he is the mediator between God and human beings and within human community.*
If life is always life in community, then mediation is constitutive of being. Life is mediated. There is mediation between the divine sphere and this world. But there must also be mediation within the community. Through initiation knowledge is handed on from generation to generation. In cases of conflict the chief mediates between the individual members of the community. Jesus Christ is 'the exemplar Ancestor, who fulfills in himself the words and deeds of the mediation of our Ancestors' (124).

There remains the question of what function is still attributed to the Bantu ancestors in this situation. The long period of the propagation of exclusivism by the missionaries certainly could not eradicate belief in ancestors, but many African Christians have internalized this position and developed a split relationship to their tradition. With its efforts to reform the liturgy, Vatican II produced further confusion. Now what for generations was regarded as taboo was suddenly to be practised.

Alongside the ancestor christology there is the attempt both to incorporate the ancestors into the church's veneration of saints, and also to develop forms of a genuinely Christian veneration of ancestors,[34] similar to what we have seen in the case of the rites of initiation.[35] However, for Kabasélé, veneration as a saint does justice neither to the Catholic understanding of saints nor to the dignity of the African ancestors.[36]

> Not having known or experienced faith in Jesus Christ, our Bantu Ancestors can perform the role neither of witnesses of nor of exemplarity for attachment to Christ (125).

By contrast, Kabasélé opts for a liturgical acceptance when he proposes integrating libations for the ancestors into the celebration of the eucharist.

African culture has a value of its own which is to contribute to the Christian community. Kabasélé uses the image of a chair which is reserved for one who comes later: 'As new cultures encounter Christ, various "vacant seats" in Christianity will be taken' (125).

4. Jesus Christ, the healer

The Guinean priest Cécé Kolié[37] makes critical comments about the three models sketched out so far. He begins his reflections on the possibility of giving Jesus the title healer with the polemical statement 'that it might be easier for African theologians to present Jesus as the Great Master of Initiation, or as the Ancestor *par excellence,* or the Chief of Chiefs, and so on. To proclaim Jesus as the Great Healer calls for a great deal of explaining to the millions who starve in the Sahel, to victims of injustice and corruption, and to the polyparasitic afflicted of the tropical and equatorial forests' (128)! For Kolié, the attempt to bestow traditional titles on Jesus Christ is an outgrowth of theology with a Western orientation following Vatican II, with no support among the people.

> Once more we impose on our fellow Africans the way of see-ing that we have learned from our Western masters. Shall we be followed by our communities, when we have finally gotten the prayers of the missal translated into these titles for Jesus whose real effectiveness has not really been tested in Africa? (142)

In turning to the socio-economic and political realities of the African context, at the same time Kolié is looking towards the Crucified One, away from the *Christus victor*. The life and suffering of Jesus come into the foreground. Kolié demonstrates this at two points:

• *Jesus Christ is the healer, because the healings were a central element in the activity of Jesus.*

• *Jesus Christ is the healer, because through his own suffering he is present in human suffering.*

However, in common with the traditional titles, addressing Jesus Christ as healer contains a reference to the community and is centred on life.

• In Africa, illness has a social dimension: 'Fundamentally, for the African person, being ill is an alteration in the equilibrium of the human organism, but it is also, and especially, a rent in the social fabric' (132).

• 'For the black African person, the aspiration to *life*, to eternity, is so primary that the persons called to administer it hold a place of eminence. . . . Accordingly, Islam and Christianity have, and will continue to have, credit with the African only to the extent that they share, side by side with the African person, *the struggle for life*' (132). Here it is not so much death which arouses fear, since the community exists beyond death, but both '*ill-living* and . . . *ill-dying*' (135).[38]

5. A comparison of models: commonalities and divergences

I have repeatedly referred to the close connection between chief, master of initiation and ancestor. All three are mediator figures between the divine and the human spheres. The chief and master of initiation have a role which is played out in this world; the ancestors to some degree transcend the community. They belong to the other world, but at the same time are present in this world. Mbiti calls them the 'living dead'.[39] The motive force is the handing on of life, which is communicated from God by way of the ancestors, through chief and master of initiation, flows into the community, and is handed on by parents to descendants. Chief and master of initiation occupy a mediating role within the human community as models and leading figures. As supreme political head the chief at the same time has a religious function. The master of initiation hands on ritual knowledge but at the same time sees to the social integration of the community. The reinforcement of the image of Christ bound up with these titles, the relationship to the community and centring on life, are at the same time its greatest weaknesses. The community in view is always only one's own tribe, even if this can embrace a whole people, as for example in the case of the Bantu. But the salvation of Jesus Christ is universal. The 'cult of life', once again to take up the term coined by Kolié,[40] excludes the sick and weak, those to whom Jesus Christ knew himself to be sent above all.

In faith in Jesus Christ, time and again there is a radical re-valuation of all values. This can be demonstrated not least by the

New Testament honorific titles. The title Messiah, which in Judaism is bound up with political and national expectations, and the title Kyrios, used in the Hellenistic sphere in the mystery religions and the ruler cult, are radically put in question by the history of the suffering of Jesus.[41] Accordingly the traditional African titles too, must undergo a revaluation:[42]

- *Chief*[43]

'The Chief analogy is dangerous because it is a *theologia gloriae*, lacking a *theologia crucis*.'[44] The office of African chief is bound up with worldly power, the claim to wealth and prestige. A distance is built up between the chief and the community which is difficult to overcome. Only through mediators can the members of the community find a hearing. By contrast Jesus calls for a radical change of position: 'Whoever among you would be great, let him be your servant, and whoever among you would be first, let him be the servant of all' (Mark 10.43f.). This revaluation finds symbolic expression in the foot-washing.

> Of course, the Bantu princes did not go as far as that. But the one who, while his royal father was yet alive, manifested tendencies to have himself served by his contemporaries, or who already treated them as slaves, thereby got himself eliminated from the scrutinies of the notables.[45]

- *Master of initiation*[46]

The master is indeed himself initiated, but he does not go the way of initiation again. It happens that he kills weak members of the community. But Jesus knew himself to be sent to the weak, and even today he is present in their suffering.

- *Ancestor*[47]

Jesus does not correspond to the vitalistic criteria of African ancestor worship. He fathered no descendants and died a violent death.

With the traditional honorific titles chief, master of initiation and ancestor, African notions are transferred to Jesus Christ. These are African names of praise which are to describe the significance that Jesus Christ could take on for Africans. They have little

Table 3. Models of African christology

Chief	Master of initiation	Ancestor	Healer[48]
pro			
• Hero • Son and envoy • 'Strong' • Big-hearted and wise • Reconciling mediator	• Has himself undergone all the phases of initiation • Representative-ness • Leads us as oldest brother • Symbolic christology	• Communicates life • Present among the living • Elder/ oldest brother • Mediator between God, human beings and fellow human beings	• Healing miracles • Presence in suffering
contra			
• Power • Wealth and prestige • Distance	• Does not go with us again on the way of initiation • Against the weak	• Vitalistic criteria; no descendants; violent death	
Commonalities			
Centred on life; related to the community			
Differences			
Christus victor; theologia gloriae			*Christus patiens; theologia crucis*
Representatives			
Kabasélé; Pobee	Sanon; Mveng; Bujo; Nyamiti	Kabasélé; Pobee	Kolié [Shorter]

support in the biblical text. Only when the new names are pronounced along with the biblical stories do they undergo a revaluation which illuminates the true meaning of Jesus Christ. By contrast, the title healer has concrete support in the text, in the stories of healings. But it describes only one aspect of christology. Here too it is the case that only by continuing to tell the story of Jesus can its whole fullness come to bear.

Christian G. Baëta (1908–1994), the grand old man of African theology, made a remark which has often been quoted: 'For, whatever others may do in their own countries, our people *live* with their dead.'[49] Moreover Bénézet Bujo sees in the model of ancestor the culminating point of the models proposed, 'for only here does Jesus Christ really emerge as source of life'.[50] The veneration of ancestors is the cornerstone of the African worldview.[51] It seems plausible to seek here the door through which the gospel can find entry into African culture. In the next section we shall look more closely at two attempts to formulate an ancestor christology.

§6 Christology in the Context of African Ancestor Worship

Charles Nyamiti (Tanzania) and Bénézet Bujo (Zaire)

Charles Nyamiti and Bénézet Bujo, both Catholic secular priests, embarked early on university careers. The son of a Christian family, born in 1931 in Ndala-Tabora, Tanzania, and given a strictly Catholic upbringing, already in his early years Charles Nyamiti was firmly rooted in the Christian faith. Soon after his ordination in 1962 the possibility opened up for him to study in Leuven, Belgium. The neoscholasticism of the Leuven school exerted its spell on him. In parallel he took a course in piano, which he completed with the final examination in 1968. The next year he presented his theological doctorate, a 'Comparison between Christian Initiation and the Initiation Rites of the African Masai, Kikuyu and Bemba peoples, with Reference to Liturgical Adaptation'. Nyamiti moved to Vienna to study ethnology and composition. There followed a second ethnological dissertation, on the 'Ancestor Cult among the Kikuyu of East Africa'. His first publications on 'African theology' also date from this time.[1] Bénézet Bujo, born in 1940 in Drodro, Bunia in Zaire, initially went to the Lovanium in Kinshasa after his ordination (in 1967), where Nyamiti had also studied, and then to Würzburg for his doctorate (in 1977) and his habilitation (in 1983).

The two obtained academic qualifications mainly in Europe, and after their return were appointed to theological colleges. Nyamiti first became Professor of Systematic Theology at the seminary in Kipalapala (1976–1981). From 1978 until he was appointed to the newly-founded Catholic Higher Institute of Eastern Africa (CHIEA) in Nairobi, Kenya, he also worked partly in parallel as a community pastor. At CHIEA he soon became head of the department of dogmatic theology. Bujo for several years (1978–1989) held a chair in moral theology in the theological faculty in Kinshasa, Zaire. In 1989 he accepted a call to be Professor of Moral Theology at the University of Fribourg, Switzerland. Whereas Nyamiti's interest was always in dogmatics, Bujo turned to moral theology. Nyamiti wants to give the whole of Christian doctrine an African expression; for him ethnology is the 'handmaid of African theology'.[2] Bujo investigates the African contribution to ethics. From different perspectives they come up against the problem of African ancestor worship and go on to speak of an ancestor christology.

1. Jesus Christ, the brother-ancestor (Charles Nyamiti)[3]

Although there is no uniform ancestor religion among the black African tribal societies, 'there are enough beliefs shared by most of these societies to enable one to affirm the presence of common ancestral beliefs in black Africa' (15). On this basis Nyamiti mentions two elements which are characteristic of 'the African conception of ancestorship': (1) *'natural relationship* between the ancestor and his earthly relatives', and (2) *'supernatural or sacred status* acquired by the ancestor through death' (15). The natural relationships of kinship can be based on a blood relationship with parents, and more rarely with brothers and sisters, or on the common membership of a clan, tribe, secret society, etc. In order to attain the supernatural or holy status of the ancestor the dead person must have led a morally unobjectionable life,[4] so that he can do justice to his future role as a model. As ancestor he is source and store of the tribal tradition. He performs a function as mediator between God and his earthly kinsfolk. If these do not pay sufficient attention to him, unpleasant consequences can result.

In connection with a Christian veneration of ancestors, Nyamiti distinguishes four types (143f.): (1) The traditional ancestors who take part in the Christian veneration of ancestors

Table 4: Jesus Christ and the African brother-ancestor (Nyamiti)[5]

African brother-ancestor	Jesus Christ	
	Commonalities	Divergences
• Blood relationship • Supernatural status through death	• Blood relationship through descent from Adam	• Christ transcends all limitations of kinship by his God-manhood • Supernatural status through death and resurrection
• Supernatural powers • Mediation between God and living relatives	• Supernatural powers • Mediation between the father and his human brothers	• Mediation salvation
• Ethical model • Source and store of tribal tradition	• Ethical model • Source and store of the Christian tradition	• Christ is the inner source and living principle of Christian life
• Regular supernatural communication between ancestors and the living through prayers and ritual sacrifices • Benefits on the part of the ancestors	• Regular supernatural communication between Christ and his followers through prayers and ritual sacrifices (mass) • Benefits through Christ	• Through the Holy Spirit • Christ communicates salvation
• Bodily hardship as a result of neglect • Prayers and ritual gifts as compensation	• Bodily or spiritual hardship as a result of neglect • Prayers and ritual gifts as compensation	• Sin against God – call for repentance
• Visits his living relatives in other forms of life (snakes, hyenas, etc.) • Preferred places (trees, cemeteries)	• Visits his living followers through other living beings (priest or other fellow-Christians) • Preferred places (church, tabernacle)	• At best a preparation for the gospel
• Common physical parents	• The first person of the Trinity is father and mother at the same time for Christ and the members of his body	• Divine descent

through incorporation into the body of Christ; (2) The saints in heaven and in purgatory who through belonging to the body of Christ are brother-ancestors of the African Christians; (3) Jesus Christ, the brother-ancestor; and finally (4), God himself, as the parent-ancestor of the human race.

Although as a rule the natural relationship between the African ancestors and their earthly relatives is based on parenthood, for his ancestor christology Nyamiti takes the sibling relationship, which he concedes to be rarer. Jesus Christ is the brother-ancestor of human beings.

> A brother-ancestor is a relative of a person with whom he has a common parent, and of whom he is mediator to God, archetype of behaviour and with whom – thanks to his supernatural status acquired through death – he is entitled to have regular sacred communication. (23)

Nyamiti sees a structural affinity in this relationship between the African brother-ancestor and his earthly relatives to that between Jesus Christ and the members of his earthly body. However, these relationships are on different levels. 'Christ's Brotherhood is revealed as the divine exemplar of its African counterpart' (23). The abiding difference is grounded in the unity of God and man in Jesus Christ and his mediation in salvation. The natural affinity through a common descent from Adam is transcended by the God-manhood of Jesus Christ. But at the same time that means that in fact Christ is the brother-ancestor of men and women only when these are in a state of habitual grace attained through adoption (17, 24, 30). Thus the natural kinship which is characteristic of the African conception of ancestors is *de facto* transcended and done away with at a higher level. It is the same with the second characteristic mentioned at the beginning, the attaining of the supernatural status of ancestors through death. 'Viewed from the angle of His divinity, Christ's Ancestorship appears as one with His eternal, immanent Descendancy' (25). Regarded from the perspective of his humanity, his status as ancestor grows with the incarnation (27). Thus the title ancestor to some degree becomes a synonym for divine sonship and incarnation. All that is left of the African conception of ancestor is the name. In this connection Nyamiti also speaks of 'the analogy of proportion so as to identify it [the African category of ancestor] formally with Christ'.[6]

Despite assertions to the contrary, Nyamiti's dogmatic remarks which follow the construction of an analogy between Jesus Christ and African brother-ancestor are substantially independent of the title ancestor. This remains 'formal translation' at one point. It seems to me to be questionable whether Nyamiti's 'ancestor christology' can be described at all adequately with the categories of accommodation and inculturation. The African notion of ancestors and the gospel do not enter into an inner dialogue, nor does he give the latter even an African garb.[7]

2. Jesus Christ the proto-ancestor (Bénézet Bujo)[8]

As we have seen, Bujo is basically a moral theologian. He seeks to ground his African ethics in an ancestor christology. As distinct from other schemes, Bujo designates Jesus Christ the *proto*-ancestor. This is meant to emphasize the difference from the African ancestors. In this connection he also speaks of the need for a 'cleansing of culture' (297). He is well aware of the 'negative sides of pre-Christian religion – views, customs and usages – which are incompatible with the Christian message' (ibid.).[9] In the specific case of ancestor theology, that means that only the good ancestors can be considered for a Christian veneration of ancestors. Whereas these are incorporated into the body of Christ, the evil ancestors are 'conquered through the Logos of the cross and the resurrection and put in chains' (301). No one need fear them any longer. But already in traditional religion the good ancestors have served as an ethical example or model.[10] By retelling 'the gestures, rites and words which were characteristic of the ancestors, a living remembrance of these . . . is aroused' (295f.). Belief in ancestors links the modes of time – past, present and future – in which the communion of the living with their dead exists. Life flows from God through the ancestors to those who live now and is handed on by these to the coming generations.

If Nyamiti's thinking is strongly stamped by neoscholasticism, in Bujo the influence of the new political theology of J. B. Metz[11]

can be noted. With recourse to his concept of a narrative theology, Bujo speaks of a *memorative-narrative soteriology* which,
in his view, can be based on belief in ancestors.

If Jesus Christ is Proto-Ancestor, source of life and happiness,
our task is to bring to realization in our lives the memory of his
passion, death and resurrection, making of that Saving Event
the criterion for judging all human conduct.[12]

In the last resort Bujo argues in terms of a theology of
fulfilment when he postulates 'that Jesus did not only realize the
authentic ideal of the God-fearing African ancestors, but also
infinitely transcended that ideal and brought it to new com-
pletion'.[13]

Bujo thinks that he can find help for his theological argument
in Christ's descent into hell,[14] as this is attested in the Apostles'
Creed. As early as 1960 Bengt Sundkler[15] quotes the essay of a
Zulu theological student in which he says that the missionaries
'missed the open gate for Christianisation' when they did not
connect the preaching of the death and descent of Jesus Christ
with African belief in ancestors. Bujo seeks the origin of this
doctrine of the descent into hell, which exegetically stands on
feet of clay, in the 'mission theology' of the church fathers. The
biblical basis is essentially I Peter (3.19f.; 4.6).

In the early church, as soon as it began a mission to whole
pagan peoples, there was no lack of voices who understood the
biblical text mentioned in the sense of the liberation of the
righteous who lived before Christ.[16]

As key witnesses Bujo refers to Clement of Alexandria and
Origen.[17]

Bujo's pressing interest is in the formulation of a negro-
African-christocentric morality;[18] his ancestor christology remains incidental. The good ancestors are incorporated into the
body of Christ. Jesus Christ as the proto-ancestor is the criterion
for the church and for African society.

Nevertheless Bujo shows himself to be more aware of the
problem than many of the authors reported on so far. (1) The

neologism 'proto-ancestor' already signals the discontinuity from the traditional ancestors. Bujo clearly works out the revaluation needed in the transference of the title ancestor to Jesus Christ. (2) To the latent vitalism he opposes Jesus' concern for the sick and weak, the poor and oppressed.[19] (3) Whereas exponents of African theology have repeatedly expressed unusually sharp criticism of black theology,[20] in his account of African theology Bujo argues for a 'new synthesis' between the two streams of tradition in contextual theology.[21] In so doing he meets the demands of the South African liberation theologians, who understand themselves to be part of African theology.

Let us return once again to our starting point, Mbiti's clear-sighted perspectives of 1967. Essentially developments have proved him right. At the centre of African theology stands the *Christus victor*. Where the cross really comes into focus, it appears as a place of glorification.

> The Africans do *not* explain the significance of the cross primarily as the sacrificial action of Christ. For them the cross, in so far as it relates to the human life of Jesus, is not a sign of shame and humiliation, but a symbol of perfection.[22]

This *theologia gloriae* is challenged when the suffering of the Africans from their socio-economic and political conditions becomes a theme. It happens if Christ is depicted as, say, a healer, and particularly in the black theology of South Africa, which proclaims Christ as the liberator in a comprehensive sense. We shall pick up these threads again in a later chapter. In the following sections, however, we shall first be concerned to trace out parallel thought structures to African theology in the Asian theologies of inculturation and dialogue.

C. 'I and the Father are one'
Christology in the Context of the
Pluralism of Asian Cultures and Religions

Creation of sun and moon; batik (Nyoman Darsane, Indonesia)

The artist portrays Christ as the mediator at creation, who dances before the Father. Nyoman Darsane, who in his youth was brought up as a Hindu together with a Balinese prince, here draws iconographically on the world of Hindu images. Shiva, the cosmic dancer, is at the same time creator, sustainer and destroyer of the universe; he can keep people in ignorance or lead them to knowledge. Depictions of this dancing god are omnipresent in Hindu art. Darsane has been stimulated by the notion of danced creation. However, the ambivalence of the figure of Shiva, who is creator and destroyer in one, does not fit his image of Christ.

As if at play, the dancing Christ lets the bright ball of the sun glide from his left hand. Spellbound, he looks directly into the source of life. In his right hand the sickle of the waxing moon is already extracting itself from a lump of earth. The dancing figure is swinging with his whole body, on the verge of throwing the moon up high. There is no gravity in this movement – it is of great vigour. His white garment of light, a simple loincloth, and his hair blow in the breath of the Spirit. Everything is bathed in the gliding ray of the sun, which makes God's light radiate over his creation.

§7 Christology in the Context of Hinduism

M. M. Thomas and Stanley Samartha (India)

1. Theological existence in the new India

With M. M. Thomas (1916–1996) and Stanley J. Samartha (born 1920), we turn to the two grand old men of Indian theology. Their theological biographies are equally closely bound up with the efforts of Christianity towards emancipation in post-colonial India and the ecumenical movement.

Madathilparampil Mammen Thomas[1] was born in Travancore in 1916. His father was a junior employee, his mother a teacher. His family belonged to the Syrian Mar Thoma church.[2] Brought up in this tradition of piety, the son was involved early in the life of the church, following the example of his parents. During his college training in Trivandrum (1931–1935), as well as being active in the youth association of the Mar Thoma church he also made his first contact with the Student Christian Movement (SCM). After a degree in chemistry (1935) he first worked for two years as a teacher before he fully devoted himself professionally to church work. At the Christian Institute in Alleppey he became responsible for the subject of liturgy. Interreligious dialogue and social commitment were already linked in the work of this institute under the direction of Sadhu Mathai. After only a year, however, Thomas went back to Trivandrum where, inspired by Sadhu Mathai, he developed a home for street children and co-operated with the urban social work. Although Thomas had arranged his work on an interreligious basis, the state authorities insinuated that he wanted to use it for evangelization. The project finally came to grief because of this.

In the following years Thomas worked in varying spheres of responsibility in Christian youth and student work, interrupted by a year's study leave in Bangalore (1941/42). On the prompting of the pastor R. R. Keithahn, who was a follower of Gandhi, he studied the relationship between Christianity and Communism in the context of Indian nationalism. His decision which resulted from this, to join the Communist party and at the same time to be ordained, was rejected by both bodies concerned, though for opposite reasons. Thomas had thus to some degree put himself between all the stools. However, in 1945 the church government appointed him the first professional youth secretary of the Mar Thoma church. Only two years later he was promoted to Asia Secretary and in 1949 also Deputy Chairman of the World Student Christian Federation (WSCF, 1947–1953); his international career was beginning. For Thomas, however, this meant a temporary separation from his wife Pennamma, who remained behind in India with their new-born son. Endowed with a WCC scholarship, in 1954 the lay theologian Thomas spent a sabbatical year at Union Theological Seminary in New York, where he devoted himself primarily to the study of social ethics with Reinhold Niebuhr, Paul Tillich and John C. Bennett, his supervisor there.

His Geneva colleagues and sponsors hoped that after his academic year he would be available for new tasks in the ecumenical movement. However, Thomas decided to return to India. Although there was no specific offer and he had to spend some years in a variety of jobs, he nevertheless did not want to alienate himself too much from his context. His focal points continued to be the problems of rapid social change and the social revolution, as well as the question of Christian participation in the process of nation-building. In spring 1957 the Christian Institute for the Study of Religion and Society (CISRS) was founded, an amalgamation of various programmes of the National Council of Churches. Paul D. Devanandan (1901–1962)[3] became its first director (1956–1962) and Thomas his associate director. He was also to be the editor of the newly-founded journal *Religion and Society*.[4] The two central themes of Indian theology came together in the aims of the institute: the role of the Christian churches in the process of nation-building and dialogue with the newly awakened religions, especially the Hindu Renaissance. Previously more interested in questions of social ethics and politics, under the influence of the dialogue theologian Devanandan Thomas quickly gave up his initial scepticism towards this combination. This is indicated not least by his important book on the christological attempts of the neo-Hindu reform thinkers (1969).[5] Without necessarily considering a transition to Christianity, here a whole series of Hindu intellectuals had grappled with the person of Jesus Christ. This was a phenomenon to which Samartha devoted a book almost at the same time as Thomas.[6]

The CISRS, of which Thomas was made director (1962–1975) after Devanandan's death, became the basis for his manifold ecumenical commitment, which culminated in his election as chairman of the Central Committee of the World Council of Churches for the period 1968–1975. In 1990 Thomas again made himself talked about when at an advanced age he was appointed governor of Nagaland, a province with a large proportion of Christians among the tribal population (Adivasi). However, this was a position which he was to occupy for only a short time because of the political tensions.

Stanley Jedidiah Samartha[7] was born in 1920, the oldest son of a Christian family closely connected with the Basel mission, in the village of Karkal in the Kanara district (present-day Karnataka). His father Lucas Jonathan Samartha (1891–1959) spent his childhood in an orphanage of the Basel mission, studied at its theological seminary in Mangalore and then spent his life in various posts as an evangelist, headmaster of an elementary school, pastor, and finally head of the orphanage in which he had grown up. Stanley's mother Sahadesi (1901–1982) worked as a primary school teacher. Stanley first went to the senior school of the Basel Mission (1933–1937), then had a four-year college training (1937–1941) and began his theological studies at UTC in Bangalore (1941–1945). Like M. M. Thomas, whom moreover he met for the first time in this connection, Samartha also came early into contact with the Student Christian Movement. In 1940 he was elected SCM Secretary for Mangalore:

It may be that it was the SCM which taught me very early that Christian life can be lived pluralistically, even as the religious life in our country has always been pluralistic, both in vision and reality.[8]

Samartha went on to be assistant pastor in Udipi, a famous Hindu pilgrimage centre (1945–1947). He taught Bible at the senior school of the Basel Mission. Here he also met his wife Edna Iris Furtado, whom he married in 1947. There were three children of the marriage. In 1947 Samartha was appointed lecturer at the seminary of the Basel Mission in Mangalore. Behind the scenes he was one of the driving forces in its affiliation with Serampore University.

Through the support of P. D. Devanandan, his former teacher at UTC, who at this time was visiting professor at Union Theological Seminary, New York (1947/48), Samartha was given a scholarship for the USA (1949–1952). He studied at Union with Paul Tillich and Reinhold Niebuhr. After taking his MA with a work on the Hindu view of history in Radhakrishnan (1950),[9] which was supervised by Tillich, Samartha got a scholarship from the Hartford Seminary Foundation where he enrolled for the doctoral course. At the invitation of the Basel Mission he was able to study for another six months in Basel, among others with Karl Barth and Oscar Cullmann. Here Samartha also met Hendrik Kraemer, who at that time was Director of the Ecumenical Institute in Bossey. After three years of intensive studies, in 1952 Samartha returned to Mangalore as rector of the Theological Seminary. In 1958 he presented his doctoral thesis on the view of history in Hinduism.[10] There followed a call to the UTC in Bangalore (1960–1966), to the chair of P. D. Devanandan, who also consulted him as advisor to the neighbouring CISRS. In retrospect Samartha sees his time as director of Serampore College (1966–1968) more as an inter-mediary stage.

At the WCC Kandy Consultation on Dialogue with People of Other Faiths (1967), Victor E. W. Hayward, the Secretary of the Division for Mission and Evangelism, took note of Samartha. The next year he brought him to Geneva as Associate Secretary. He was to give new impulses to the work on the WCC study 'The

Word of God and the Living Faiths of Man',[11] which had got stuck. Under his aegis this developed into the dialogue programme which in 1971 was established as a separate sub-unit,[12] with him as the first Director. Together with the chairman of the newly-founded division, Hans Jochen Margull, Professor of Mission and Ecumenics in Hamburg, Samartha played an important part in the formulation of the 'Guidelines on Dialogue with People of Living Faiths and Ideologies', which was accepted by the Central Committee in 1979 after long struggles. This is still the position of the WCC on problems of dialogue.[13] The theme of his life, dialogue with other religions, did not let go of Samartha even after his return to India. He continued to speak as visiting professor at UTC and adviser to CISRS.

M. M. Thomas has always criticized in his alter ego the neglect of the addition '. . . and ideologies' in the name of the dialogue division, here at the same time a cipher for the socio-economic and political dimensions of the context.[14] Conversely, for Samartha Thomas has not gone far enough in questions of interreligious dialogue. However, whereas Thomas became open to the dialogue with Hinduism, at the bottom of his heart Stanley Samartha, has always been a dialogue theologian, even if he concedes the justification for social questions. To take it positively, their theological contributions are to some degree complementary; each is in his own way a 'disciple' of Devanandan, who sponsored them both. Invitations to guest lectures and visiting professorships both at home and abroad and the award of honorary doctorates[15] attest the international recognition of the two founding figures of Indian theology after independence.

2. Christ-centred humanism and syncretism (M. M. Thomas)

From the very beginning of his theological thinking, M. M. Thomas was less concerned with the material formulation of a genuinely Indian christology than with a Christian transformation of the pluralism in the 'universe of faiths'[16] and the 'secular ideologies'[17] of India. He was ready 'to risk Christ for Christ's sake', to quote the provocative title of one of his last books.[18]

He felt personally fortified for this in his faith in the cross and resurrection of Jesus Christ.[19] As in the liberation theologies, for Thomas salvation history and the history of the world are one.[20]

> The Cross, or the self-emptying redemptive love of God revealed in Jesus, has been the central dynamic of all history.[21]

However, for Thomas the cross is not just the motive force of history but at the same time also the hermeneutical key for disclosing the action of Jesus Christ in history.

> Christ makes use of worldly and non-worldly forces for this purpose. The notion that Christ is at work only in the church and Christians is foolish and nonsensical. But it is the church and the Christians who can recognize Christ in the efforts and events of our time.[22]

In a theology-of-history scheme Thomas incorporates the cross into the span of 'creation, fall and redemption'.[23] From here it would have been only a short step to give theological support to this view of history with the mediation of Jesus Christ at creation and thus to develop a cosmic christology. Following the Third General Assembly of the WCC in New Delhi in 1961, the doctrine of the cosmic Christ was prominent in ecumenical discussion, stimulated by a lecture by Joseph Sittler, a systematic theologian from Chicago. However, Thomas touches on this theme in his keynote address given in New Delhi[24] only in passing and does not go back to it later. The christological argument in his New Delhi lecture is correspondingly brief. First of all he states 'that the gospel of Jesus Christ should not be identified with any particular culture, political order, social ideology or moral system'.[25] Thomas explains why he nevertheless seeks traces of God's action in history by referring to the universal efficacy of Jesus Christ for salvation, which is 'social and cosmic', and the resultant doctrine of the kingly rule of Christ. Evidently he sees no need for a further substantive elaboration.

Although in his lecture Thomas himself alludes to the misuse of conceptions from the theology of history in the Third Reich and dissociates himself from them,[26] he was sharply attacked by

Hans Heinrich Wolf who associated him with the German Christians.[27] In the face of such 'neo-orthodox nervousness'[28] on the part of his critics, Thomas appeals to Barth himself.

Strange as it may seem, the dialectical theology of Karl Barth, Emil Brunner and Hendrik Kraemer, which emphasizes the transcendence of the Word and Deed of God in Jesus Christ over all religions and quasi-religions of mankind, has provided the basis for a radical relativization of all religions including Christianity and also of Atheism; and its understanding of Jesus Christ as the humanism of God rejecting and electing all mankind in Jesus Christ points to a transcendent power which can renew them all.[29]

With his belief in the possibility of transforming cultures and religions christologically, Thomas is close to H. R. Niebuhr. Christ permeates the cultures and religions and through this at the same time makes them capable of linking up with christological discourse:

Today we recognize universally the possibility and even the necessity of Jesus Christ taking form in different cultures and re-forming them from within. That is, we have come to see Christ as transcending the culture of Western Christendom and able to relate Himself creatively to other cultures. Since cultures are traditionally moulded inwardly by the spirit of their respective religions, the idea of Christ's transcendence has to be extended to include religions . . . Herein we are acknowledging the theological validity of attempts at expressing the meaning of the cross in terms of the indigenous religious traditions other than Christian, and in that process renewing the indigenous traditions themselves to become the vehicle of Christ.[30]

Accordingly, for Thomas christology is at the same time both the inner structural principle and the criterion of history. Thomas's programmatic article about Christ-centred humanism and syncretism, which I shall now analyse more closely, is to be read against this background.[31]

Thomas wants to use the formulation 'Christ-centred' to replace the controversial term 'absoluteness of Christianity', which is in constant danger of taking to an absurd degree any conceptions of the world or creation and human history.

> We can then speak of other realities of the world and life as real as they are centred in Jesus Christ. Even various apprehensions of the totality of the world and life, i.e. religious and secular faith, need not be denied validity so long as they can be redefined or transformed in the light of the centrality of Christ. (387)

Thomas gives a theological foundation to his commitment to the overcoming of socio-economic and political problems in a 'Christ-centred humanism' (391).[32] In parallel to this, in respect of the cultural-religious dimension he argues for a 'Christ-centred syncretism' (387, etc.).[33] This last combination of words implies a rehabilitation of the term syncretism, with its negative connotations; he wants it to be understood neutrally in terms of the phenomenology of religion. Thomas refers to H. Kraemer's classic book *The Christian Message in the Non-Christian World*.[34] Written in preparation for the World Missionary Conference in Tambaram in 1938, this book has exercised a persistent influence on the debate so far. Granted, Kraemer defined syncretism as an 'illegitimate mingling of different religious elements' (389), but originally used the term as the opposite of 'adaptation'. By adaptation he describes the translation processes which he also recognizes to be necessary in contexts that are stamped by the non-Christian religions. Kraemer explicitly concedes the legitimacy of different 'incarnations' of Christianity.

However, only the negative term syncretism was taken up. Kraemer's insight into the need for processes of adaptation was suppressed by the 'Kraemerism' of his successors. Thomas understands the 'Christ-centred syncretism' which he propagates decidedly as a 'post-Kraemer theology of inter-religous relations' (388). Here he allows himself to be guided by his specifically Indian experience. The Christian involvement in the process of nation-building led to co-operation with people and groups of other religious traditions in the socio-economic and political sector. And as we have seen, Neo-Hinduism had already opened itself to Christianity. Its form is to be described as 'more elliptical, with two foci in tension, rather than circular with one centre' (391). In the descriptions of the Christ of the Hindu Renaissance Thomas has sketched out in exemplary fashion the *Sitz im Leben* of Christ-centred syncretism. Accordingly, he sees 'all religions and cultures . . . in various stages of disintegration and reintegration' (392). In this context the adaptation of Christianity is an open process. 'Syncretism with a sense of Christian direction is all that we can now realize' (392). Thomas does away with Kraemer's distinction between adaptation and syncretism. For him syncretism means the necessary process of adaptation in a multireligious context. However, the use of the term 'adaptation' is obsolete.[35] Thomas himself emphasizes the dynamic and reciprocity of the processes that he describes:

> The expression 'translation' for the incarnations of Christianity in Asian and African cultures is not an adequate one. There has to be a reciprocity in interaction between the gospel of Christianity and the existential self-understanding of Asian and African cultures for proper incarnation to happen. It is a more creative process than mere 'translation'. (395)

Although Thomas notes such problems, one must take exception to considerable terminological vagueness generally. Adaptation or accommodation, the term I prefer for what is meant, denotes a model for describing the processes which take place in the encounter of gospel and culture. Interreligious dialogue is an open event between the representatives of different religions, whether at the level of so-called living dialogue in the daily communal life of people belonging to different religions or in institutionalized dialogues. Mission is once again to be distinguished fundamentally from this.[36] When Thomas speaks of a 'Christ-centred syncretism as the goal of interfaith dialogue' (387), then for him mission and dialogue are obviously the same thing. Like Karl Rahner with his talk of 'anonymous Christians',[37] Thomas seems to start from the premise that all religions and ideologies are always already centred on Jesus

Christ. He does not develop a material christology. His concern should rather be termed one of fundamental theology, when he seeks to formulate 'the theological criterion and goal of the meeting of Christianity with other religions and secular faiths' (387). Christ-centred syncretism is a hermeneutical concept, not a christological programme.

3. Theocentric christology (Stanley Samartha)

Whereas Thomas remained a convinced inclusivist all his life, today Samartha tends towards the pluralistic theology of religion.[38] In his Utrecht dissertation, Eeuwout Klootwijk has demonstrated that in his theological thinking 'Samartha has moved from a christocentric to a theocentric or Mystery-centred approach to religious pluralism'.[39] Here Samartha was guided by an insight into the impossibility of communicating Christian claims to absoluteness or exclusiveness in the context of the religious pluralism of India.

> In no other country, does the claim for the uniqueness of one particular religious tradition or the assertion of the normativeness of one particular faith over others sound so rude, out of place, and theologically arrogant as in India.[40]

Without wanting to speak of a complete break with the Western theological tradition on the part of Indian theology, Samartha argues for a Christian reception of 'the Hindu response to religious pluralism'.[41]

In his book about the christology of Neo-Hinduism,[42] aiming to sketch the outlines of an Indian christology he showed a clear preference for the advaita philosophy of Shankara.[43] Samartha regards the Upanishads[44] 'as Protestant movements within Hinduism, seeking to liberate the essence of religion from priestly authority on the one hand and outmoded beliefs and practices on the other' (170). In Shankara's interpretation they have developed their greatest clarity, in that he drew 'together God, world and man in a single conception of unity [advaita]' (170).

To legitimate his procedure Samartha refers to the primitive church, which in first crossing a cultural boundary gave expression to its faith 'in terms of Greek philosophical thought' (167). By the adoption of 'the categories of *advaita* in its classical and modern interpretations' (146) in the Hindu Renaissance, Samartha wants to make room for faith in Jesus Christ in Indian pluralism and overcome the traditional claim of Christianity to absoluteness. This basic decision for the advaita as a frame of reference sets the direction for the further course of his thought. Initially he still shows an awareness of the hermeneutical circle: christology and advaita are to be mutual correctives:

> the insights of Christian faith in Jesus Christ as Lord and Saviour would help in recovering the sense of the personal, the historical and the social in the structure of Hindu spirituality. (171)

If Christianity introduces the dimension of the historical to the Hindu world of ideas, the encounter with Hinduism reverses this very historicity through the 'insight into the larger unity of all life' (171).

In his late work *One Christ – Many Religions,*[45] Samartha countered normative exclusivism with the possibility of a *relational distinctiveness* of Jesus Christ.

> It is *relational* because Christ does not remain unrelated to neighbours of other faiths, and *distinctive* because without recognizing the distinctiveness of the great religious traditions as different responses to the Mystery of God, no mutual enrichment is possible. (77)

Corresponding to the doctrine of non-duality (advaita, 108), he opposes addressing Jesus Christ as God (123, etc.). The New Testament authors, he says, never went this far.[46] 'Jesus himself was theocentric' (87) and by analogy Samartha wants to speak of a 'theocentric christology' (86). Certainly there is no christology without a theology, but the opposite is not the case. Other religious traditions also have theologies without necessarily developing a christology. Samartha seeks to ground the unity of reality in the divine mystery and in so doing consistently also dissolves the personal notion of God: 'Mystery lies beyond the theistic/non-theistic debate' (83).

Samartha does not accept the criterion of Christ-centredness propagated by M. M. Thomas. Without following the current Hindu praxis which sets Jesus as the incarnation of a god (avatar) against other avatars, Samartha notes that in the religious pluralism of India there is no avoiding a comparison of Jesus Christ with other 'saviours'. He cites Buddha, Rama and Krishna as examples: 'there can be no credible christology today without trying to understand not only their theological significance, but also their devotional meaning and ethical guidance to millions of people' (125). In conclusion Samartha mentions three points of comparison (130f.), a paraphrase of which I give here:

• In the life and work of each of these three personalities, revelation and liberation stand in a direct connection.
• Exclusivist tendencies are by and large avoided.
• The development from original humanity to later deity takes place over a lengthy span of time and is generally open-ended.

Samartha avoids a direct comparison with Jesus Christ. But this can be supplemented on the basis of his other statements.

• The close connection between revelation and liberation also exists in the case of Jesus Christ (89f.).
• Samartha wants to break up the normative exclusiveness disseminated in Christianity by a critical discussion with the Hindu tradition, which in his estimation is more open in dealing with other religions (76f.).
• He sees virtually the roots of the Christian claim to absoluteness in the veneration of Jesus Christ as God, which in his view cannot be attested explicitly in the Bible (123f.).

But in that case, what comprises the distinctiveness of Jesus Christ for Samartha? His arbitrary interpretation of the incarnation as the self-relativizing of God in history (76) can only issue in a dead end. The communicative and hermeneutical potential which is suggested particularly in the theological pattern of kenosis is unnecessarily given away. God does not relativize himself in the incarnation, but puts himself in relation to the world. At the same time, with God's revelation in Jesus Christ we are given the hermeneutical key to God's action in history. Samartha misses the opportunity of grounding the 'relationality' of Jesus Christ which he propagates in the incarnation, because he misunderstands it as 'relativization'. But the way through cross and resurrection[47] which he also pointed out earlier ends now in a broad field: 'It is therefore within the larger horizon of the activities of the Creator and Redeemer God that the cross and resurrection have to be interpreted. Christology is larger than soteriology, and theology larger than christology' (137)

There is no dispute that christology and the doctrine of creation must be linked. The doctrine of the cosmic Christ with which Samartha initially still sympathized[48] offers good points of contact for this, particularly in the Asian context. In his concern to dissociate himself from christocentrism, however, Samartha is wide of the mark. Whereas earlier[49] he still presented clear reservations about the designation of Christ as avatar,[50] he now states:

The theory of multiple *avatars* seems to be theologically the most accommodating attitude in a pluralistic setting, one that permits recognizing both the Mystery of God and the freedom of people to respond to divine initiatives in different ways at different times. (131)

Despite all assertions to the contrary, christology slips between his fingers. What is left is Jesus of Nazareth as one avatar along-side others. Whereas in M. M. Thomas the christology to some degree becomes a hermeneutical instrument for preserving Christian identity in the pluralism of Asian religions, in Samartha it dissolves in the hermeneutical field of reference which he has chosen, the advaita philosophy of Shankara.

§ 8 Christology in the Context of Buddhism

Katsumi Takizawa and Seiichi Yagi (Japan)

1. Conversions on the boundary of Buddhism and Christianity

In age, a generation lies between Katsumi Takizawa (1909–1984) and Seiichi Yagi (born 1932). Moreover in a way they stand in a teacher-pupil relationship. However, in their theological existence they both still belong to the same generation, conditioned by the circumstances of the time. The older one was born on 8 March 1909 in Utsunomiya near Tokyo, the sixth child of the lacquer-ware merchant Saichi Takizawa. He had two brothers and three sisters. His parents came from a mountain village in the central region of Honshu, the main island of Japan. Originally Zen Buddhists, later they turned to the nationalistic Hokkeshu sect.[1] Seiichi Yagi was born in a Christian family in Yokohama in 1932. His father belonged to the circle around Kenzo Uchimura (1861–1930).[2]

Having first enrolled in the faculty of law at Tokyo University (in 1927), following his father's wishes, a year later Takizawa changed to the imperial Kyushu University in Fukuoka, to study philosophy far from the distractions of the capital. He himself describes how already at the age of twelve he was struck by the question of human existence:

When I was still very young, around twelve years old, I saw on the way back from my school, which was in the country far away from our city, an old peasant treading a little water mill with bare feet to wash the potatoes in it. It was a hot afternoon, as it always is with us in the late summer. And it was a countryside which was familiar to me. Nevertheless suddenly a strange notion came to me: why in the end that old man was going on with his work. The sun shone brightly and the way home was there as usual. Nevertheless it was as if I had been transposed – I did not know how – into the deep unknown forest, surrounded by thick cloud, and was all alone there. Soon I continued my way home. I did not mean to keep the strange moment in my mind for long. But its echo did not disappear; it became ever greater, until I could no longer get rid of the question: Where am I really? Where have I come from? Where will I finally go?

After that, life so to speak lost its reality and its meaning for me. I could no longer work without secretly having the feeling of making an aimless effort. When I spoke to my friends it was always as if I was separated from them by thick glass.[3]

His legal studies had not been able to give him an answer. On the contrary, the lack of concern with which his professors thought that they could get by without any reflection on the foundations of their legal theory irritated him extremely.[4] But initially the study of philosophy, too, primarily of German origin, proved unsatisfactory. It was only his encounter with the writings of Kitaro Nishida (1870–1945) which brought about a change.

They were written in an unspeakably refined style, but with a strictly logical terminology. However, to my dismay I could not understand a line of them . . . So after my final examination I concentrated on the works of Nishida. It was very difficult, and sometimes I got through only two pages a day. I learned almost by heart on which page of which book this or that word or expression stood. After eighteen months of almost stifling reflection, one day a point suddenly dawned on me to which all Nishida's laborious thinking and unprecedented remarks related . . .

The oppressive dividing wall which had tormented me more and more since that strange experience, cutting me off from all realities, suddenly disappeared. With unspeakable joy I felt that I was on firm ground, where only childlike play was allowed me and asked of me; despite the difficulties which were such an effort, this would basically always be congenial and interesting for me. That a man is only a man and remains so, that I have nothing special in which I could boast above others, that I myself cannot determine where I come from or where I am going, all this has no longer tormented me since then, but rather freed me to do my best in whatever given situation.[5]

Just after graduating, Takizawa summed up his insights in an article which as a result of the support of his professor was published. Something quite unusual in Japan happened. Nishida, at the height of his career, wrote a letter of acknowledgment to the young scholar; he felt that Takizawa had understood him. Takizawa, who was preparing to study in Germany on a Humboldt scholarship, then visited the revered master in Kamakura. On being asked for advice, the Buddhist philosopher surprisingly recommended that he should study with the theologian Karl Barth:

He replied to me: 'Today it is better to study with theologians than with philosophers, as the former are far more interesting than the latter. For the moment something needed in truth, namely God, is lacking even in Heidegger. So it is best for you to go to Karl Barth, who is also the firmest of the theologians.'[6]

While Takizawa had already started his academic career in the final phase of the Second World War, Yagi took up his study of philosophy at Tokyo University after the end of the war (in 1950). Reading Kierkegaard's *The Sickness unto Death* led him deliberately to turn to Christianity.

It was as if I had seen myself in the mirror, in a mirror which visibly showed the invisible in me. I found the description of despair and pride in the book apt. After that I fell sick. In bed I continued to read Kierkegaard. So I first had time to concern myself seriously with Christianity, although I had already been baptized at school. In bed I also learned Greek and read the

New Testament in the original. I read it from Matthew 1.1 on. When I got to Romans, the word of the apostle spoke to me: 'For we hold that man is justified by faith without works of the law' (Rom. 3.28). Through this word I believed in Jesus Christ, who was nailed to the cross for our sin and rose. With this faith I also adopted all the premises and conclusions of faith, from the creation to the eschatological advent of the kingdom of heaven. So I became a Christian of orthodox Protestant belief.[7]

Yagi's study of the New Testament did not let him go again. After completing his MA course he enrolled for a doctorate, but first went to Germany to prepare for that.

Takizawa and Yagi both intensified their studies in Germany, Takizawa as a Humboldt scholar between 1933 and 1935 in the initial years of the Third Reich, Yagi in 1958/59 in the Federal Republic, when it was still young. On the advice of his Buddhist mentor Nishida, Takizawa went to Bonn to hear Karl Barth. After Karl Barth was driven out, he then changed to Rudolf Bultmann in Marburg Yagi studied historical-critical exegesis with Ernst Käsemann in Göttingen. But he too grappled intensively with the theology of Bultmann. For both, their stay in Germany marked a decisive shift in their theological thinking. Takizawa thought that in Barth he had found a thinker congenial to his Japanese teacher Nishida:

In the great lecture hall in which almost 500 students were gathered, I took a place right at the front, in the fifth row and immediately before the desk, so that I did not miss a word of the teacher. Around me there were perhaps 20 students from Switzerland. When Professor Barth entered, around ten SA students got up with a jingling of spurs and shouted out 'Heil Hitler!' Karl Barth stood rock-steady like an oak behind the desk, prayed briefly, and sang some verses from the hymn book with the students. Then he began to lecture. The topic this semester was 'The Virgin Birth'. I listened as though I had become an ear, body and soul. I do not know what happened to me, but an unspeakable joy filled me. Nowhere else, in no philosophical lecture room or seminar, did I feel so free as I did here. Despite my ignorance and my linguistic difficulties his explanation of the creed, 'conceived by the Holy Spirit, born of the virgin Mary', was not wholly alien to me, but as clear and familiar as if it were going directly to me and my very soul.[8]

By contrast, Yagi in Germany, time and again asked about Buddhism by his fellow students, as a result came up against the world of religious ideas in his Japanese homeland which had hitherto remained alien to him. By his own confession, his inability to understand them provoked an existential crisis in him. On the occasion of a visit to Wilhelm Gundert (1880–1971),[9] the missionary to Japan and later professor of Japanology in Hamburg, who was living as an Emeritus in Ulm, gave him an offprint of the German translation of the *Bi-Yän-Lu*,[10] a classic Zen text, which he had edited. During his time in Japan Gundert had been in contact with Uchimura's No-Church Movement and in this environment had got to know Yagi's father. Yagi describes his reading of the text as an awakening (*satori*) in the Buddhist sense.

I read the text in the express train to Göttingen. Fortunately the train was empty; I could sit by myself in a corner and steep myself in reading undisturbed. I read it with such zeal and such concentration that finally I grew tired. Exhausted and relaxed, I looked at the country scene near Kassel; the rain had just stopped and the clouds were breaking up. The rift in the clouds expanded so that blue sky became visible. Then suddenly the saying flashed through my mind: 'Open expanse – nothing holy.'[11] I got up and looked around. Something had happened to me which I could not immediately understand. All the things that I saw looked quite different from before, although they remained the same. The first words I said to myself were: 'I took the tree for the tree. How wrong that was!' What I took to be a tree was in reality only the public concept 'tree'. I first introduced it into the 'object' without being aware of it, and when I saw it, I expounded only what I had put into it beforehand, and I called only that 'knowing an object'. So I was simply recognizing again what I had already long known. But that was no seeing, no encounter with being. However, now I saw the 'tree' as it originally showed itself, before the formation of any concept.[12]

On their return to Japan both took up academic careers. Takizawa first became an assistant at his former university. After an interlude as lecturer in the Merchant College in Yamaguchi (1937–1943) he became a lecturer at his *alma mater,* where from 1947 until his retirement in 1971 he held a chair in philosophy. He had married Toshi Ogasawara, by whom he had four children, in 1932.

Initially Yagi taught New Testament at the Kanto Gakuin University. However, because of controversies over his theological views he left this as early as 1965. He became a professor of German at the Tokyo Technical College (1965–1988) and was active as a theological author with great public success. Only after he had become quite well known for his publications was he also invited by the Christian side to give lectures and teach.

Visiting lectures and lectureships meant that Takizawa and Yagi did not lose contact with German theology. Takizawa became visiting professor at the Kirchliche Hochschule in Berlin (1965/66) and at the universities of Heidelberg (1974), Essen (1975 and 1979) and Mainz (1977). The theological faculty of Heidelberg awarded him an honorary doctorate on his seventy-fifth birthday, but this could be bestowed only posthumously. Yagi taught in Göttingen and Hamburg.

In their biographies Takizawa and Yagi embody almost the ideal intellectual. Whereas Takizawa gained much recognition for his public support of the rebel students of the generation of 1968,[13] Yagi was caught in the cross-fire of left-wing criticism because it was believed that his thought was too elitist and 'here the burning needs of a social and political kind which are shaking Japan and even more the world community can no longer be found'.[14] Both raise the question of the common basis of Buddhism and Christianity. Each in his way here goes in search of structural parallels, against the general trend to demonstrate agreements in content. The younger indeed learns from the older, but at the same time has persistently argued against him. Their scholarly dispute has long since gone down in the history of Japanese theology, which is still young, as the Takizawa-Yagi debate.

2. Christology as the-anthropology (Katsumi Takizawa)

Pupil of two teachers

Kitaro Nishida, whom Takizawa calls his teacher,[15] though he never studied with him, is similarly already a go-between, moving between Eastern and Western thought. Originally appointed Professor of Western Philosophy at the imperial Kyoto University, he became 'the "patriarch" of modern Japanese philosophy'[16] and founder of the so-called Kyoto school. Himself a practising Zen Buddhist, at the same time Takizawa wanted to give expression, with the aid of Western categories of thought, to the truth underlying his Zen experience. However, to describe him as a 'Zen philosopher' implies an intrinsic contradiction, since Zen Buddhism seeks to overcome intellectual reflection and thus the split between subject and object, and to break through to pure or immediate experience.

> They say that Zen forms the background to my thought. That is absolutely correct. . . . Zen is about the authentic grasp of actual reality. Impossible as it may seem, I want to bring this together in some way with philosophy. That has been my dream since my thirties.[17]

In Nishida's doctrine of *absolutely contradictory self-identity*[18] Takizawa finds a first answer to his existential question.[19] Starting from the effort to define the relationship between individual and universal or, to put it in theological terminology, between human beings and God, Nishida arrives at this formula, which sounds paradoxical from the perspective of Western logic.

> At the point of this world where a real person arises and exists, there is always something which is in no way his I-self, but is eternal and lives. The link between this something and a

human I-self, which exists in the beginning, here and now, in the ground of the origin and existence of this I-self, is not a relationship which it produces with other things or people only after it has come into being as a human subject. Rather, the association grasps someone at the point where he stands, as it were right from behind; indeed, it has already grasped him there and will never let him go . . . In biblical faith one may give the name of Yahweh (I am who I am), God the almighty Lord, the Creator and the immeasurably merciful God, to this something which despite and in the absolute difference from this I-self is completely one, and which distinguishes itself absolutely from this I-self precisely in being directly one with this I-self. And in Zen Buddhism one will call the same something 'the true self' or 'the absolutely formless subject', which is directly one with the I-self in the ordinary sense, but at the same time is in no way this I-self.[20]

The paradox that in the primal point of his self the human being is always already identical with God, which is formulated in this way, is the quintessence of Nishida's thought.[21] Takizawa now thinks that he can recognize his master's notion of the *absolutely contradictory self-identity* in Barth's primal fact Immanuel ('God with us').[22] This has remained a constant thorn in the flesh for his theological teacher. Takizawa criticizes in Nishida's conception the fact that in the concept of 'identity' he makes it possible to blur the impossibility of reversing the relationship of God and human beings which was first demonstrated clearly to him by Karl Barth.[23] What he finds fault with in Barth is that he does not know how to distinguish between 'Christ, the eternal son of God', the primal fact Immanuel, and 'Jesus in the flesh'.[24]

Expressed in his own terminology, he (Karl Barth) does not distinguish between the Immanuel in the first sense, who exists in each and every human being completely independent of historically contingent reflections, and the Immanuel in the second sense, as he takes place among us Christians, certainly only through the Holy Spirit, but as a kind of self-determination of our fleshly subject.[25]

Takizawa terms the point of contact between God and any human being which is always already given (Immanuel I) the primary contact. However, it is not the case that human beings are always already aware of this contact. It must first awaken in them, as Takizawa puts it in Buddhist conceptuality. The state of not being awoken can be described in Christian terms as persisting in sin.

> This split, this contradiction in the self which we all bear within ourselves from birth without any of our doing, regardless of whether or not we are aware of it, which from of old in Buddhism has been called 'ignorance' and in Christianity 'sin'.[26]

Awakening is not an autonomous act, but the indwelling of something which is always already given. The secondary contact of God with human beings (Immanuel II) takes place in awakening. In Christian terms, God who always already embraces the human being from behind, in Jesus Christ depicts himself from the front. Christ is the side of God which is turned toward human beings. In this connection Takizawa speaks at an early stage of a *theo-anthropology*.[27] The notion of an atoning death has no place in this conception.

> If that is the case, however, sin can never be eradicated by a human figure, however exalted. That is even true – in Christian teaching – of the figure of Jesus who with his 'atoning death' in no way has exterminated sin itself in this its original sense. Therefore according to Christian teaching even the 'reconciled human being' must come before the 'Last Judgment'.[28]

Consequently Takizawa's whole effort is to produce a synthesis of the thought of his two great teachers. From a Western perspective his fixation on this one point is rather like monomania. In constantly new approaches he attempts to demonstrate the universal foundation of Buddhism and Christianity in the primal fact Immanuel.

Buddhism and Christianity

When Takizawa speaks of Buddhism, he has in view the originally divergent schools of Zen and Jodo-Shin, both of which reached Japan via China and here received their specifically Japanese stamp. The founder of Jodo-Shin is Shinran (1173–1262), himself a pupil of Honen (1133–1212), whose Jodo teaching he to some degree democratized and made accessible to lay people. Anyone who takes refuge in Amida Buddha by pronouncing the formula 'Nembutsu (*Namu-Amidabutsu* = Amen, Amida Buddha)'[29] will attain rebirth in the 'Pure Land' regardless of his moral status. This is made possible by the chief vow of Amida, who vowed to enter Nirvana only when the possibility had been given to all human beings to enter his land by calling on his name.

> If I become Buddha and all human beings who believe in me joyfully with all their heart and with the longing for blessed rebirth call on my name, though only once, and if nevertheless they cannot be born in my land – I will never become Buddha.[30]

Whereas the roots of Amida Buddhism reach back to India itself, Zen (Chinese Ti'an) is regarded as a Chinese creation. It was made native to Japan in its two currents by the monk Eisai (1141–1215) and his pupil Dogen (1200–1253). Both had themselves been instructed in Ti'an in China. Eisai brought to Japan the Rinzai sect, which seeks to encourage sudden enlightenment (*satori*) through contemplation of *koans*.[31] Dogen established the Soto sect, which concentrates exclusively in meditative sitting (*zazen*).

Jodo and Zen Buddhism are generally distinguished by their soteriology. If the effect of the power of the wholly other (Japanese *tariki*) is seen in turning to the Amida Buddha, in Zen there is only the power of the self (Japanese *jiriki*). However, contrary to the tradition and religion as it is lived out, Takizawa puts forward the thesis that the same truth underlies both schools. For the legitimation of this hermeneutical construct he refers to his teacher Nishida and Daisetz Suzuki (1870–1966), probably the best-known Zen thinker in the West, with whom he

had been friends since his schooldays. According to their interpretation, the power of the wholly other is at the same time the
power which brings about the awakening to this very self in the
human self.

> According to Shinran's belief, the power of the Wholly Other
> does not harm the power of its self in any way but forms its
> sole ground and inexhaustible source. Amida's beyond gives
> the person who believes in it the unshakeable courage to 'go
> back' into this world, into the midst of this dark world of
> which he himself is a part, to live with all his power out of
> sheer love for all others.[32]

But then it is also true of Zen Buddhism that this power of the
wholly other is at work in the power of the self. 'The self, which
is all that matters in Dogen, is none other than the wholly other
in this sense.'[33]

Francis Xavier (1506–1552), the co-founder of the Jesuit
order and pioneer of Jesuit missionary activity in Asia, was
already struck by the proximity of Jodo Buddhism to the
Protestant doctrine of justification. On his arrival in Japan
he is said to have remarked, 'The accursed Lutheran heresy is
already there!' Takizawa begins his article on '"Justification" in
Buddhism and in Christianity' with a description of the story of
Hozo-Bosatsu, handed down in the main sutra (Daimuryojukyo)
of Jodo Buddhism. It tells of a king who after a sermon by the
Buddha Sejizai-Obutsu decided himself to attain Buddhahood.
He left home and became homeless, from then on called himself
Hozo-Bosatsu,[34] and sought enlightenment under that Buddha.
But instead of going to Nirvana himself, he pronounced the
vow of the Amida Buddha that we already know. Despite or pre-
cisely because of this vow, Hozo becomes Amida. According to
Takizawa this is not to be understood in the sense of a transformation of any kind, since for him Amida is only a further
designation of the primary contact of God with human beings.

Tradition attributes this story to the historical Buddha
Shakyamuni in the form of a sermon. It reflects the course of his
own life. But in this case a strict distinction is also to be made
between the eternally present Buddha and the mortal man

Shakyamuni. The relationship of Shakyamuni to Buddha is to be understood in analogy to the relationship between Jesus and Christ or Immanuel in Christianity. However, in reversing the sentence 'Hozo became Amida' into 'Amida became Hozo', Takizawa is interpreting it in Christian terms from the perspective of the incarnation. As he himself concedes, this reading has no direct support in the Buddhist scriptures.[35]

So Takizawa undertakes a twofold re-reading of Jodo Buddhism, in that he first describes it in a way shaped by Christian notions and makes tacit use of categories from Zen Buddhism in his comparison with Christianity. The framework of interpretation is formed by his theory of primary and secondary contact, which Takizawa plays through time and again by means of the distinction between Amida and Hozo, the eternally present Buddha and the ordinary man Shakyamuni, both Christ in the first and Christ in the second sense.

Christ in the first and second sense

For Takizawa, by his own confession christology is the central concern: '. . . for me personally it is one of the most important tasks, or rather the one great task, to grasp and depict as clearly as possible with body and soul, with my whole personality, "the person of Jesus Christ".'[36] As we have already seen, for this he takes over Nishida's notion that the contact between God and human beings has always come about at the place in which a person is put.

> In that case it is necessary to distinguish between 'Christ' in a first, original sense and 'Christ' in a second, symbolic sense. Jesus as the 'Christ in the second sense' is *the first Christian, the perfect norm of all Christians.* We must bear his cross together with him. By contrast, 'Christ in the first sense' *is* at the basis of being of the human Jesus, and precedes all his activity, works unceasingly in him and in every human being before he, indeed before Jesus himself, does or says something.[37]

Takizawa describes the relationship between God and man in

Jesus Christ in a way reminiscent of the christology of the early church as being absolutely *inseparable*, but without being *capable of confusion*.[38] With his theological teacher Barth, he designates the point of contact which at the same time marks the boundary between God and man as the primal fact of Immanuel, God with us. The boundary between God and man cannot be crossed and, as Takizawa asserts with Barth[39] against Nishida, the relationship between God and man is *irreversible*.

In Jesus Christ the possibility of secondary contact has become manifest. He is the primal image of the true God-man and in this is the criterion for our own humanity. As such an example[40] Christ is our signpost. But, and here Takizawa turns against his teacher Barth, 'As a sign the figure of Jesus is to be distinguished strictly from the matter itself.'[41] The disciples were already wrong when they saw the primary contact first realized through the person of Jesus.[42]

> By contrast, pure the-anthropology lets itself be helped and guided by the contingent and unique figure of Jesus of Nazareth or the Bible, but never fettered. Rather, it is led precisely by it as the living signpost, turns exclusively to the way, the truth, the Logos in the beginning, to use Barth's term, the primal fact Immanuel, the eternally new, absolutely indivisible, irreversible relationship between God and human beings which cannot be confused. Therefore it cannot, may not and will not contain any specific historical figure as its real content.[43]

For Takizawa, christology is ultimately an expression of this pure the-anthropology, no more but also no less.[44] Here soteriology is to some degree taken back from the second article of faith into the first.

3. The I in Jesus (Seiichi Yagi)

From the New Testament to Zen

In his first major publication *The Origin of New Testament Thinking* (Japanese 1963),[45] Yagi still stood wholly in the tradition of existentialist interpretation. As a foundation for his orientation on the question of the New Testament understanding of human existence, however, he already refers to his encounter with Buddhism.

> His recognition of the Buddhist understanding of existence parallel to the views in Christianity led him to the conviction that the origin of Christian faith, including the Easter faith, is not to be thought of as a supernatural process but has to be followed historically – not simply in terms of the history of religion, but above all existentially.[46]

Very much along the lines of Bultmann's programme of demythologizing, Yagi therefore makes a fundamental distinction between what he calls 'religious psychology', e.g., the miracle stories and the virgin birth, and those texts which are of 'genuinely religious significance'.[47] For the latter he distinguishes between three types or structures of New Testament thinking,[48] which theologically reflect 'the three basic forms of human relationship, namely the we-relationship, the relationship to oneself and the I-Thou relationship' (86).

• Type A is the classical *salvation-historical* theology of Jewish-Christian origin with its central themes of the election of the people of Israel, the old covenant, law and human failure, the atoning death of Christ and the justification of men and women, the new covenant and new people of God, resurrection, last judgement and kingdom of God. At the centre stands the *social nature* of human beings (the 'we-relationship of human beings before God'). The *righteousness* of God becomes the existential category. 'Cross and resurrection' are interpreted in the atoning death of Jesus Christ. In the justification of sinners the existential shift takes place from the old to the new man, which is the basis of freedom from legalism (nomism). The earliest testimony of this trend of thought has been handed down with the use of I Cor. 15.3–5.
• Type B is of Hellenistic origin and can perhaps best be described as *incarnational* theology. Yagi himself gives no name to it. The pre-existent Son of God is the mediator at creation. Sent into the world, he empties himself and becomes flesh. Jesus'

death on the cross is an act of obedience and the consummation of his earthly way. By God he is 'raised, exalted and appointed cosmocrator' (83). 'The cross and resurrection of Jesus Christ are now understood in the sense of the victory over the powers of sin and death.'[49] The believer has died and risen with Christ. He lives in Christ and belongs to the body of Christ. The issue here is essentially the *individuality* of human beings, their 'relationship to themselves'. The existentialist category is 'life'. The existential shift comes about in the freedom from care about existence. Yagi refers to the Philippians hymn (2.6–11) and the Johannine prologue (John 1.1–18).

• Type C is about the *co-humanity* of human beings, the 'I-Thou relationship' as Yagi puts it, referring to Martin Buber.[50] 'Herein has the love of God become manifest to us, that God has sent his Son into the world' (84; cf. John 3.16). Human relations, too, must be shaped in analogy to God's loving relationship to human beings. 'The salvation which has taken place in Christ is here understood as the expression of the love of God for human beings.'[51] Love is the existential category. The existential shift is interpreted as liberation from a 'love shut in on itself'. For example I John 4.7–10 serves Yagi as a reference.

Table 6: Types of New Testament theology (Yagi)

	Type A	Type B	Type C
	Salvation-historical theology	Incarnational theology	Theology of love
Existential setting	Social nature of human beings (we-relationship)	Individuality of human beings (relation to themselves)	Co-humanity of human beings (I-Thou relationship)
Existential category	Righteousness	Life	Love
Existential shift	Freedom from nomism	Freedom from care about existence	Freedom from love shut in upon itself

These three types do not occur in a pure form in the New

Testament but are interwoven in many ways. However, New Testament theology thus proves to be pluralistic. Attempts to force it, say, into the scheme of salvation history do not go far enough (86).[32] Nevertheless they have a common point of reference in 'Christ the risen Lord' (86).

Yagi now also finds the types which have been worked out in the preaching of the earliest community in the preaching of Jesus. He distinguishes between four groups of sayings of Jesus: (1) sayings about the law, (2) sayings about life, (3) sayings about love and (4) sayings about the kingdom of God. If the first three groups correspond to the types of earliest Christian preaching, the sayings about the rule of God are to some degree their point of convergence. 'In Jesus the rule of God is the transcendent determination of how the human being is to be' (88).

The complete focus on human existence had already led Yagi to suspend the question of the reality of God. Under the impact of Takizawa's criticism, however, he undertakes a radical shift in his thinking. He appropriates Takizawa's insight into the grounding of human existence in the primary contact which in his own terminology he designates the human *self*, and consequently turns against Bultmann: 'Unfortunately we fail to find in Bultmann's interpretation the adequate conceptuality for transcendence or the self in our sense, although he had an existentialist orientation.'[53]

Yagi now once again makes a critical examination of the three types of earliest Christian preaching. They relate to the preaching of Jesus in such a way 'that "rule of God" and "Christ the risen Lord" ultimately designate the same thing' (89). Bultmann coined the formula of the 'proclaimed proclaimer' for this. The decisive mistake of earliest Christianity, to which Bultmann has also succumbed, lies in this link between christology and soteriology in the reinterpretation of the Jesus event. The disciples 'identified with Jesus himself the ground of authentic existence which has now appeared to them' (89). However, a distinction has to be made between Christ as the transcendent ground of human existence and the historical Jesus. 'The Godhead and manhood of Christ cannot be separated, but are to be distinguished' (94f.). Yagi sees the really basic obstacle to understanding the New Testament in faith in the saving efficacy of Jesus

Christ. It contradicts the central maxim of Bultmann's hermeneutics: it is not the pre-understanding of the matter which
makes it possible to understand it, but the *immediate experience*
of the matter itself.

Whereas initially Yagi took over the distinction between the
kerygmatic Christ and the historical Jesus from historical-critical
exegesis as he had learned it from his teacher Käsemann, he now
interprets the proclaimed Christ as a misunderstanding of the
first Christians and asks about the self-understanding of Jesus the
proclaimer: 'What is the "I" in Jesus?' This question leads him to
a new interpretation of the sayings about the Son of man and the
antitheses.[54] The sayings, traditionally divided into three groups,
about (1) the coming Son of man, (2) the suffering and rising Son
of man and (3) the Son of man active in the present, had time and
again been the subject of controversies. If the sayings in the
second group are generally seen as *vaticinia ex eventu*, Bultmann
sees those which belong to the third group as simply a translation
mistake:

> In Aramaic, 'the son of man' in these sayings was not a
> messianic title at all, but means 'man' or 'I'. So this group
> drops out of the present discussion.[55]

That leaves only the first group of sayings, which speak of the
coming Son of man in the third person, as a source of possible
original sayings of Jesus. By contrast Yagi thinks that the sayings
about the Son of man active in the present, which speak in the
first person, are also fundamentally authentic.

> With the sayings of the third group, therefore, Jesus declared
> his work and words to be those of the son of man in him . . .
> the son of man is for Jesus both *das ganz Andere* and his ulti-
> mate self. (126)[56]

Yagi here assumes 'that the figure of the son of man as used in the
words of Jesus is the personification of the reign of God' (125).

The consequences of this thinking become clearer in Yagi's
answer to the question of who is really speaking in the antitheses
of the Sermon on the Mount (Matt. 5.21–48).

In the antitheses – really, in the words of Jesus in general –

something divine (the reign of God or the son of man as its personification) spoke through the mouth of his empirical person. (127)

Yagi postulates a double structure of the I.[57] The human *ego*, which in our terminology is constantly threatened with succumbing to egotism, is to be distinguished fundamentally from the self, which corresponds to Takizawa's notion of the Immanuel or the primary contact. If the ego awakens to this self, the self-ego is constituted, as happens in Jesus in an exemplary way. With Takizawa, Yagi can also call this self Christ, or, as in the present case, Son of man.[58] But he emphasizes more strongly than Takizawa has done how the wholly other at the same time stands over against it.

This becomes clear when we turn to Yagi's picture of Paul. Here the half-verse Gal. 2.20 has become central: 'I live, yet now not I, but Christ lives in me', which Zen Buddhists often regard as a kind of Christian *koan*. Yagi also recognizes the double structure of ego and self in Paul's 'I' (Illustration 5).

The relation of Jesus to the Son of Man is the same as the relation of Paul to Christ in him.[59]

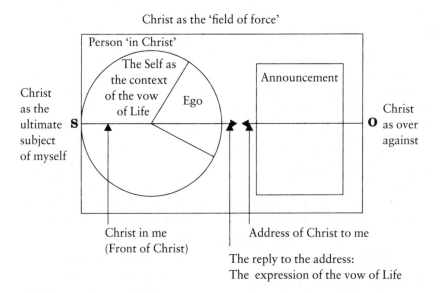

Illustration 5: The Front Structure (Yagi)[60]

In Gal. 2.20 Paul then depicts his awakening to Christ. However, Christ is not only 'in me'; I am also 'in Christ'. 'Christ as the object of faith and Christ as the ultimate subject of the believer are, paradoxically, identical' (118). In Romans 7 he gives a negative description of the state before the awakening as being under or 'in sin' and the working of 'sin in him' (Rom. 7.17).[61]

Referring to the Gospel of John, Yagi can say 'that the relationship between Christ and his believers reflects the relationship between Father and Son' (121). Paul is an example for all believers, 'For all human beings are so constituted, in their very natures, that the divine and the human are at the same time one and two' (122f). This basic assumption about human existence applies equally to Christianity and Buddhism.

Christ and Buddha

Unlike Takizawa, Yagi personalizes the comparison between Christianity and Buddhism.[62] He regards Jesus Christ and Gautama Buddha as founders of a religion 'who, in each situation and tradition, found and realized religious truth common to all humanity' (25). Their teachings become comparable through an analogous understanding of human existence. Both saw this constantly threatened by the arrogance of the ego. Whereas Gautama recognizes the cause of suffering in the absolutizing of the alienated ego, Jesus attacks the absolutizing of the relative in the form of the law as the cause of sin. 'For Gotama (sic), the result of arrogance was pain; for Jesus, it was sin. Pain centers in the self, sin is a matter of personal relations' (28). Accordingly, what is common to the Buddhist and Christian understanding of existence is the openness of the self to transcendence and the constant threat to it posed by a self-absolutizing of the ego. For New Testament thought and the proclamation of Jesus, Yagi demonstrates the differentiation into three basic forms of human relationship. 'By contrast, Buddhist thinking concentrates on the relationship of the human being to himself. Communal or interpersonal relationships are mentioned relatively rarely.'[63] The social character of Christian faith distinguishes it fundamentally from Buddhism, whose urgent interest is 'to clarify the matter of being a self'. Whereas Gautama taught as the highest goal the ultimate entry of the individual into Nirvana, where the individual is extinguished like a candle, Jesus proclaimed the approach of the kingdom of God, where human beings take up their abode with the Father (28f.).

The first followers of Buddha were to be reckoned essentially among the educated upper class; Jesus proclaimed the kingdom of God to the ordinary people (30). Buddha's teaching was philosophically abstract, Jesus' proclamation narrative and concrete (28f.). If after his illumination Buddha could still go through the country for more than thirty years and develop his teaching, the public activity of Jesus was restricted to one up to three years at most. Buddha died at a great age, as the result of food poisoning, in the circle of his disciples; Jesus suffered a violent death on the cross at an early stage, abandoned by all (31). The followers of Buddha were to leave their master behind on their way to enlightenment like a ferry on the other bank of the river, whereas primitive Christianity attributed to Jesus the role of a mediator of salvation. The essential difference between Buddhism and Christianity is in their relationship to their founder figures. Whereas Christians believe in the person of Jesus Christ, the Buddhists base themselves on *dharma*, 'the eternal cosmic law of the world',[64] not on the person of Gautama (31).

Table 7: Christ and Buddha (Yagi)

Teacher (founder of religion)	Gautama Buddha	Jesus Christ
Content of the teaching	Absolutizing of the alienated ego → Suffering ← Dharma/Nirvana	Absolutizing of the relative → Sin ← Kingdom of God
Nature of the teaching	Philosophical	Narrative/historical
Followers	Educated upper class	'ordinary people'
Faith	in Dharma	in Jesus Christ
Duration of teaching activity	Dies in the circle of his disciples; active to a great age	Early, violent death; only about one to three years of public activity

The Front Structure as a bridge from Buddhist to Christian thinking

Altering Descartes' dictum, Yagi's basic assumption can be summed up as 'I exist in relationships, therefore I am'. The starting point of his thought, as we have seen, was the structuring of New Testament thinking by means of the 'three basic forms of human relationship'.[65] Yagi thinks that in the New Testament he has found an understanding of existence analogous to Buddhism. At first he excludes the question of the reality of God. Only on the basis of Takizawa's criticism does he ask 'Must we really speak of God?'[66] Yagi's critical discussion with Takizawa has made him take over the latter's distinction between primary and secondary contact. Unlike Takizawa, however, he does not think of these contacts in terms of points but develops his own theory of the Front Structure, again in a critical discussion with Buddhist thought.[67] Yagi resorts above all to three terms to explain the Buddhist understanding of existence: *sunyata* ('the non-substantiality of all existing beings'), *pratitya samutpada* ('mutual dependence and relatedness'), and *muge* ('in one another without hindrance'). Apparently his translation of this conceptuality is stamped by existential philosophy. *Sunyata* and *pratitya samutpada* ultimately describe the same situation from different perspectives.

> While *Sunyata* negatively means that nothing has a sufficient basis of its being in itself, *Pratitya Samutpada* means positively that one event is dependent on others. One concept is implied in the statement of the other. On the contrary, substance, which is dependent only on itself, excludes both *Sunyata* as well as *Pratitya Samutpada*. Therefore, Buddhist thought recognizes no substance. (146f.)

Accordingly, all being is being-in-relationship. Yagi quotes Martin Buber: 'In the beginning was relationship.' This understanding of existence is the presupposition for being 'in one another without hindrance' (*muge*):

> that which is found outside of me is transformed into a consti-

tutive part of me in that what now belongs to me still continues to remain a part of that which is outside of me. (76)

According to this basic existential assumption, that the being-in-relationship is constitutive of being, Yagi distinguishes between the individual, who is always dependent on relationship, and the existing being, which is first constituted in relationship.

Since the living being cannot exist as an individual for itself alone, it is not an existing being. In order to become an existing being, however, it needs another whose Front it can appropriate to itself (94).

The individual   The existing being

Wall (W)

A   B

Illustrations 6 and 7: The Front Structure (Yagi)

Yagi illustrates this distinction (Illus. 6) with a rectangle open on one side (the individual) and a closed rectangle (the existing being). As a further illustration of what he means, Yagi takes over a picture of the dividing wall (W) between two rooms (A and B), which is shaped by Nishitani Keiji; this wall, belonging to both, depicts the one in the other (a/b) and at the same time constitutes them (Illus. 7). Yagi describes this understanding of existence which is common to Buddhism and Christianity as the Front Structure of all beings. 'The Front is that in which we encounter the other' (77). With his Front the individual combines with another individual; there is a giving and appropriation of Front which is thought of as a reciprocal process and accordingly can also be termed a Front Exchange. At the same time Yagi sees this as the basis of the need for individuality and difference, for there can be no exchange of Front between the same. However, this is not a singular process; the Front Structure hides a great potential for pluralization. Yagi makes this clear once again with the help of his rectangle. Even if a random number of individuals are put side by side, a rectangle always remains open (Illus. 8). Only when the last attaches itself to the first in a circle does a closed circle result (Illus. 9). However, to do justice graphically to the plurality of possible relationships the sphere would be more appropriate (96). But often there are false developments in which the individuals are put in hierarchical strata (Illus. 10).

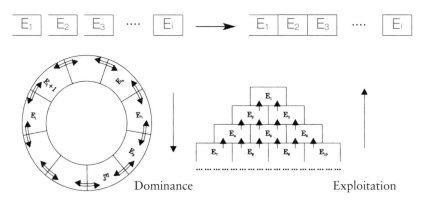

Illustrations 8–10. The Front Structure (Yagi)

Yagi distinguishes three types of Front Structure. Alongside the substantial type, which can be neglected in our context, and in which there is material exchange, there are the wave-type and the field-type. The effect of the sayings of Jesus on those born later can be explained by the wave-type. The Front-Expansion makes it possible that 'the words of Jesus reach us and continue to address us although he himself died 2,000 years ago' (82). But Yagi's christology is developed fully only by the construct of the field-type. Unlike Takizawa, who sees the contact between transcendence and human being realized in a point, Yagi imagines this relationship as a *field of force*.[68] This makes it possible for him to reconstruct the counterpart. I find myself in the field of influence of Christ or, to put it in terms of the tradition, I am 'in Christ', and at the same time Christ is active 'in me'.

4. Interreligious christology as an intellectual borderline experience

The Takizawa-Yagi debate

The external circumstances are quickly told. Takizawa began a review of Yagi's *The Discovery of New Testament Thought* (Japanese 1963), which he expanded into a book of his own entitled *The Biblical Jesus and Modern Thought* (Japanese 1965). Yagi reacted to this with a further book, *The Biblical Christ and Human Existence* (Japanese 1967), which Takizawa thereupon followed with his *Immanuel, The Place of the Origin of Freedom* (Japanese 1969). Despite the ongoing disagreement, Takizawa accepted both of Yagi's books as philosophical dissertations (1967). The two scholars initially continued their debate in the Japanese journal *Gospel and World*.[69] However, they did not reach agreement here. Takizawa criticized Yagi for arguing purely existentially and in terms of the history of ideas, and claiming to remain philosophically neutral.[70] This, he said, leads to indifference over the question of truth or God. 'Yagi does not speak appropriately of transcendence, as is also the case in Bultmann.'[71]

After reading Takizawa's main work *Buddhism and Christianity* (Japanese 1964), which had appeared a year previously, in his second 1967 book Yagi takes over his grounding of human existence in the Immanuel and his distinction between the primary and secondary contact. This adoption represents a complete U-turn in Yagi's thinking. As a result he shapes his own terminology and develops a system. According to Kenzo Tagawa he turns from being an existentialist into an essentialist.[72] However, Takizawa seems never really to have done justice to this shift of Yagi in his argumentation. For his part he takes over the distinction between the historical Jesus and the kerygmatic Christ which is mediated through Yagi, but uses it in the sense of his own thought. The historical Jesus is then the model of the secondary contact which is realized in human beings. The kerygmatic Christ is the great error of the community.

Over against Takizawa's ontological view of the primal fact Immanuel, Yagi emphasizes that the primary contact is only a potential one which is first realized in the secondary contact.

Insofar as the divine does not reveal itself to the ego – that is, insofar as we are not aware of it – this reality is virtually nonexistent and in this sense we are not united with the divine.[73]

Here the conception of immediate experience taken over from Zen Buddhism becomes sharper.

From the beginning Yagi had the impression that Takizawa himself did not know 'immediate experience' and therefore he did not argue from immediate experience but on the basis of the imprecise description of Nishida. But this impression is heightened, the more often and the longer Yagi carried on conversations with Takizawa.[74]

Takizawa and his pupils accused Yagi of putting in question the irreversibility of the primary and secondary contact. Yagi counters this allegation with his field theory. If he reinterprets Christ as the field of activity, we are always already 'in Christ', even if the self-identity of the 'Christ in me' is given only potentially and realized only in the secondary contact which ultimately is none other than the direct experience of the primary contact.[75] Christ as the counterpart of the human has always remained alien to Takizawa. But Yagi, too, explicitly maintains the distinction between Christ in the first and second senses. What he means is likewise the side of God turned to human beings.

Interreligious christology

Werner Kohler, himself a pupil of Barth, who as a missionary in Japan has relied deeply on Takizawa's thinking in his theology,[76] calls him a 'Buddhist who is a Christian'.[77] Kohler's Mainz assistant Ulrich Schoen, in his habilitation thesis, has coined the term *'interreligious existence'*[78] for this state of affairs. But these characterizations do not get to the heart of the problem. In Takizawa and Yagi intellectual religion rather than lived religion is in the foreground. With their reflections they adopt a standpoint outside the two religions and in so doing construct a meta-religion.[79] Contrary to the maxims of his teacher Barth that only 'the Christian religion is the true religion',[80] for Takizawa the primal fact Immanuel is the common ground for Buddhism and Christianity. 'To confuse religion with the ground of religion is ruled out.'[81] Yagi has taken over this approach of Takizawa. However, whereas Takizawa has vehemently resisted the designation philosopher of religion,[82] Yagi calls the philosophy of religion his third area of work alongside the New Testament and dialogue with Buddhism.[83] Both are concerned to deabsolutize Christianity. Their common starting point is christology. If christology and soteriology are radically separated and the latter is taken back into the first article of faith, the doctrine of God,[84] what is left is first of all a christology of the primal image or model. At the same time there is an immense revaluation of anthropology. That human beings are created in the image of God is here ultimately interpreted in such a way that God represents himself in any human being.

§9 Christology in the Overall Asian Context

Kosuke Koyama and Choan-Seng Song

1. Telling the stories of the gospel in Asia

Kosuke Koyama and Choan-Seng Song fall somewhat out of the framework of our gallery of contextual theologians. Theologically, they go beyond the context of their homelands and address the whole horizon of Asia. Moreover they have spent a good part of their lives, initially as students and then later as ecumenical officers and theological teachers, abroad in the West. Unlike the specific theologies of dialogue presented in the two previous sections, Koyama and Song represent the whole spectrum of the theology of inculturation.

Kosuke Koyama[1] was born in 1929, the son of a Christian family in Tokyo. His grandfather on his father's side had been converted from Buddhism to Christianity under the influence of the British lay theologian Herbert George Brand (1865–1942), who carried on a mission in Japan and Korea on his own initiative (1888–1921). The respect which this man showed to Japanese culture and Buddhism had convinced Koyama's grandfather of his message of the gospel. Koyama's theological account of himself in *Mount Fuji and Mount Sinai*[2] is dedicated to Brand's memory. His father, utterly impoverished by the great earthquake of 1923 and with acute inflammation of the lungs, was admitted into a benevolent Buddhist hospital, where he succumbed to the consequence of his illness. He died when Kosuke was five years old. Unlike many new converts who completely deny their own culture under the influence of the Western missionaries, on the basis of his family history as a Christian in the third generation Koyama had a quite open attitude to his cultural heritage. However, in the heated mood of the time his baptism in 1942, in the middle of the war, was regarded as a confession to the enemy's religion.[3] Despite repeated servile addresses on the part of the church government, the Christian minority (around 1 per cent) was regarded with scorn by the government.

The defeat of Japan in the Second World War which Koyama consciously experienced as a sixteen-year-old in bombed-out Tokyo left a lasting impression on him. He speaks of it repeatedly:

> It was 25 May 1945. All night Tokyo was bombed by the American B29s. Our tiny wooden house was reduced to ashes together with the whole of Tokyo.[4]

> The night . . . began with an ominous silence, but by midnight our section of Tokyo became a sea of fire as the fire-bombs rained upon it. The raids continued until early morning. I was alone, running from one shelter to another. I heard the screech of a bomb coming towards me. In a panic, I ran as fast as I could in what proved to be the wrong direction. Had I run a little faster, my head would have been crushed by the impact of a huge bomb which landed in front of me and by some chance did not explode. It disappeared into the ground. I jumped over it and ran towards another shelter where I hoped to find the other members of my family.[5]

> The morning came as though nothing had happened. I knew the morning came because I saw the sun rising over the devastated wilderness that had been Tokyo. I saw the sun . . . but it was a sun I did not know. The sun I knew did not come up *that* morning. It was a different, strange sun that came up over the wilderness. Overnight Tokyo was changed. I felt homeless. I felt misplaced and lost. I felt an intolerable loneliness encircling me. Tokyo was a forsaken city and I a forsaken person. I was orphaned. I felt as though I had been deserted by time . . . as though submerged into lifeless timelessness.[6]

Koyama's resolve to study theology was also determined by a

longing to work through the bitter experiences of the war years. In this respect, however, study at the Tokyo Union Theological Seminary proved frustrating for him. The question of guilt for the war and the war crimes committed by Japan was not a topic of discussion in the seminary. Probably out of disillusionment with this, Koyama decided against parish work and left Japan to study abroad. Unlike his two fellow-countrymen Takizawa and Yagi, his way did not take him to Germany, by whose theological tradition Japanese theology was strongly influenced – at this time it was likewise destroyed by war – but to the United States, the land of the victors. After a BA at Drew University (1954) he enrolled at Princeton, where he gained an MA in 1955 and four years later (1959) presented his doctoral thesis on Luther's exegesis of the penitential psalms.[7] Koyama shrouds the experiences of these years of study in unusual silence. With his American wife Lois Rozendaal, whom he had got to know as a fellow-student at Princeton, he returned to Japan. The United Church of Christ in Japan (Kyodan)[8] sent them to Thailand as missionaries. From 1960 to 1968 he taught systematic theology at Thailand Theological Seminary in Chiangmai. Koyama rediscovered Asia as his theological sounding board. Alongside his war experiences, these years were to serve as the second great experience to which his theology refers. He outlines the vision of a 'theology from below' which empties itself and works with the 'raw materials' and the 'raw situations' of Asia. The collection of articles, *Waterbuffalo Theology*,[9] which appeared in 1974, documents his first steps in this direction. It made him known at a stroke. In the introduction he explains his programme in a very poetic way:

On my way to the country church I never fail to see a herd of waterbuffaloes grazing in the muddy paddy field. This sight is an inspiring moment for me. Why? Because it reminds me that the people to whom I am to bring the gospel of Christ spend most of their time with these waterbuffaloes in the rice field. The waterbuffaloes tell me that I must preach to these farmers in the simplest sentence-structure and thought-development. They remind me to discard all abstract ideas and to use exclusively objects that are immediately tangible. 'Sticky-rice', 'banana', 'pepper', 'dog', 'cat', 'bicycle', 'rainy season', 'leaking house', 'fishing', 'cock-fighting', 'lottery', 'stomach-ache', – these are meaningful words for them. 'This morning,' I say to myself, 'I will try to bring the gospel of Christ through the medium of cock-fighting!'[10]

In 1968 Koyama moved to Singapore as Director of the Association of Theological Schools in South East Asia and Dean of the South-East Asia Graduate School of Theology. Here he could implement institutionally what he proclaimed theologically. His new tasks also included the editorship of the *South East Asia Journal of Theology*,[11] which over the years developed into the most important theological journal in Asia. Now Koyama travelled all over Asia. He was one of the co-initiators of the Programme for Theology and Culture in Asia (PTCA) of the South East Asia Graduate School.

The year 1974 brought yet another decisive change. Koyama left Asia and became Senior Lecturer in the Phenomenology of Religion at the University of Otago in Dunedin, New Zealand (1974–1979). In 1980 he accepted a call to Union Theological Seminary in New York, where until his retirement he taught as Professor of Ecumenics and World Christianity.

Born in the same year as Koyama (1929) in Taiwan, which was occupied by Japan (1895–1945), Choan-Seng Song[12] is in many respects his theological twin brother. He is the son of an old-established family of Chinese origin which at a very early stage was converted to the Presbyterian church. In Taiwan, as in Japan, Christianity is a disappearing minority (c.1 per cent), but enjoys sympathy among the population. The Presbyterian church is by far the largest denomination.

On the advice of his mentor Hwang Chong-Hui, better known as Shoki Coe (1914–1988), Song first studied philosophy at the Taiwan National University (1950–1954, BA). Then he moved on to study theology in Edinburgh (1955–1958), New York (1958–1959) and Basel (Winter 1959/60). After an interlude as lecturer in Old Testament at Tainan Theological College (TTC, 1960–1962) he returned to New York to Union Theological Seminary, where in 1965 he gained his doctorate with a work on the relationship between revelation and religion in Karl Barth and Paul Tillich.[13] As successor of Shoki Coe he was then dean of TTC and professor of systematic theology (1965–1970) until leaving Taiwan for good.

Like Koyama, Song had first to rediscover the cultural and religious world of his homeland after the long years abroad. But already in parallel with his doctoral work in New York he formulated first thoughts on a contextual theology.[14] He also repeatedly made critical remarks against the Nationalist Chinese regime. He was by no means alone in holding this position within the Presbyterian church.[15] When in 1971 Taiwan lost its seat in the United Nations in favour of the People's Republic of China, and the normalization of relationships as a result of the state visit of the American President Nixon to China was striking, the church made a 'Public Statement on Our National Fate'. As a reaction to the one-China policy of the USA, in 1977 there followed the church's 'Declaration on Human Rights'. Self-determination, democratization and human rights are the central demands of these declarations. For Song this shows 'God's politics of construction at work through the Presbyterian Church in Taiwan'.[16]

Song's self-chosen exile again took him first to the USA, where he worked as Asia Secretary of the Reformed Church (1971–1973). In 1973 he went to Geneva as Deputy Director of the Faith and Order Division of the World Council of Churches (1973–1982). This was followed by activity as Study Secretary of the World Alliance of Reformed Churches (WARC) (1982–1987). In 1985 there followed a call to be Professor of Theology and Asian Cultures at the Pacific School of Religion in Berkeley, California. At the same time he was Dean of the Programme for Theology and Culture of the South East Asia Graduate School of Theology, which has already been mentioned, and again, in an honorary position from 1990 to 1992, rector of TTC.

Choan-Seng Song and Kosuke Koyama cross the frontiers between Asia and the West. For a long time they have been at home in both traditions. Or have they become homeless? Whereas Song was granted recognition in Taiwan, which is evident from his (further) nomination as honorary rector of TTC (1990–1992), there has been no reception of Koyama's work in Japan.[17] Their books are not monographs in the academic sense but compendia of theological everyday texts – occasional writings, the genre of which oscillates between meditation and essay. However, it becomes clear from footnotes and interspersed excursuses that they are very familiar with academic theology. Both have also had a training in cultural anthropology and the history of religion. Therefore their rejection of academic convention is quite deliberate.

The motive force behind their theological reflections is the question of the definition of the relationship between gospel and culture. However, both have also grappled critically with the politics of their homelands. Whereas Song collaborated actively in the organization of the Taiwanese exiles, Koyama's protest manifested itself theologically in his constant warning against any form of idolatry of the kind he had to experience in Japanese emperor worship. Therefore the socio-economic and political dimension is present in their writings alongside the cultural and religious dimension.

In terms of method Koyama already refers to the Theological Education Fund (TEF) and its programme of contextualization. But he uses the conceptuality without any differentiation.[18] In the same breath as contextualization he speaks of critical accommodational prophetism and prophetic accommodation (21), incarnation (23) and indigenization (ibid.). But he can also speak of Third World theology (3), inculturation (87, 123), in-localization (123) and Hebraization (156). Koyama thinks throughout in dialectical terms. Any missionary must practise two kinds of exegesis: 'exegesis of the Word of God, and exegesis of the life and culture of the people among whom he lives and works' (91). In connection with his interpretation of the 'theology of the pain of God' of his teacher Kazoh Kitamori[19] he speaks of a penetrating correlation of gospel and culture (123).

For C. S. Song, the linking of stories from the rich treasure of Asian culture and religions with the biblical stories is the principle behind the composition of his rich *oeuvre*:

> In this interaction neither the word of God nor the reality of life remains static.[20]

Certainly, referring to Juan Luis Segundo, Song occasionally speaks of the 'hermeneutical circle',[21] but all in all he seems to mistrust the current terminology.[22] When he does introduce it, he uses it in the same undifferentiated way as Koyama.[23] This is the case although the origins of the contextualizing debate point to Taiwan, and Shoki Coe played an essential part in the formulation of the Third Mandate programme of TEF.[24]

Song's own terminology, 'third-eye theology' and 'transpositional theology', once introduced, is not taken up again. 'The term "third eye" is derived from Buddhism.'[25] Song refers to the Zen master and philosopher Daisetz Suzuki:

> Zen . . . wants us to open a 'third eye', as Buddhists call it, to the hitherto unheard-of region shut away from us through our own ignorance. When the cloud of ignorance disappears, the infinity of heavens is manifested where we see for the first time into the nature of our own being.[26]

The 'third-eye theology', at the same time the title of the book with which Song achieved an international breakthrough, opens up the perspective for the activity of God in the sphere of a particular culture.[27] It is important to transpose Christian theology into this context, from 'Israel to Asia', to quote the title of an early programmatic article.[28] Song defines this 'transposition' more closely as (1) transition in space and time, (2) communication and (3) incarnation.[29] Incarnation is the term which runs through his whole work as a theological cipher for the processes of contextualization.

However, apart from a few passages, Song's work is not conceptual but narrative. He has taken story theology seriously. But whereas Song, even where he speaks of Taiwan, largely retreats behind his stories, the theme of Koyama is always also Koyama. What he writes in the introduction to his last book also applies to all those which preceded it:

> This book, then, is a report of my personal pilgrimage, how I have brought together my historical experience and my confession of faith, or, more truly, how I have been brought, by grace of God, to dialogue between my own historical experience and the theology of the cross.[30]

Both authors equally accord a high status to christology in their theology, though from different central perspectives and with different functions.

2. No handle on the cross (Kosuke Koyama)

Koyama's theological thought is cross-centred. The fact that the cross has no handle symbolizes for him the unwieldiness of this Christian symbol and the way in which it cannot be controlled. God has emptied himself in the cross of Jesus Christ: 'He established his centrality by going to the periphery.'[31] The cross symbolizes failure, suffering and death before any resurrection. 'The biblical truth is not an *intact* truth but a *suffered* truth. The truth suffers because it is deeply in *contact* with man.'[32] Discipleship of Jesus Christ is discipleship of the cross. For that, Christians need a *crucified mind*.[33] 'The crucified mind is the mind shaken by the "foolishness and weakness of God".'[34] What is meant by this is an attitude of respect towards God and fellow human beings, particularly also towards those of other cultures and religions.

God for Koyama is a slow God, who adapts to human beings at their speed of 'three miles an hour'.[35] 'The crucifixion of Jesus Christ the Son of God, means that God went so slowly that on his search for people he was nailed to the cross.'[36] When God meets people in history, he treats them with respect for the autonomy in which he dismissed them. In accordance with this behaviour of God, men and women must approach him equally slowly, thoughtfully and with respect. At the same time this relationship with God finds its image in relations with fellow human beings. Koyama attacks a *'crusading mind'*[37] which scorns the other.

> We regard all those who differ from ourselves as *nons*. We look at humanity as a whole, and then classify all those who are not Christians under the heading 'non-Christians'.[38]

Attacking such an attitude, Koyama proclaims a radical change of perspective with his concept of *neighbourology*.[39] In the encounter with the neighbour, including the one who belongs to another culture and religion, God encounters us.

> Our sense of the presence of God will be distorted if we fail to see God's reality in terms of our neighbour's reality. And our sense of our neighbour's reality will be disfigured unless seen in terms of God's reality.[40]

We must therefore do our theology to some degree from the perspective of the others and together with them. We and our religion will also be assessed by others by the way in which we act towards them: 'Our neighbours are not concerned with our christology, but they show, from time to time, their interest in our "neighbourology".'[41] In accordance with this concept of neighbourology Koyama directs his attention less to the religious system, the -ism, or the doctrine, the -logy, than to the lived religion and its concrete adherents.[42]

Here Koyama in no way endorses syncretism. By syncretism he primarily understands, in terms of the phenomenology of religion, the processes which take place in the encounter and interaction of religions.[43] 'The question is whether such inter-action of the gospel with any religion or culture produces an enrichment or a distortion of the gospel.'[44] Like M. M. Thomas, Kosuke Koyama advocates an inclusive position:

> When we bring all to bow at the name of Jesus we are not syncretistic. But if we place the name of Jesus with any other name and say that there is really no difference between it and the other names, we become syncretistic.[45]

In Koyama the beginnings of an understanding of mission becomes visible as indicated in Matt. 5.14–16. Behind the meta-phorical language of being 'light of the world', 'city on the hill', stands the claim of the followers of Jesus to be present among men and women and give them a model by their behaviour. '"Neighbourology" is in fact the best vessel to convey Christ.'[46]

> Christian faith does not and cannot be spread by crusading. It will spread without money, without bishops, without theo-logians, without planning, if people see a crucified mind, not a crusading mind, in Christians.[47]

As an Asian Christian, Koyama in person embodies the dilemma of cultural contact. Moreover at the beginning of his theological *magnum opus, Mount Fuji and Mount Sinai*, he asks the rhetor-ical question: 'How can I appreciate the thought world of Mount Sinai without bringing it into a dialogue with the culture world native to myself?'[48] Here Koyama reviews his cultural and religious heritage. He emphasizes that his 'theology' 'begins with a deep sense of respect for these memories'.[49] But just as the cross is the critical authority for one's own behaviour towards others, so too the others must be measured by the claim of the cross.

> I would suggest that this [the cross] should become the criterion of the symbols of all religions. This is a scandalous criterion because it is a crucified criterion, a criterion of radical self-denial. It is the criterion that *theologia crucis* upholds.[50]

The state Shintoism which hurled Japan into the war is unmasked as idolatry. Koyama interprets the Japanese defeat as God's punishment.[51] Over against this trauma of his youth stands the rediscovery of Asian culture and religions during his time as a missionary in Thailand and as a theological official in Singapore.

Koyama's picture of the world recalls Troeltsch's theory of cultural circles.[52] Asia has been enriched by two great currents of tradition, '(1) India-China tradition and (2) the Judaeo-Christian-Islamic tradition'.[53]

Table 8: Asian and biblical spirituality (Koyama)

Asian spirituality	Biblical spirituality
Cosmology	Eschatology
Nature (cyclical)	History (linear)
Turned away from the world (cool)	Turned towards the world (hot)

Asian spirituality is cosmological, orientated on nature, and generates a cyclical picture of the world. By contrast biblical spirituality is eschatological and based on a linear view of history. Asian piety is turned away from the world, its gods are cool. The Christian God is hot, turned towards the world.

Koyama breaks through this contrast in three respects.

• In terms of the *phenomenology of religion* he seeks parallels between Christian and Asian spirituality. Koyama attributes historical thinking to Buddhism, which he regards with great sympathy and which is generally characterized as unhistorical.[54]

He sees this primarily grounded in the significance that the historical Buddha has as a founder of religion. Moreover there are emancipatory features in his teaching: he rejects sacrifice, magical thinking and the caste system. Even such a central statement as the doctrine of co-dependent origination (*pratitya samutpada*) implies historical thinking. 'Buddhism takes history seriously because it takes the problem of *tanha* [greed] seriously.'[55]

• With the striking remark that 'there is no fundamental difference between East and West',[56] Koyama brings an *anthropological* argument into play. Human beings as such have a primarily cosmological orientation. The real 'cultural revolution' was sparked off by the intervention of God in history. 'Some cultures historically have been more exposed to this God than others.'[57] 'It is the depth of exposure to this critical element that distinguishes the West from the East.'[58] The transitions to the third, theological framework of argument are fluid.

• That 'God came earlier than the missionary' can also be perceived clearly in Koyama: 'Often I am reminded that Jesus Christ was present among the peoples of the world even before the arrival of missionaries, Christians and churches.'[59] Koyama sees his prime task as seeking traces of this historical action of God in Asia. Here he is well aware of the fundamental character of this undertaking as response.[60]

For Koyama, the criterion for this quest in the context of the pluralism of the cultures and religions of Asia is the cross. I have already emphasized how close this is to the hermeneutical concept of the 'Christ-centred syncretism' of M. M. Thomas. As a creed Koyama postulates: 'No one can isolate incarnation from crucifixion, crucifixion from resurrection . . . We have no compartmentalized theology of incarnation, theology of cross and theology of resurrection.'[61] Mindful of these premises, he can then himself argue throughout from the perspective of the cross. Whereas the incarnation serves for him as the theological foundation of the processes of inculturation, to the criterion of which he has elevated the cross, the resurrection must be presupposed as belonging to the event of the cross, though it does not become a further theme. In Koyama's theology the stories of Jesus play a more subordinate role. Things are different in Song, who combines the perspective of the incarnation with the theology of creation.

3. Theology of incarnation in Asia (Choan-Seng Song)

Song develops his argument along two lines. God has created the world and since the very beginning has been entangled in a history with it. In Jesus Christ he has become man and entered this history. 'That is why history – the history of all nations and all peoples – must be the subject matter of theology.'[62] Song wants to make his premise that God is active in the cultures and religions of Asia theologically plausible by closely interlinking creation and redemption:

> Creation and redemption are in reality two sides of the coin. Where there is creation, there is redemption. Conversely, where there is redemption, there is creation. Or to put another way, creation is God's redeeming act, while redemption is God's creating act.[63]

But Song thinks that the doctrine of God is quite inappropriate as a way into theology.[64] He has retained a remnant of a positivism of revelation from his time as a pupil of Thomas F. Torrance in Edinburgh and his later doctoral work on Barth. 'God is already in Jesus Christ. That is why we know how to begin with Jesus Christ.'[65] Nevertheless, he by no means wants to constrict theology by a christocentrism. Rather, the life, death and resurrection of Jesus Christ are the hermeneutical key for discovering the traces of God's action in history in Asia.

> What we have in Jesus Christ is the concentration of God's creating and redeeming power. In him we are redeemed and created anew. In him an old history comes to an end and a new history begins. In the light of this supreme concentration, which is Jesus Christ, we encounter the God who created and redeemed over the long centuries before the historical event of Jesus Christ.[66]

It is, therefore through this person and work that we must try to understand God's salvation in the contexts of Asian cultural and religious experiences.[67]

By comparison, in Song, too, for a long time the pneumatology has been weak. Only in the framework of his trilogy with a trinitarian orientation, *The Cross in the Lotus World*, does he devote a separate volume to it.[68] It is the Spirit of God which empowers Jesus to perform his actions (70, 134). In this Spirit the Risen Christ is present among us (227). The Holy Spirit is the medium of communication both *ad intra* and *ad extra*.

> And if the Spirit enables Jesus crucified, dead and buried to be present with us in the world, as Jesus risen, living and working, that same Spirit also makes Easter happen to us who have to face the powers of corruption, destruction, and death each day of our lives. (305)

By retelling and inter-relating countless stories, biblical, Asian and also Western, Song reconstructs the history of the triune God. Behind the kaleidoscope of stories is concealed a dialectical mind which time and again confronts readers with surprising shifts in perspective. I shall briefly sketch out the theological consequences of three of them here.

• *Identification versus representation*

The suffering Jesus is present in those who are 'economically exploited, politically oppressed, culturally and religiously alienated, sexually, racially, or class-wise discriminated against'. '*Jesus, in short, is the crucified people!*'[69] The death of Jesus on the cross is not primarily to be interpreted as representation and certainly not at all as sacrifice. On the cross God has shared the suffering of the ordinary people in Jesus Christ. God has become man to the point of a cruel death on the cross.

> The God who is crucified on the cross is not so much the God who vicariously suffers and dies for the world as the God who suffers and dies *with* the world. Here vicariousness is replaced by identification. The crucified God is the God who identifies all the way with us in our suffering and death. God suffers with us and dies with us.[70]

This change of perspective cannot fail to have consequences for hamartiology. 'There is no theological ground for a causal relationship between sin and grace.'[71] Sin is human failure before God and fellow human beings or the community. For Song, the cross becomes a cipher for the dark sides of creation, for the violence which people are capable of doing to others. The cross means 'human beings abandoning human beings.'[72] At the same time sin against fellow human beings and sin against God are interlocked in the cross. Thus the cross becomes the embodiment of sin.

> The scandal of the cross is the scandal of humanity. That scandal is too much even for God. In that deep silence God must be protesting the scandal of human beings committed against God's 'beloved Son'.[73]

For Song, the silence of God implies his compassion for his creation. However, Song at the same time opposes an interpretation of the cross as an event within the Trinity, as it was put forward by Jürgen Moltmann and in Asia by Kazoh Kitamori.

> What we have in Kitamori and Moltmann . . . is a theology that loses sight of human beings by trying to say too much about God.[74]

• *Reign of God versus kingdom of God*

Song speaks of the reign of God, distinguishing it polemically from hope for the kingdom of God orientated on the other world.[75] The reign of God stands at the centre of the proclamation of Jesus Christ (ix).

> Strictly speaking, Jesus did not bring God's reign into the world, for it is already there. What he did was to engage people in the manifestation of it, to enable them to know it is there, to open their minds' eye to see it. (162)

Jesus' vision of the reign of God grew out of living together with the ordinary people (4). At the same time it is the hermeneutical principle for understanding his life and work (2). Message and person stand in a direct connection (xii).

- Missio Dei *versus* Missio ecclesiae

God is active in his creation from the very beginning. This action of the triune God in history can also be described as *Missio Dei*. The *Missio ecclesiae* represents only a limited realm in this. Any attempt to absolutize it turns it against God. At the same time that means that salvation and thus the presence of God cannot be restricted to the church:

> one particular culture alone, even that which is called Christian culture, cannot reveal the entirety of God's thoughts for the world. Until Hindu culture or Confucian is consulted, the God of Christians remains a partial God.[76]

It follows from this approach that Song is opposed to any proselytizing.[77]

> A Christian ecumenical vision should not be translated into a Christian missionary enterprise too quickly. This word of caution is necessary lest we, in the name of Jesus, practise a 'Christian ecumenical imperialism' and are blind to what we and others really are. An ecumenical vision, if it is to be true to its name, contains many local visions – a Hindu vision, a Buddhist vision, a Confucian vision, a Islamic vision, and so on. A Christian vision is one of these local visions. It is part of the ecumenical vision.[78]

But Song's attitude to mission ultimately remains ambivalent. Critical tones[79] stand right beside a theology of mission which is quite comparable with that of Koyama.[80]

Even if in Song's extensive *oeuvre* there is the permanent danger that readers will lose the scarlet thread in the fabric of the stories, unlike Koyama he succeeds in developing an open but quite coherent christology. For him the theology of incarnation and cross or the paradigm of creation and redemption and death and resurrection, as he himself has once named them,[81] fuse together.

> The cross shows how a new creation must come into being through intense pain and suffering. The whole being of God aches in Jesus Christ on the cross. And the God who suffers is the God who redeems.[82]

The span of the incarnation holds the life, death and resurrection of Jesus Christ together. Christology at the same time becomes the hermeneutical key for the action of the triune God in history. Song achieves a synthesis of a theology of inculturation and a liberation theology. All this is concentrated for him in the title of his trilogy, *The Cross in the Lotus World.*

> The lotus is to Buddhists as a religious symbol what the cross is to Christians. Radically different in every way, these two symbols point to a crucial quest of human life – deliverance.[83]

Under the aegis of christology, Song spells out yet again what he has developed in a variety of articles and books since the early 1960s. Here we begin to see the contours of the way in which a future ecumenical theology, at the centre of which stand the life, death and resurrection of Jesus Christ, could speak of the triune God.

4. Models of Asian christology

At the end of our journey through the Asian theologies of inculturation or dialogue, three basic models of Asian christology are crystallized. M. M. Thomas and K. Koyama represent a *christocentrism* which elevates christology to be the criterion of the encounter of culture and religion. The goal of inter-religious dialogue is mission, but to some degree a post-colonial mission, which wants to preserve the culture identities of the others. The inner contradiction of the inclusive model, which sees the other as always already standing under the salvation of Jesus Christ and thus in the last resort cannot take the other religions seriously, remains. However, the question is whether it is possible to think out coherent theology in any other way.

At any rate the attempt to remove this contradiction by a theocentric model, of the kind put forward by S. Samartha and K. Takizawa, is doomed to failure. They seek the common ground of salvation of Hinduism or Buddhism and Christianity in the doctrine of God. Here Samartha even gives up the notion of a personal God. In the best case, what remains is a christology of the primal image or model.

A way out seems to be suggested in the sketches by S. Yagi and

C. S. Song. They similarly locate soteriology in the doctrine of God. Despite the repeated criticism that they have a defective pneumatology, they both tend to adopt a trinitarian course towards a solution. Therefore I speak here of a *christocentric theology*. Whereas Yagi's field model, according to which people always already find themselves in the field of the side of God which is turned towards them, is ahistorical (synchronous), Song brings people into the history of the triune God (diachronous).

The stamp of a *theologia gloriae* which is characteristic of the theocentric model displays a certain nearness to African christology. However, the drifting apart of Christ as the side of God turned to human beings and the man Jesus Christ, makes the image of *Christus victor* fade, as was still found in cosmic christology.

Table 9. Models of Asian christology

Christocentrism	Christocentric theology	Theocentrism
Jesus Christ as the criterion of difference	Jesus Christ as the hermeneutical key	Christology of the primal image or model
Jesus Christ as mediator of salvation	Soteriology located in the doctrine of God	
Revelation of God in Jesus Christ		• Jesus a man • Christ as the side of God turned towards human beings
Thomas, Koyama	Song, Yagi	Samartha, Takizawa

In the christocentric model the *theologia crucis* serves as a formal criterion of difference over against the other cultures and religions. By contrast C. S. Song puts forward a material christology which sees Jesus present in the crucified people. Here he takes up a central theme of the liberation theologies, to which we shall now turn again.

D. 'What you have done to the least of these my brothers . . .' Christology in the Context of Poverty and Oppression in Africa and Asia

Refugees from East Pakistan; woodcut (Solomon Raj, India)

At the centre of the picture is a mother crouching on the ground, holding her child tightly to her. Diagonally behind the two of them, the father is sitting in an almost meditative position. The woman is wearing a sari, the man a loincloth and turban; around his neck hangs a simple leather ornament. The child's clothing cannot be determined more closely. Mother and child are barefoot. All three have their eyes closed out of exhaustion. From the background, structured with irregular, short cuts, the upper part of the body of Christ appears, putting his left arm round the father, and holding his shoulder in his left hand. The right arm extends beyond the border of the picture. Christ seems to be bowed forwards, as if he wanted to protect the three. A mighty crown of thorns stands on his head. His face too is marked with exhaustion and his eyes are shut. His lower body, clothed only with the loincloth of the coolie, merges with the hatching of the background. In the right foreground is a clay pot, the family's only possession. God's Son came into the world as a child of ordinary people. Solomon Raj has repeatedly portrayed them as a refugee family. Christ is present among the poor and oppressed, and at the same time he constantly encounters them as one of theirs.

§10 The Black Messiah – Christology in the Context of Racism

James H. Cone (USA) and Allan A. Boesak (South Africa)

At around the same time as Latin American liberation theology but independently of it, a liberation theology likewise developed among the black minority in the United States. It has its roots in the Civil Rights Movement and the Black Power Movement with their two congenial protagonists, the pastor Martin Luther King and the Muslim Malcolm X.[1] While in harmony with the movement as a whole their exponents initially described themselves as negroes, and then as blacks; today the term African-American has largely become established, a reference to their understanding of themselves as an African Diaspora.

Reflection on its African roots has led in parts of the movement to the rejection of Christianity as the religion of the white slave-owners. This attitude favoured the advance of Islam, prominently represented by Malcolm X and his Black Muslims. Just as in Latin America Gutiérrez became the founder figure with the publication of his book *Theology of Liberation* (1971/1972), so in the USA James H. Cone became the figurehead of this theological movement through his two books *Black Theology and Black Power* (1969)[2] and *A Black Theology of Liberation* (1970),[3] which appeared in close succession.

In his Kampen dissertation *Farewell to Innocence*,[4] the South African Allan A. Boesak has critiqued Cone's sketch of a 'Black Theology'. Cone is the unloved godfather of South African Black Theology, whose representatives do not weary of asserting their independence.[5]

1. Jesus is black (James H. Cone)

James Hal Cone[6] was born in 1938, the child of a black family in Fordyce, Arkansas, a small town in the south of the USA. When he was one year old, his parents moved into neighbouring Bearden, a village with 1,200 inhabitants, a third of whom were black. The domestic circumstances of the family of five – there were two other sons in addition to James Hal – were poor, but the father showed a certain pride, and opposed the latent racial discrimination. Occasionally,[7] Cone describes two contrasting impressions which he remembers from Bearden: the piety and fellowship in the black church, the African Methodist Episcopal Church (AME), and the racism of the whites. He decided at an early stage to study theology. At the age of sixteen, on leaving high school (1954), James Cone, together with his brother Cecil, at first went to a seminary of the AME, Shorter College, which was not recognized by the state. Later the brothers moved to Philander Smith College, which also belonged to the Methodist Church but was recognized. After gaining their BAs, the two again went together to Garrett Biblical Institute (later Garrett Evangelical Theological Seminary) in Evanston, Illinois. Cone's description of the harassments which he had to endure in those years as a young gifted student is depressing.[8] Nevertheless, even among the whites he found teachers who encouraged him, and in 1965 he was able to gain his doctorate with a thesis on Barth's anthropology. As early as 1964 he was appointed a lecturer at Philander Smith College, but after only two years he was removed from this post by the white administration of the seminary. Cone then changed to Adrian College in Adrian, Michigan (1966). This was the time of the Civil Rights Movement and racial unrest. In summer 1966 a statement from the National Committee of Negro Churchmen (later the National Conference of Black Churchmen) appeared in the *New York Times*, openly supporting the Black Power Movement.[9]

For a long time Cone himself sought possibilities of relating his black experience to his theological work. Already during his time as a lecturer at Philander Smith College he had begun to doubt the relevance of the academic theology taught at the white seminaries to the situation of black Christians. He wrote in retrospect:

> But what did Barth, Tillich, and Brunner have to do with young black girls and boys coming from the cotton fields of Arkansas, Tennessee and Mississippi seeking to make a new future for themselves? . . . I had spent six years studying theology, and now I found it irrelevant to the things that mattered most to me.[10]

This remark of Cone's is symptomatic of the epistemological break which precedes the formulation of any liberation theology. It is always also a biographical break. Theology and biography are interlocked in a similar way as theology and context.[11] The two hermeneutical circles are somehow related as micro- and macro-structure. I by no means want to identify theology and biography, but the dialectical relationship between text and context propagated for the theological process does not stop at one's own life, especially as participation is explicitly required. The liberation theologians in particular have a special existential involvement in their theology.

Following an invitation to Elmhurst College, for the first time Cone collected his thoughts together in written form. He eloquently describes the origin of his lecture manuscript *Christianity and Black Power*.[12]

> I will never forget the event of writing that essay. It seemed that both my Christian and black identity was at stake. My first priority was my black identity, and I was not going to sacrifice it for the sake of a white interpretation of the gospel that I had learned at Garrett. If Christ was not to be found in black people's struggle for freedom, if he were not found in the ghettos with rat-bitten black children, if he were in rich white churches and their seminaries, then I wanted no part of him. The issue for me was not whether Black Power could be adjusted to meet the terms of a white Christ, but whether the biblical Christ is to be limited to the prejudiced interpretations of white scholars. I was determined to set down on paper what I felt in my heart.

> I decided to write a brief manifesto identifying Black Power
> with the gospel of Jesus . . . From Barth and others I knew all
> about ideological dangers of my procedure. Identifying the
> gospel with historico-political movements was anathema to
> anyone who bases his theology on divine revelation. But I
> purposely intended to be provocative in much the same way
> that Barth was when he rebelled against liberal theology. As
> Barth had turned liberal theology up-side-down, I wanted to
> turn him right-side-up with a focus on the black struggle in
> particular and oppressed people generally.[13]

Cone's reminiscence of Karl Barth is an impressive documentation of his struggle with the Western, white theological
tradition. He himself claims to be the better Barthian: 'I have
always thought that Barth was closer to me than to them [the
Barthians].'[14] Cone has been much criticized by his clientele for
this alleged Barthianism, but the theological parricide has long
since been committed. More radically than most liberation
theologians, Cone takes the rejection of Jesus Christ into
account, should it prove that he is not present in the suffering of
the blacks.[15] The question which moves him existentially is:
'How can I as a black nevertheless be a Christian?' This problem
of identity is the hermeneutical key to his identification of the
Black Power Movement and the gospel of Jesus Christ. The
Black Power Movement is an expression of the reconstruction of
a black identity. In a comparable way to Latin American liberation theology, here it creates its own myth of its origin.[16] For
centuries the blacks have internalized the discrimination of their
white oppressors. They took over the latter's definition of them
as not-white and regarded the blackness of their skin as inferior.
The overcoming of this self-negation is concentrated in the
slogan 'Black is beautiful'. Cone contradicts those activists who
think that in this process the significance of Christian faith for
the black community can be neglected or can even be disqualified
as a religion of the white man. He sees in the preaching of
the black church a parallel structure to the Black Power message.
In the same way as we could already note in the liberation theology of Latin America, belief in the presence of Jesus Christ in
their suffering gives the blacks, contrary to the reality of their

suffering, their own dignity before God and restores their self-respect.

> After being told six days of the week that they were nothings by the rulers of white society, on the Sabbath, the first day of the week, black people went to church in order to experience another definition of their humanity.[17]

The identification of the poor and oppressed, in this case the black slaves and their descendants, with the suffering of Jesus Christ creates identity. This is a further parallel to Latin American liberation theology. This understanding of the cross is diametrically opposed to the white reading. So on closer examination the provocative identification of the Black Power movement and the gospel has a functional basis. Both seek structurally to promise the same thing, which is to give to the blacks their human dignity. Cone's remarks make the black church positively the forerunner of the Black Power Movement. Black Theology for its part transcends the aims of Black Power and shows that it is rooted in faith in Jesus Christ.

With the publication of the two works on Black Theology already mentioned at the beginning, Cone had attained a certain popularity and received several offers from famous schools. In 1969 he accepted an appointment to Union Theological Seminary in New York, where he still teaches. A key factor in this decision was not least the immediate proximity of the seminary to Harlem.

In terms of method Cone's initial question – 'what has the gospel of Jesus Christ to do with the black struggle for justice in the United States?'[18] – suggests a hermeneutical approach. The sources of Black Theology which he mentions can be divided into the two groups of our two hermeneutical categories: revelation, scripture and tradition to the *text* and black experience, black history and black culture to the *context*.[19] Cone wants to relate these dialectically, very much in the sense of the hermeneutical circle.

> The dialectic relationship of the black experience and Scripture is the point of departure of Black Theology's Christology.[20]

A christology comparable to that of Boff or Sobrino does not appear in Cone's numerous publications. But he repeatedly emphasizes that the life, death and resurrection of Jesus Christ are the centre of his Black Theology, as they are of any Christian theology.[21]

> *The norm of all God-talk which seeks to be black-talk is the manifestation of Jesus as the black Christ, who provides the necessary soul for black liberation.*[22]

Around this are grouped a set of themes which can be demonstrated with different emphases in all liberation theologies and are therefore described here by way of example. As a comparison I use Gutiérrez's *Theology of Liberation*.[23]

(1) The unity of history

Belief in the historical action of the triune God leads the liberation theologians to overcome the distinction between salvation and world history, which they regard as artificial (C, 44; G, 86). God's history with the world begins with its creation, has reached its climax so far in the new creation in Jesus Christ, and is orientated on his return. 'There is only one history – a "Christo-finalized" history' (G, 86). The temporal modes of past, present and future are closely linked together. What J. B. Metz calls 'the dangerous memory' of the exodus and Jesus event at the same time opens up hope for the future in the present.[24] The ordinary people become subjects of history (C, 117; G.30), for the new creation in Jesus Christ, his presence in their suffering, is the foundation of their identity and restores their own dignity to them.

(2) The partisan God

From the very beginning of his history with the people of Israel to the present day God takes the side of the poor and oppressed. Cone demonstrates that paradigmatically by means of the exodus event, the appearance of the prophets and the life, death and resurrection of Jesus Christ (C, 43–47; G, 86–97).[25] God has freed his people from oppression in Egypt. When the poor in

Israel are oppressed by the rulers, prophets emerge and remind them of this liberating event. They proclaim God's anger at the existing conditions. In the exile the remembrance of the exodus becomes the source of hope of a new liberation by God. Just as the exodus is the basic datum of the history of God with his people and a hermeneutical key to its understanding, so the Jesus event discloses his universal promise of salvation. In Jesus Christ, his only-begotten Son, God has revealed himself in history. However, he was not born of a royal family but as the child of ordinary people. God's son came into the world as one of them. From this acceptance by Jesus Christ of their suffering, the poor and oppressed are given the promise of their own dignity before God, contrary to the facts of the conditions in which they live. The birth narratives (Matt. 1–2; Luke 1–2), the Magnificat (Luke 1.46–55), the inaugural sermon in Nazareth (Luke 4.18f.), the answer to John the Baptist's question (Luke 7.18–23; Matt. 11.2–6) and time and again the parable of the judgment of the world (Matt. 25.31–46) are the repertory of biblical stories which are brought as evidence.

(3) Individual and structural sin

Without wanting to deny the individual sinfulness of human existence, the liberation theologians have given the concept of sin a new dimension. Sin is initially, in keeping with the tradition, a turning away from God and fellow human beings; here in particular once again the poor and oppressed neighbours are in view. Not only are people sinful, but also the structures in which they are entangled (G, 23f., 85, 102f., 113).[26] Oppressed and oppressor equally need liberation. But whereas the ordinary people are promised the kingdom of God in a particular way, the oppressors are called on to repent. The poor and oppressed are those who are sinned against. Raymund Fung has spoken in this connection of 'sinned-againstness'.[27]

(4) A new person in Christ

Referring to Paul, Cone speaks of the 'new black man' (C, 53) whose 'new-found identity [is grounded] in Christ'. It is the overcoming of the sin of self-denial by internalizing the alien perspectives which produce discrimination, and the status of 'sinned-againstness', whether as a black person or a poor person. The function of christology in creating identity (C, 149) is the impulse for a tremendous anthropological optimism which leads Gutiérrez to talk of the creation of 'a new person / humanity' (G, 20–22, 56, 90). The 'anthropophany' (G, 121) which he virtually conjures up is nevertheless not a divinization of human beings. What is meant in Gutiérrez as in Cone is the '"new creature" in Christ' (C, 53).

(5) Church as community

The specific church community, whether that of a black church in the USA or a Latin-American base community, is the place where the poor and oppressed experience themselves in the community of Jesus Christ. It can represent something of a counter-society. The liberation theologians are well aware of the ambivalence of the church as institution. All too often the church conformed with the system and stabilized it, despite all declarations to the contrary. They therefore remind the church as a whole of their prophetic ministry (C, 2; G, 68f.), which they themselves exercise as theologians towards society and church equally.

(6) Kingdom of God and eschatology

Contrary to a widespread prejudice, the liberation theologies do not give up the eschatological proviso. The tension between the 'now already' and the 'not yet' is preserved (C, 40; G, 92). But in the old dispute over eschatology they certainly stand on the side of present or realized eschatology. The emphasis on the preaching of the kingdom of God lies on its anticipation in the life, death and resurrection of Jesus Christ. Jesus promised the kingdom of God to the poor and oppressed; his healings and feedings are already a pledge of this. The overcoming of death in the resurrection is the basic datum of the hope of liberation. At the parousia the poor and oppressed will follow Jesus Christ in this and enter into his kingdom. But this process has already begun now, with the promise of their own dignity and in their newly-found identity in Jesus Christ. The call to discipleship is essentially also a call to the work of the kingdom of God (G, 46), which for many people in Latin America has become a call to discipleship of suffering and even martyrdom.

The generative themes mentioned echo traditional dogmatic topics like the doctrine of God, hamartiology, anthropology, ecclesiology and eschatology without making a claim to deal with them in all their breadth. The concern, rather, is for a re-orientation within the network of themes in liberation theology. Linking together the different strands of thought here gives rise to a coherent fabric of texts. Anyone who attempts to separate out the christology destroys it. Conversely, without the ensemble of themes which surrounds it, christology loses its significance.

2. Black and white reconciled in Jesus Christ (Allan A. Boesak)

The *oeuvre* of the South African Allan A. Boesak for the most part consists of occasional writings like lectures and sermons.[28] He too has not put forward any christology in the classical sense. But with Cone he confesses the centrality of Jesus Christ. For the blacks, Jesus Christ is the Black Messiah (42) who is present in the suffering of the poor and oppressed blacks of North America and South Africa and who restores to them their own dignity before God.

> Black Theology is not prepared to separate the reality of the historical Jesus from the reality of his presence in the world today. (41)

The abolition of the artificial difference between historical Jesus and kerygmatic Christ in the doctrine of the *Christus praesens* is, as I already noted in the chapter on Latin America, one of the key statements of a liberation-theological christology.

> Black Theology is a theology of liberation . . . Black Theology believes that liberation is not only 'part of' the gospel or 'con-sistent with' the gospel; it is the content and framework of the gospel of Jesus Christ. (9)

The importance of the concept of the Black Messiah is that it expresses the concreteness of Christ's continued presence today. (42)

Allan Aubrey Boesak[29] was born in 1946, the son of a black primary school teacher and his white wife in Kakamas (Cape Province). According to the South African race laws which applied from 1948 on, he thus belonged to the 'coloureds', who occupied a position in between black and white. Allan's father died when he was six years old. His mother brought him and his seven brothers and sisters up by working as a seamstress. She reared her children in the pietistic faith of the Dutch Reformed mission church. Boesak began his study of theology in 1962 at the seminary of this church and completed it in 1967 at the University of the Western Cape, an educational institution especially for coloureds. His first years as pastor of the Emmanuel Community in Paarl (1968–1970) and confrontation with the system of apartheid in the daily work in the community made him feel clearly the defects of this education.

> Brought up by white theologians in the Dutch Reformed Church who were regarded as 'missionaries' in our church, my years at seminary were a time of frustration. The professors were incompetent; their theology was a strange mixture of a Dutch Calvinism deriving from the nineteenth century, which provided the basis for the theology of apartheid represented by the white Dutch Reformed Church, and a pietistic theology related to the world beyond, which aimed at spiritualizing the gospel. They taught us a theology which was utterly irrelevant to our situation.[30]

That made the euphoria all the greater when it became possible for him to study for a number of years in the USA and the Netherlands (1970–1976).[31] His doctoral thesis, presented in 1976, is essentially an intensive critical discussion of the Black Theology coming from North America. The Black Theology of South Africa is generally regarded as an American import. Certainly its representatives tried to claim independence for themselves, but they would never completely succeed in this. The literary advantage of the Americans was simply too great. A quotation from an early article by Basil Moore can be regarded as symptomatic of these efforts at demarcation:

> While the slogan 'Black Theology' has been imported from the United States into South Africa, the content of American Black Theology has not been imported with the title.[32]

It is evident that there are differences between the situation of blacks in South Africa and blacks in the USA. But the context is only one constitutive element. The text which is to be expounded in the different situations remains the same. And the fact that there are many striking 'parallels between the situation of the black men in America and South Africa',[33] as Moore also concedes, must be reflected in the particular interpretations of the text. Here the desire for independence has disturbed the perspective. Boesak was also in this dilemma. Here his secret *alter ego* in writing his dissertation was James Cone, to whom he keeps referring.

Their theological starting points are structurally the same. Boesak describes himself as a contextual theologian[34] who is reflecting on the relevance of the gospel in the situation of blacks in South Africa.[35]

> Black Theology is the theological reflection of black Christians on the situation in which they live and on their struggle for liberation. Blacks ask: What does it mean to believe in Jesus Christ when one is black and living in a world controlled by white racists? (1f.)

Black Theology is a liberation theology with Christ as its centre. Boesak speaks of a 'christological theology' (13; cf. 9).

In four closely linked points Boesak attempts to distinguish himself from Cone.[36]

(1) Black Power or Black Consciousness

On the very first page of his book Boesak emphasizes that 'Black Consciousness is an integral part of Black Power' (B, 1, cf. 65). The attempt to limit the term to the pure process of forming consciousness in the sense of discovering a black identity is a contradiction in terms. The overcoming of the institutionalized alienation perpetrated by the white oppressors necessarily has consequences in the situation of apartheid. That can already be seen from the so-called SASO Manifesto of the black South African Student Organization in 1971 which clearly connects Black Consciousness and political action.[37] Boesak also concedes that 'the term Black Consciousness is interpreted [by some South African black theologians] in such a way that it really becomes identified with Black Power' (B, 75). He therefore sharpens the distinction by discussing the question of violence and of ideology.

(2) Violence or non-violence

To associate Cone directly with militant black nationalists like Albert Cleage Jr (B, 42, 116–121) and J. R. Washington (B, 127f.) does not do him justice. Boesak agrees with him in denying whites the moral right to make the question of violence a theme (B, 68, 126). Theologically Cone's critical discussion of the problem of violence remains unsatisfactory. He does not apply Bonhoeffer's embracing of violent resistance as a matter of incurring personal guilt, which is perhaps the most convincing thing that can be said here.[38] But his own remarks make it credible that for him violence is only the last possibility (C, 138–143).[39] Boesak ultimately adopts a similar position; he too does not reject violence generally. He remains similarly vague in his theological argumentation.

(3) Ideology or theology

Boesak claims that Cone *de facto* is open to the suspicion of ideology in three respects: he (1) gives the situation of blacks the character of revelation (B, 12) or virtually identifies Black Power and gospel (B, 73); (2) one-sidedly emphasizes racism (B, 148–151); and (3) commandeers God '*solely* for the black experience' (B, 143f.). None of these arguments stands up to close examination.

- Primacy of the situation

As we have seen, Cone is well aware of the hermeneutical circle. Situation and gospel are to be related dialectically.[40] His interpretation of the Black Power movement as 'Christ's central message to twentieth-century America' (C, 1) certainly walks along the razor's edge. He focusses his claim 'that the goal and message of Black Power . . . is consistent with the gospel of Jesus Christ' (C, 48) on the question of the discovery of identity. In this respect his argument has great plausibility (C, 1f., 48, 117). Boesak follows him in this respect.

- Primacy of racism

The striking feature of Cone's theological new departure was that he branded racism as being incompatible with the gospel of Jesus Christ. The charge that he only wants his share of the cake of the American way of life does not apply to Cone, though it does apply to others, as Boesak rightly works out (B, 133). It is perhaps in the nature of things that Cone's first manifestos are silent here. Later he certainly criticized capitalism. But he could also point out that the American white Marxists were similarly not free of racism.[41]

- Primacy of the blacks

As I already remarked at the beginning, Black Theology was a parallel development to liberation theology. Cone in fact understands his theology as a particular exegesis of the gospel by blacks, with blacks and for blacks.[42] The use of the attributes *black* and *white* is a metaphorical way of speaking. In Cone's context the poor and oppressed of the gospel are the ordinary people of the black community, whereas the black social climbers have allowed themselves to be corrupted by the whites.

At the time when Boesak was finishing his book, Cone and he were already among the founding members of EATWOT, an ecumenical forum in which over the following years he was time and again to bring Black Theology into dialogue with the other Third World theologies.

(4) Repentance or reconciliation

'Liberation and reconciliation presuppose one another' (B, 92). Reconciliation is certainly the great theme for Boesak, as it is in South African Black Theology generally.[43] By contrast Cone issues a distinct call for repentance. He does not preach racial hatred (C, 13), but points out that the statement that for a rich man – in his metaphorical idiom, Cone would say a 'white' man – it is difficult to enter the kingdom of God is a saying of Jesus which many find uncomfortable. Despite all the verbal radicalism, however, Cone closes his very first and most controversial book with an explicit profession of reconciliation:

> Black Theology is a theology which takes seriously God's reconciling act in Jesus Christ. In fact, the heart of the New Testament message is the gospel of reconciliation. (C, 147)[44]

Accordingly on this point, too, Cone and Boesak are closer than the latter would have us believe. Correspondingly, in both there are two presuppositions for reconciliation between black and white, even if Cone emphasizes that the conditions are laid down by the blacks and calls on the whites to repent to the blacks.

• The blacks must drop their internalized slave mentality and accept themselves in their blackness. Theologically they are promised their own dignity before God as new men and women in Christ (B, 28, 92f.; C, 149).
• '. . . reconciliation is possible only after the establishment of righteousness and social justice' (B, 93; cf. C, 144). White racism must be abolished. The whites must learn 'to address black men as *black* men and not as some grease-painted form of white humanity' (C, 147).
   Speaking metaphorically, Cone calls for reconciliation with the poor and oppressed: in this case, for reconciliation with the blacks:

> Reconciliation makes us all black. Through this radical change, we become identified totally with the suffering of the black masses . . . Being black in America has very little to do

with skin colour. To be black means that your heart, your soul, your mind, and your body are where the dispossessed are. . . . Therefore, being reconciled to God does not mean that one's skin is physically black. It essentially depends on the colour of your heart, soul and mind. (C, 151)

In Black Theology 'blackness' is a metaphor for 'being poor and oppressed':

The 'blackness of Christ', therefore, is not simply a statement about skin colour, but rather, the transcendent affirmation that God has not ever, no not ever, left the oppressed alone in struggle. He was with them in Pharaoh's Egypt, is with them in America, Africa and Latin America and will come in the end of time to consummate fully their human freedom.[45]

Because Jesus Christ has identified with the poor and oppressed, conversely the blacks can identify with him. Through the presence of Jesus Christ in their suffering they are promised dignity before God as human beings which is contrary to the facts of the conditions in which they live.[46] Through this they learn to accept themselves. It is here that the function of christology lies in creating identity in the context of poverty and oppression.

If in the two previous chapters about the African and Asian theologies of inculturation the acceptance of a particular cultural identity is seen in analogy to incarnation and strives for the creation of a Christian-cultural bi-identity, the liberation theologians begin at the even more elementary position of human dignity.[47] This theme runs like a scarlet thread through the next sections.

§11 Encountering Jesus Christ in the Minjung – Christology in the Context of a Development Dictatorship

Ahn Byung-Mu and the Minjung Theology of South Korea

Alongside K. Takizawa and S. Yagi, the Korean Ahn Byung-Mu (1922–1996)[1] is one of the few Asian contextual theologians of the first generation to have studied in Germany. He was born on 23 June 1922 in Shinanju, South Pyong-yang province, in present-day North Korea, the son of a doctor who practised traditional Asian medicine. When Byung-Mu was one year old, the family fled from Japanese-occupied Korea[2] to Manchuria.[3] Brought up a Confucian, he converted to the Christian faith in his youth. This led to a final rift with his father, who drank and kept a concubine. When Ahn's mother left her husband, her son contributed to her support by doing temporary work. He went to the Canadian Presbyterian mission school in Yongchang. But then in 1941, like many Koreans of his generation seeking education, he went to the land of the hated colonial lords. After completing college education at Taisho University in 1943, he enrolled in sociology in the philosophical faculty of Waseda University. To avoid the threat of being conscripted into the Japanese army, that same year Ahn broke off his study and went underground in Manchuria. For a while he worked as a lay preacher in a community. After the end of the war he initially assumed duties in self-government and negotiated with the Russian occupying forces. However, the hopes of the Koreans for national autonomy were not fulfilled. Korea was divided along the thirty-eighth parallel into an American and a Russian zone, each of which were soon to develop their own states. In 1946 Ahn fled from the increasing reprisals of the Communists, particularly also against Christians, to Seoul, where he first scraped a living for himself and his mother as an English teacher. At the same time he resumed his study of sociology; he studied religion as a second subject. His election as chairman of the Korea Student Christian Federation (KSCF) is an indication of his continuing Christian commitment. The person of Jesus exercised a great fascination on him. He taught himself ancient Greek and read theological literature. His encounter with the writings of Rudolf Bultmann left a lasting mark on him.

> Bultmann was the only teacher who had a great influence on me, as a theologian and at the same time as a New Testament scholar . . . Had I not encountered Bultmann I would never have begun theology. He showed me a way of doing theology.[4]

With friends, Ahn founded a Christian community. They emphasized the lay element and wanted to demonstrate an alternative to the established church. This was also the impetus in founding the Chungang seminary, which was to provide theological education for laity. At first Ahn taught sociology and ancient Greek. His first New Testament teaching was centred on the historical Jesus. When there were increasing tensions in the community and failure was foreseeable, Ahn resolved to deepen his Jesus studies in Germany. As Bultmann himself had been retired since 1951, he went to Heidelberg to Bultmann's pupil Günther Bornkamm (1905–1990). Ahn continued primarily to teach himself. But abroad he turned to his own tradition and began to read the Confucian classics.

> I had to redefine my standpoint as a Korean or an Asian . . . I wanted to liberate myself from Western theology and investigate from another angle. With deliberate scepticism I wanted to ask whether my enthusiasm for Jesus was fortuitous.[5]

In 1965 he gained his doctorate with a work on *The Understanding of Love in Kung-tse and Jesus*. On his return, Ahn at first again taught at Chungang Seminary, of which at the same time he became president (1965–1971). In 1971 he was called to Hankuk Theological University in Seoul.

At the beginning of the 1970s the political situation in South Korea increasingly came to a head. After the fall of the first president of South Korea, Singman Rhee, in 1960 following student unrest, in 1961 Park Chung-Hee seized power by a military coup. The short spring of democracy was nipped in the bud. In a series of five-year plans the new strong man transformed the south from an agricultural region into a modern industrial state. This process was favoured by low wages, long working-hours and the suppression of independent trade unions. The impoverishment of the rural population through the regulation of food prices by the state was regarded acceptable. In 1963 Park had himself confirmed in office in 'free' elections, and in 1967 he was re-elected. In order to be able to be a candidate for a third term in office he changed the constitution (1969), but in 1971 barely defeated the opposition candidate Kim Dae-Jung in an election the legitimacy of which was contested. In foreign policy the regime was increasingly isolated by the closer relations between the USA and China and the end of the Cold War in the Pacific which these signalled. In domestic policy, for the first time since the introduction of the five-year plans the country was shaken by an economic crisis. Park responded to this with the introduction of the Yushin constitution (1972), which gave him unlimited power. Resistance grew against the development dictatorship, which was becoming increasingly repressive.

Ahn became involved in human rights work. External circumstances had some influence on his theological thought. He became increasingly alienated from the German tradition, which he had once lapped up so eagerly. In retrospect he speaks of the 'German captivity' of Korean theology.[6]

> Yes, and for a long long time I lived in Germany. When I came back, I began to teach German theology here, and I discovered that our question was a Western question and the answer was again the Western answer. This removed the questioner, who simply disappeared . . . So we must honestly ask what we want and who we are. And the answer must come from us; we must be involved in it.[7]

The intellectual circles in which the opposition formed discovered the Minjung, the 'ordinary people', as the real subjects of Korean history. In a quasi-theological interpretation they reconstructed this history as the history of the suffering of the Minjung. This is a procedure which we already know in a comparable form from Latin American and Black liberation theology.[8]

The sociologist Han Wan-Sang describes the Minjung more closely as a group of people 'who are oppressed politically, exploited economically, alienated sociologically, and kept uneducated in cultural and intellectual matters'.[9] The Sino-Korean term Minjung is composed of 'Min', 'people', and '-jung', 'mass', i.e. 'mass of people'. But the representatives of the Minjung movement keep emphasizing with some solemnity that it cannot be translated. They deliberately do not want to define the Minjung, so as to keep its membership as open as possible. However, the demarcation from the Marxist concept of class is clear. This can be explained not only by the repression of the military, who wanted to muzzle the opposition with the anti-communism laws. What went far deeper was their own painful experience of the bloody civil war of 1950–1953. Practically every Korean had to mourn losses in his family or his circle of close acquaintances.

The Minjung movement was a political reform movement which in domestic politics stood for respect for human rights, social justice and democratization and, in the question of the division of the land, for national self-determination and reunification. Here it was part of a cultural renaissance that revitalized Korean culture, which had already been oppressed by the Japanese occupying forces and was further neglected under Western influence. A hermeneutical dispute developed with the military and bureaucratic elite over the interpretation of Korean history and culture. For after anti-Communism had proved to be of only limited use as an ideological cement, the state leaders again sought to ground their legitimacy in a common Korean identity. The government took massive steps against the opposition. The Minjung theologians too were removed from their posts and arrested; some of them were tortured. Ahn himself was imprisoned on 1 March 1976 as a co-signatory of the

'Declaration on the Democratic Deliverance of our Nation'[10] and condemned to many years in prison. However, through international pressure he was released as early as December of the same year. But his rehabilitation, which made it possible for him to return to Hankuk University, did not take place, like that of many college teachers, until 1984, in a phase of relative *détente*.

The Minjung theologians keep stressing that they are only part of a larger movement in which as Christians they represent a minority. What individual theologians have been formulating since the early 1970s was for the first time presented to a wider public at the invitation of the Christian Conference of Asia (CCA) and the National Council of Churches Korea (NCCK) in 1979 at a conference with the harmless title 'The People of God and the Mission of the Church'. While the consultation was actually taking place, Park Chung-Hee was murdered by the chief of his secret service. The hopes for democratization which were again budding were bloodily stifled in the Kwangju massacre of 1980.[11]

The conference volume[12] remains the theological manifesto of the movement. Everything that has appeared since then is basically just a reminiscence. There is no monograph, just a few articles, theology as a fragment, spoken in a particular situation with no claim to abiding validity. Minjung theology has always remained a minority position in the church, but its protagonists have had an incomparably greater influence in church politics and politics generally.

Like Black Theology, Minjung theology too has produced no explicit christology. Yet here too Jesus Christ is implicitly also the centre of gravity on which the argument focusses. Access again is through the question of the relevance of the person of Jesus for the Korean context. It is to the credit of the New Testament scholar Ahn that he has added a specifically Korean variant to the interpretations of Jesus in liberation theology.[13] In the *ochlos*, the crowd of people around Jesus as they are described in the Gospel of Mark, he discovers a reference group for a theological interpretation of the situation of the Korean Minjung. With *ochlos* the evangelist has adopted a term for 'mass of people' which in the Hellenistic-Jewish literature of the time has predominantly pejorative connotations, in order to denote a group of people which is central in his Gospel. Publicans, sinners and the sick apparently belong to this, as do women and children. It is these people who are socially and religiously despised, the weak and those forced to the periphery, in short the poor and oppressed. This amorphous group of members of the Galilean lower class, the composition of which varies, is the direct concern of Jesus. They stream together wherever Jesus appears and are those to whom his mission is addressed. For them Jesus performs his miracles to demonstrate the nearness of the reign of God. To these 'ordinary people' he promises the kingdom of God. At the same time their proximity grants him a certain protection, for the rulers fear the people. Jesus' unconditional concern for the 'ordinary people' is here already signalled at a linguistic level. With this social kerygmatic interpretation of *ochlos* Ahn corrects the view of form criticism, which merely saw this grouping as a stylistic figure in the sense of the ancient 'chorus'.

The betrayal by the *ochlos* in Jerusalem stands in crass con-tradiction to the close relationship between Jesus and the people in Galilee which had been depicted hitherto. But the passion narrative as a whole is shaped as an increasing process of the isolation of Jesus. Peter, James and John, those disciples who have a particular relationship of trust to Jesus, keep falling asleep in Gethesemane. Then all flee at his arrest. The *ochlos* loudly calls for his death. On the cross even God himself seems distant. Jesus' cry 'My God, my God, why have you forsaken me?' rings out from a deep feeling of human loneliness. But the women stand afar off. They were the only ones who remained.

Mark the evangelist bases his account on oral tradition. Ahn goes this far with traditional exegesis. However, in this con-nection he says that the ordinary people handed on the Jesus event in the form of rumours. Rumours are the form of commu-nication in situations of oppression. The rumour is subversive. The people preserved the stories of how Jesus had lived with them in Galilee, proclaimed the reign of God to them, healed their sicknesses and fed them, and handed these stories on. The representatives of the official church as it consolidated itself acted quite differently. They formulated the kerygma of the meaning of the death and resurrection of Jesus Christ. The kerygma does not go on relating the event itself, but interprets it. This de-historicization serves inwardly to stabilize the institution and outwardly to reduce conflict. By contrast, Ahn emphasizes, in undisguised polemic against Bultmann: 'In the beginning there was the event, not the kergyma.'[14] He again elevates the life of Jesus so that it becomes a constitutive element of christology. The life, death and resurrection of Jesus are the *event* in which God has revealed himself to the world. For Ahn, the category of event is an expression of the historicity of Christian faith. Jesus' activity in Palestine, his death and resurrection, become the hermeneutical key to the presence of the Risen Christ in Minjung events like the self-immolation of the textile worker Chun Tae-Il or the death by torture of the student Park Chun-Chul.[15]

For Ahn, the retelling of the Jesus events is concentrated in social biography. He takes over this term from Kim Yong-Bock (born 1938), who is by far the youngest in the group of the first generation of Minjung theologians. Ahn transfers this concept, which Kim has developed in dealing with the stories of the Korean Minjung,[16] consistently to the relationship between Jesus and the *ochlos*. Jesus does not die for the Minjung but *with* them; he dies the death of the ordinary people. In their suffering the Risen Christ time and again becomes present.

The *corporate theologia crucis* which is taking shape here has brought on Ahn the charge that he identifies the Minjung with Jesus Christ and thus as it were introduces a divinization of the Minjung. This is a criticism which has time and again been made in a similar form of the liberation theologies.[17] Here, however, we must first ask the basic question, 'Who is identified with whom or who identifies himself with whom?' Jesus identified himself with the ordinary people and obeying his call to discipleship, we too should identify ourselves with them.

> Discipleship as identification with Jesus is above all about putting oneself on the side of the poor and oppressed with which Jesus identified himself.[18] 'The Minjung theologians have encountered the suffering Christ in the suffering Minjung.[19]

The emphasis lies on the presence of Jesus Christ in suffering. The Koreans speak of 'Han' and claim that this, like the term

Minjung, cannot be translated. They attribute a certain paradox to the term which runs diametrically counter to the Western conceptions of suffering. Suh Nam-Dong (1918–1984), regarded by many alongside Ahn as the second ancestor of Minjung theology, gives the following short definition:

> Han is an underlying feeling of Korean people. On the one hand, it is a dominant feeling of defeat, resignation, and nothingness. On the other, it is a feeling with a tenacity of will for life which comes to weaker beings. The first aspect can sometimes be sublimated to great artistic expressions and the second aspect could erupt as the energy for a revolution or rebellion.[20]

However, there already seems to be a christological reading of this term, which Suh has taken over from the Catholic poet and lay theologian Kim Chi-Ha (born 1941). For Suh, Han is an expression in Christian terminology of the state of those who are sinned against. '"Sin" is the language of the rulers, "Han" is the language of the Minjung.'[21]

Ahn does away with the division between historical Jesus and kerygmatic Christ in a way which is now already familiar to us from liberation theology, in the *Christus praesens*. The quest for the present Christ has allowed his face to be discovered in the Minjung. The text of the Gospel of Mark and the Korean context interpret each other reciprocally and are recognizable in each other. The presence of Jesus Christ in the suffering of the Minjung has the function of creating identity, and dignity is promised to the ordinary people, which goes against the facts. Once, when I asked him about his method, Ahn replied to me:

> To be honest I have no special methodology, no hermeneutic of my own. To begin with, we did not want to found a new theological school; we just wanted to live. Then through life we got another perspective . . . I have seen things from above, and now I see them from below. I have always looked at everything in terms of the intellect, but now I see everything in terms of the suffering of the Minjung, from the perspective of the suffering. The interpreter and the content of the text may not

be separated. Otherwise, we could easily fall victim to the subject-object scheme. I expound the Bible, and at the same time I expound myself . . . There is no text without context and no context without text. As Bultmann has already said, the exegete is also part of the story, i.e. the text. We expound a text which is two thousand years old, but as Koreans who live in the present day we expound our history. In this respect it is not the Jesus of two thousand years ago; certainly it is the historical Jesus, but he is also present now.[22]

Whereas in accordance with his profession as a New Testament scholar Ahn grounded his Minjung theology in a re-reading of the Gospel of Mark, and took the Korean context into account from this perspective of the text, his *alter ego*, the systematic theologian Suh Nam-Dong, took the opposite course. Suh was fond of speaking of the confluence of two traditions.

Now, the task for Korean minjung theology is to testify that in the Mission of God in Korea there is a confluence of the minjung tradition in Christianity and the Korean minjung tradition. It is to participate and interpret theologically the events which we consider to be God's intervention in history and the work of the Holy Spirit.[23]

In a lecture shortly before his sudden death Suh exchanged theological blows with Ahn over this question of the relationship of text to context. The discussion could not be taken further. When at the Seventh General Assembly of the WCC in Canberra the young Korean theologian Chung Hyun-Kyung (born 1956) stirred people up with a tempestuous theological performance and provoked the theological public with her dictum '*we are the text*, and the Bible and tradition of the Christian church are the context of our theology'[24] this was basically only a new version of a dispute over principles which had already been seething in the previous generation.

Suh's concepts, which still remain theoretical, are already translated into praxis by Hyun Young-Hak (born 1921), the third senior member of the movement. In accordance with his slogan, 'God was not carried piggy-back to Korea by the first missionary',²⁵ he looked for the traces of the historical action of God in Korean culture. Hyun tells stories to which he gives only a sparing theological interpretation. However, in fragmentary form the picture of a fool's christology emerges. In a central theme of the Bongsan mask dance which inspires Hyun's narrative, Malttugi, the servant of the nobleman (Yang-ban), makes mock of his masters. He is a Korean clown who becomes transparent to the figure of Jesus. Hyun also attributes a similar function to the female shaman who in the ritual (Kut) cures the suffering (Han) of her followers.²⁶ In the mask dance or in the feasts the ordinary people gain a *critical transcendence*²⁷ which makes it possible for them to laugh about their tormentor and also about their own wretched situation. Hyun's picture of Jesus, shaped by his experiences with the Minjung, remains ambivalent. Jesus encounters him in his remembrance as a spirit, as he hangs on the cross streaming with blood,²⁸ but also as Dokaebi, a kind of Korean troll, who plays tricks on people.²⁹ In order to become the priest of Han, the Minjung theologians have themselves to be willing to become fools in the discipleship of Jesus. What Ahn has worked out in a matter-of-fact way by the biblical text, Hyun achieves through a narrative staging, imagining the presence of the suffering Christ in the suffering Minjung and vice versa.

Whereas in racism Black Theology attacks an evil which can quickly be understood intersubjectively, as a political theology in the Korean context Minjung theology requires a minimum of information about more recent Korean history in order to be understood. Theologically both movements have equally found access to christology through the person of Jesus and the doctrine of the *Christus praesens*. Both can be understood as theologies of the cross in the best sense, though with different accents. Minjung theology puts all its weight on the presence of Jesus in suffering (Han); Black Theology brings the atonement in Jesus Christ more markedly into the centre. Their arguments meet where they both attribute the creation of identity to Christology.

In the meantime South Africa and South Korea have undergone great political changes. The former opposition is now the government. Whether the exponents of Black Theology and

Minjung theology manage to follow these changes through and adapt to the new challenges or whether these movements have passed their peak is a question which must remain open here. As we shall see in the following sections, however, they have still come to shape new theological departures elsewhere.

§12 Jesus with Us – Christology in the Context of New Departures in Liberation Theology in the 1980s

Indian Dalit theology and Japanese Burakumin theology are late-comers among the liberation theologies of the Third World. Although Dalit theology is referred to in a whole series of quite redundant publications, the sources for Burakumin theology in Western languages are still extremely thin. Nevertheless, the fact that I am putting these two theological movements at the end of this chapter indicates how, to some degree, structures and patterns of argumentation persist. In respect of our leading theme, that means that here too we are not to count on a completely formulated christology. Access is again opened up through the person of Jesus, who is claimed by the representatives of interests among the poor and oppressed in the different contexts as one of them. From this there follows a christological stimulus for the reconstruction of a distinctive identity. As a rule, the exponents of these theologies have read the books of their predecessors. Their network today – through EATWOT or, say, the Commission on Theological Concerns of the Christian Conference of Asia (CTC-CCA) – is far better than it was in the beginnings of contextual theologies, but this has also led to terms like Minjung, Dalit or Burakumin sometimes being used interchangeably at conferences.[1]

1. From the Dalit movement to Dalit theology

Dalit is the current self-designation of the Indian outcastes. 'Caste' is a term coined by the Portuguese for the structuring of

Indian society. The Hindus themselves speak of *varna* (colour) and *jati* (birth, profession). In religious terms the division into castes or *varnas* is rooted in a myth of origins which has been handed down in the Rig Veda:[2]

> When they divided the *Purusa* into many parts, how did they arrange him? What was his mouth? What were his two arms? What were his thighs and feet called?
> The *brahmin* was his mouth, his two arms were made the *rajanya* (warrior), his two thighs the *vaisya* (trader and agriculturist), from his feet the *sudra* (servile class) was born.[3]

These four *varnas* are once again subdivided into many thousand sub-castes by the *jatis*. Whereas as 'twice-born' the members of the first three *varnas* may read the holy scriptures, this is forbidden to the Shudras. Accordingly, the outcastes, who remain outside this system, are called the *a*-varnas. They even come below the Shudras. Since on the basis of their occupations they are regarded as ritually unclean, they are also called 'untouchables'. They must live in their own districts at the edge of the villages and towns, and may encounter the caste Hindus only at a due distance.

The English colonial administration spoke of the 'depressed classes', and later they were especially promoted as 'scheduled castes' by the programme of positive discrimination. Mahatma Gandhi called the outcastes 'children of God (Harijans)', a quite ambivalent term, as it is synonymous with the designation for the fatherless children of temple prostitutes. The self-designation 'Dalit' probably goes back to Gandhi's opponent, the founder of the modern Dalit movement, B. R. Ambedkar.[4] The term to some degree coincides with the whole semantic field of 'oppression'. The Dalit theologian Arvind P. Nirmal mentions six meanings:

> (1) the broken, the torn, the rent, the burst, the split, (2) the opened, the expanded, (3) the bisected, (4) the driven asunder, the dispelled, the scattered (5) the downtrodden, the crushed, the destroyed, (6) the manifested, the displayed.[5]

The origins of the division into castes and the segregation of the outcastes are obscure. The current theory is that around 1500 BC the so-called Aryans, Indo-European tribal peoples from Central Asia, invaded Northern India, spread through the land and subjugated the original inhabitants. However, whereas John C. B. Webster in his history of the Dalit Christians[6] remains sceptical about the evidence of the sources, which are primarily the Rig Veda and the archaeological evidence of the pre-Aryan Indus valley civilization, the Dalit theologian James Massey builds his whole argument on this.[7] Massey comes to the conclusion 'that the Dalits share their historical roots with the indigenous people, particularly groups known as the *adivasi*'.[8] Here he agrees with the pioneer Christian thinkers of the tribal societies who seek a connection with the Dalit movement.[9] As in Minjung theology and the other liberation theologies, here again we come upon a hermeneutical construct of history, to some degree a historical-theological myth of origins.[10]

By contrast, Webster soberly states that 'the quest for the origins of caste, untouchability and specific Dalit castes ends in speculation, uncertainty and frustration'.[11] He devotes four and a half pages to the problem and then turns to a description of the development of the modern Dalit movement, in which he distinguishes three phases. Webster sees its beginnings in the so-called mass movements. These are collective conversions of the Dalits to Islam, to Sikhism, but above all to Christianity, which gave them a certain amount of publicity. The Hindus saw themselves put under pressure by a reinforcement of the religious minorities. When the British in their 1909 constitution (Government of India Act) defined India not as a single nation but as a diversity of divergent interests, the Dalit movement entered its second phase. The politics of numbers by which these interests were to be regulated was primarily orientated on religious adherence. This principle was continued in the third phase, when only the Hindu Dalits came to enjoy compensatory discrimination. Thus the Christian Dalits were *de facto* doubly discriminated against, as Dalits and as Christians, and did not win proper legally guaranteed privileges as part of the preferential treatment of them as Dalits. Whereas the scope of the law had meanwhile been extended to the Sikh Dalits (1956) and the Buddhist Dalits (1990), the Christians continued to fall outside it.[12] Often mocked as 'rice Christians', who had become Christians only to improve their wretched situation,[13] they are further discriminated against within the new community of faith as well. Although the majority of Indian Christians are Dalits, estimates speak of up to 80 per cent among the Protestants and still 60 per cent among the Catholics who in their missionary activity are traditionally orientated more strongly on the upper class.[14] The Dalits do not have appropriate representation in the church governments, nor have these taken the Dalit problem on board. The church hierarchy and theology are equally dominated by converted members of higher castes who theologically sought continuity with Hinduism. In this context A. P. Nirmal speaks of a 'Brahminic tradition' of Indian theology.[15]

The pioneer thinker of the modern Dalit movement, B. R. Ambedkar, himself an outcaste from Maharashtra, studied in the USA and England on a scholarship and returned to his homeland in 1923 with a doctorate in law. He quickly advanced to become a spokesman of the outcastes. At the round table conferences in London in 1930/1931 which discussed the future participation of the Indians in the government of their country, he called for the rights of the oppressed and the minorities. A dispute with Gandhi broke out over his demand for special representation for his clientele. Gandhi's famous 'fast to the death' of 1932 was directed less against the English colonial system than against such a special regulation for the outcastes. In the so-called 'Poona pact', Gandhi conceded to Ambedkar a set of parliamentary seats for these groups in exchange for his falling into line.

Whereas Gandhi wanted to reform Hinduism, Ambedkar parted company with it:

> I had the misfortune to be born with the stigma of 'untouchable'. But it is not my fault, but I will not die a Hindu, for this is within my power.[16]

Shortly before his sudden death in 1956, with hundreds of thousands of his followers he was converted to Neo-Buddhism. Ambedkar attached great importance to education; his motto was 'Unite, educate and agitate!'[17] The educational establishments which he founded became the cells of the Dalit literature movement (Dalit Sahitya Movement). Some of its protagonists founded the Dalit Panthers in 1972. As a model they took the negro literature and the Black Panther Movement in the USA. In analogy to Black Power and Black Consciousness, there is now talk of Dalit power and Dalit consciousness. (The slogan 'Dalit is dignified' is reminiscent of 'Black is beautiful'.) Here a direct influence can be demonstrated of one emancipation movement of the poor and oppressed on another kindred movement, even at the secular level.

Dalit theology developed in the shadow of the Dalit movement, itself influenced by Black Theology. On the Protestant side a landmark was a consultation in 1986, on the theme of 'Towards a Dalit Theology', which was organized jointly by the Christian Dalit Liberation Movement (CLDM) and the Christian Institute for the Study of Religion and Society (CISRS). The conference volume published in 1988 under the same title[18] contains most of the contributions which are still normative today; in the meantime they have often been reprinted.[19]

Seen from the outside, Dalit theology bears the typical features of liberation theologies. I shall elucidate that here briefly by four points.

• *Dalit theology is a theological movement.*
Like the liberation theologies generally, Dalit theology bears very strongly the stamp of a new theological direction which is supported by a group of theologians, from which individuals often come to stand out only in retrospect.

• *Dalit theology is only part of the more comprehensive Dalit movement.*
The new theological departure is taking place in the wake of the political and cultural emancipation movement of the outcastes. In this the Christian Dalits represent a minority, just as the Christians in Asia generally are a diminishing minority. The same is therefore also true of Minjung theology and Burakumin theology. In Latin America, the USA and South Africa, which have a Christian stamp, it was secular emancipation movements, sometimes also influenced by Marxism, which gave the impetus to new theological reflection.

• *Dalit theology is part of the project of reconstructing a counter-culture.*
The Dalit movement and with it Dalit theology oppose socio-economic and political structures – the Hindu caste system – which have a cultural and religious foundation. Contrary to other liberation theologies, this is not a controversy with the late consequences of European colonialism. By contrast, Minjung theology and Black Theology were part of cultural renaissances which in the course of the reconstruction of their own identity revitalized the cultural heritage which had been suppressed by the Japanese colonial rulers or the white slave-owners and colonists. Such tendencies developed only late in Latin American liberation theology. Here for a long time the emphasis lay one-sidedly on the socio-economic and political question. Through the conversation with the African and Asian theologies of in-culturation and dialogue a change of consciousness took place here. Today popular religion, and the culture of the indigenous and Afro-Latin Americans, are being rediscovered.

• *Dalit theology is a counter-theology.*
Dalit theology is also specifically opposed to another contextual theology, the dialogue theology of the theological establishment, most of whom belong to the higher castes. Similarly, the South African Black theology was opposed to the exodus theology of the Boers.[20] Latin American liberation theology and Black Theology are also opposed to a liberal theology which does not go far enough for them in their concern for reform.[21]

2. Jesus was a Dalit – Arvind P. Nirmal (India)

Arvind P. Nirmal (1936–1995),[22] who died early, regarded himself as the founder of Dalit theology. In a lecture given at United Theological College (UTC) in Bangalore in 1981 he claims to be the first to have referred to the need for such a theology.

> In 1981, therefore, when called upon to deliver the valedictory address to the Carey Society of the United Theological College, Bangalore, I entitled my address 'Towards a Sudra Theology'. It provoked a great deal of discussion. It was

pointed out that the word 'Sudra' as well as 'Harijan' were resented by those to whom they were applied. I found out that the so-called Sudras preferred to be addressed as dalits. I further discovered that there was already a dalit or Dalit Panther movement for liberation. While still in Bangalore, I heard that in Maharashtra, towards the end of the sixties, a new trend in Marathi literature known as Dalit Sahitya movement had captured the imagination of dalit writers. When I moved to Pune in 1981,[23] I decided to study this movement closely.[24]

Nirmal still speaks here of a Shudra theology. Shudra is really the designation for the lowest caste whose members, themselves at the bottom end of the Hindu social order, still look down on the Dalits. Even if Nirmal points out that in Mahashtra 'the terms "Shudra", "Ati Shurdra" and "Dalit " are interchangable',[25] this terminology would still blur clear boundaries in the lower spectrum of the caste system.

Whoever the spiritual father of Dalit theology may have been, at all events Nirmal was the first occupant of a newly-created chair of Dalit theology at the Lutheran Gurukul College, Madras (1987–1994), and his inaugural lecture 'Towards a Christian Dalit theology' (3 November 1987)[26] can with some justice be regarded as the theological manifesto of the movement.[27]

Arvind Nirmal was born the son of a pastor from a small town in South India. His parents' marriage had remained childless for fourteen years. Nirmal contributed to the formation of myths about himself when he bandied around the following 'pre-birth story':

One day a pupil of Sadhu Sundar Singh came to my home town. He prayed for my parents and announced to them the birth of a son and a daughter. But the son had to be given to the service of the church. Before I was born, my fate was already determined. However, my parents did not think that one day I would become a theological teacher.[28]

Nirmal indeed studied theology. After he passed the examination with distinction his church authorities first sent him to the countryside. Here Nirmal had to learn that even as an academic he continued to be exposed to discrimination as an outcaste. He might give English lessons to the children of members of higher castes, but he might not draw water from their wells. Like the other Dalits he had to keep a distance of 200 metres from the wells of the Hindus and drink the brackish water of the Dalit well. Even if Nirmal later says that this experience left a mark on him, initially it does not find expression in his theology. After study in Oxford,[29] his academic career began as lecturer in systematic theology at UTC in Bangalore (1976–1981).

The collection of his articles from the years 1970–1990, which appeared in 1991 under the title *Heuristic Explorations*,[30] clearly shows two interests in the research of these years: as is already indicated by the title, a grappling with scientific and epistemological questions which in his view previously had played no role in Indian Christian theology,[31] and the religious pluralism of India. Nirmal shows himself most familiar with the hermeneutical discussion.[32] Even if later he is fond of quoting a 1978 article,[33] in which he goes critically into the 'Brahminic tradition' in Indian Christian theology, Nirmal assigns dialogue theology an important place in theological education and himself plays a lively part in this discussion.[34] Only at the end of the collection is his inaugural lecture for the chair of Dalit theology at Gurukul reprinted.

Nirmal[35] characterizes Dalit theology by means of an exegesis of the Deuteronomistic confession (Deut.26.5–9), to which he attaches paradigmatic significance (220f.).

• *Dalit theology is a theology of identity*
Unlike liberation theology, which has elevated the exodus event to be the basic datum of the history of God with his people, Nirmal enquires into the origins of the people of Israel. Like the 'wandering Aramaean' who came to Egypt with a few people and only there, in a foreign land, grew into a great people, from being 'no people' the Dalits have become 'God's people'. But this comparison is lame in so far as according to the Dalit movement's picture of history the Dalits were in fact among the original inhabitants of India and were robbed of their identity by the invading Aryans. Here too the real point of comparison

remains that the Dalits' dignity is restored by God through the promise of God's election, contrary to the facts.

• *Dalit theology is a theology of the people*
The wandering Aramaean was the patriarch of the exodus community; Dalit theology too seeks the origin and identity of the Dalit community. 'The question of identity and roots is inseparably bound with the sense of belonging to a community' (221).

• *Dalit theology is a theology of suffering*
Here too the comparison with Israel, which has already been seen to go wrong, must be maintained. Just as the Israelites suffered in Egypt, so too the Dalits suffer discrimination from the caste system.

• *Dalit theology is a liberation theology*
Liberation takes place with a strong hand and has intrinsic value. The settlement is a second step. The Dalits have to organize themselves and develop a Dalit consciousness. They were not just 'no-people' but 'no-men and no-women' before they became 'God's people'. Here Nirmal clearly dissociates himself from liberation theology of Latin American origin. Its acceptance in India (Nirmal uses the vague terminology 'Third World theology') is doomed to failure from the start, as the class analysis inspired by Marxism fails in the controversy with the caste system, which has religious and cultural sanctions (216f.).[36] By contrast, the Dalit problem first gives the theme of 'liberation' its specifically Indian ring.

Alongside the general characterization as a theology of the people and liberation theology, with identity and suffering two themes are mentioned which are familiar to us. Moreover, for his argument that Jesus was a Dalit Nirmal works with these elements from liberation theology. Jesus identifies himself 'with the Dalits of his day' (cf. e.g. Mark 2.15f.); in his 'Nazareth Manifesto' (Luke 4.16f.) he promises them liberation (227). He is the Son of man who must suffer. But the central symbol is the cross.

On the Cross, he was the broken, the crushed, the split, the torn, the driven asunder man – the dalit in the fullest possible meaning of that term. (229)

Nirmal gives christological overtones to the sixth meaning of Dalit mentioned at the beginning, "manifested" or "displayed".

It is precisely in and through the weaker, the downtrodden, the crushed, the oppressed and the marginalized that God's saving glory is manifested or displayed. This is because brokenness belongs to the very being of God. (230)

Again it is Jesus' presence in suffering, the fact 'that the Jesus of Palestine or more immediately, the Jesus of India is in the midst of the liberation struggle of the dalits of India' (223), in which, contrary to the facts of the conditions in which they live, the dignity of the Dalits before God is grounded.

However, Nirmal labours to demonstrate 'that Jesus Christ whose followers we are was himself a Dalit – despite his being a Jew' (225). Unlike the liberation theologies that we have investigated so far, he goes beyond the mere construction of an analogy which is to be legitimated theologically by the doctrine of the *Christus praesens* and wants to transfer the caste system directly to Palestine in the time of Jesus. In the case of the order of castes this concordistic[37] way of proceeding, with which perhaps initial success is to be achieved among the peasants of Latin America or the nomads of Africa, is doomed to failure from the start; the conditions are simply too different for it.

The reference to Jesus' genealogy, too (226), is hardly convincing; that among his forebears there are some morally dubious figures – Nirmal mentions Tamar, Rahab and Solomon – can, to put it casually, happen in any good family; a reference to the caste order is hard to get from these morally offensive features. Finally, the attempt to connect the thesis that by driving out the merchants and money-changers from the Court of the Gentiles Jesus restored their religious rights to the non-Jews with the Hindu prohibition on Dalits entering the temple seems to me equally unfortunate. The cultural and religious limitations of the caste system are transcended by Jesus Christ's universal message of salvation. Nirmal's thinking here remains imprisoned in Hindu categories.

It is in keeping with this observation that Nirmal transfers to God the servant of God typology which in the Christian tradition is mostly referred to Jesus Christ. God himself is a Dalit God. 'He is a servant God – a God who serves' (224).

> Are we prepared to say that my house-maid, my sweeper, my *bhangi* is my God? It is precisely in this sense that our God is a servant God. He is a waiter, a *dhobi*, a *bhangi* traditionally, all such services have been the lot of dalits. This means we have participated in these servant-God's ministries. To speak of a Servant God, therefore, is to recognize and identify Him as a truely Dalit Deity. (224)

So as we have seen in S. J. Samartha, the most prominent representative at the time of the Brahman tradition in Indian theology which he fought, Nirmal advocates a decided theocentricity. Here the doctrine of God and christology are notably fused; at the same time the divinity and manhood of Jesus drift apart. What is left is Jesus, the Dalit.

3. The Burakumin wear Jesus' crown of thorns – Teruo Kuribayashi (Japan)

By comparison with Dalit theology, Burakumin theology is still right at the beginning of its development. It is carried on above all by pastors who work among the Burakumin. Their commitment has found a record not least in church documents.[38] The theologian Teruo Kuribayashi has put the Burakumin problem in the wider Asian context in his doctoral thesis written at Union Theological Seminary in New York.[39]

The discrimination against the so-called Burakumin or Eta goes back to the class order of the Japanese Middle Ages under the Tokugawa shogunate (1600–1867).[40] Teruo Kuribayashi translates *buraku* by 'off the village'; he derives the suffix '-min' from the Japanese word for 'eye' and gives the composite the meaning 'people whose eyes are pierced by a needle and blinded'.[41] This form of almost mythical connotations of conceptualities could already be observed in Minjung and Dalit theologies. Eta is rendered in an essentially more sober way as 'much filth'[42] or 'covered in filth'.[43] Further below the Burakumin or Eta are the Hinin, 'beggars, prostitutes, itinerant entertainers, mediums, diviners, religious wanderers, and fugitives from justice',[44] but their status is not hereditary. As leather workers, skinners or grave-diggers the Burakumin were regarded as unclean because of their occupations. Like the Dalits they had to settle on the edges of the villages and towns. Once they were separate, the occupational status and thus the social status was hereditary. The Burakumin are 'from an ethnic perspective pure Japanese',[45] so the discrimination against them 'is neither racial, ethnic nor religious in nature'.[46] That in contrast to the other Japanese they have no link to the genealogy of the imperial family is a later mythological construct.[47] Although in the course of the Meiji restoration[48] after 1871 they were officially given equal status, the discrimination against the Burakumin lasts to the present day. This is a fate that they share with the Korean minority, who were taken off to Japan during the Japanese colonization and the Second World War; with Japan's original inhabitants the Ainus; and with the population of Okinawa. In 1922 the Burakumin initiated a liberation movement, Zenkoku Suiheisha (1922–1940). As a banner this secular emancipation movement, without having a majority of Christians, chose the scarlet crown of thorns against a black background, fixed to a bamboo spear, the symbol of the Japanese peasant revolt. The manifesto of the Founding Assembly states:

> Burakumin throughout the country, unite! . . . Brothers and sisters! Our ancestors sought after and practised liberty and equality. But they became the victims of a base contemptible system developed by the ruling class. These became the martyrs of industry. As a reward for skinning animals they were flayed alive.
>
> As a recompense for tearing out the hearts of animals, their own warm, human hearts were ripped out. These were spat upon with the words of ridicule. Yet all through these cursed nightmares, their blood, still proud to be human, did not dry up. Yes! Now we have come to the age when men and women,

pulsing with this blood, are trying to become divine. *The time has come, when the martyrs' crown of Thorns will be blessed.* The time has come when we can be proud of being ETA. . . . Let there be warmth in the hearts of people, and let there be light upon all humankind. From this, the Suiheisha is born.[49]

The crown of thorns symbolizes the presence of Jesus in suffering. It replaces the symbol of the cross, which is all too often misused in an ideological way.[50] Again the motif of the revaluation of a stigmatization here becomes a self-designation. Here the Eta or Burakumin are promised through the messianic symbol of the crown of thorns a dignity contrary to the facts, in a way that we have already seen among the poor of Latin America, the blacks, the Minjung and the Dalits. The element of the presence of Jesus in suffering which creates identity can be demonstrated throughout. On the occasion of the second General Assembly of the Suiheisha in 1923 the exodus was accepted in a similar way.

March 3rd of 1922 shall be remembered as the glorious foundation day of the National Suiheisha. It was the day when our three million brothers and sisters under curse chose the path towards liberation. It reminds us of the people of Israel who used to be despised in Egypt, tried to be free from oppression, led by day in a pillar of cloud and by night in a pillar of fire, and marched into the desert of Paran. Since then a year has passed, and now our day of the Second National Convention has come. Though the wilderness is endless and the promised land of Canaan is still far, our marching tone is even higher and more brave. History is a process of liberation. Three million brothers and sisters and six thousand un-liberated Buraku, unite under the flag of the crown of thorns![51]

Teruo Kuribayashi (born in 1948), today professor at Kwansei Gakuin University, gained his doctorate in 1986 at Union Theological Seminary, New York, with a thesis entitled *A Theology of the Crown of Thorns: Towards the Liberation of the Asian Outcasts.*[52] As the title already indicates, Kuribayashi surveys the whole Asian context; he explicitly mentions 'India,

Burma, Nepal, Korea and Japan' (vi), but then concentrates essentially on India, Japan and initially Korea. His central thesis is that the situation of the outcasts in Asian societies is not to be explained by socio-economic and political theories, but is the consequence of 'religio-cultural sanctions' (14) in dealing with 'dirt, blood and death' (9), behind which are 'concepts of uncleanness and desecration' which presuppose a knowledge of the Asian religions and cultures and their history (15). However, the description and analysis then remain very superficial. That is also true of the Japanese context and the situation of the Burakumin themselves. Instead of this, Kuribayashi offers a broad, socially kerygmatic interpretation of the Bible, for the 'context and the biblical text relate dialectically' (115). Unfortunately the story theology praised by the author (70) similarly remains a postulate. Text and context stand side by side with relatively little connection.

The structure of Kuribayashi's argument follows a formula with which by now we have already become familiar:[53] (1) The group discriminated against is mentioned and its members are identified with the poor and oppressed of the biblical writings.[54] (2) In this context, with reference to the New Testament, sin is understood as a social and not a moral category.[55] (3) An attempt is made at connection with a secular emancipation movement which in the case of the Suiheisha in fact already works openly with Christian symbols: 'it was the Burakumin themselves who first took Jesus' crown of thorns as the symbol of their suffering and liberation'.[56] (4) Jesus is present among the Burakumin as at the same time a fellow-sufferer and liberator.[57]

Kuribayashi's ethical appeal to the churches to exercise their prophetic office meets up with an initiative from the National Japanese Council of Churches which as early as 1976 at its twenty-sixth General Assembly published a statement and appointed a special committee for questions of discrimination against the Burakumin.[58]

If Dalit theology is influenced by the Black Theology of the USA, Minjung theology was godfather to Burakumin theology. Kuribayashi quotes at length the Catholic poet and lay theologian from Korea, Kim Chi-Ha. Moreover James Cone is not unknown in Japan and Korea.[59]

Neither theological movement is to be underestimated in the stimuli and correctives that they provide. They bring into awareness problems which have long been kept silent about and correct a one-sided picture communicated by the older contextual theologies. However, theologically they are only slight innovations compared with the state of discussion arrived at so far. The question is whether that is intended at all or if their protagonists are satisfied with raising the problem. Note that here I do not want to speak of the formation of a theological system in the classical sense of the word. But it is important for the contextual theologians to link the themes further if they are to both engage in international discussion and replace the existing paradigm of theology which time and again they have sharply criticized.

That brings us to the end of our way through the contextual theologies of Africa, Asia and Latin America. The final part investigates what they have in common and where they differ, and the opportunities for ecumenical learning. It attempts a systematic summary and shows the possibilities of dialogue with the contextual theologies.

III. THE FORMS TAKEN BY JESUS CHRIST

§13 Models of Contextual Christology – Commonalities, Divergences and Opportunities for Ecumenical Learning

Despite the cultural differences, the biographical portraits of the contextual theologians presented in the previous sections prove to have striking features in common. Most of the theologians have a 'middle-class background', though this term is useful in the Third World only with qualifications and is hardly compatible with our notions of the middle class. But at any rate often the fathers and mothers already enjoyed a formal education, perhaps as teachers, and saw to it that their children also had access to higher education. The outcome was therefore assured. Among the Catholic representatives life usually followed more peaceful courses, since on entering an order or being ordained as a secular priest they came under the obligatory protection of their superiors or the church authorities, who furthered their gifts and opened up opportunities of further education. These conditions are certainly also a reason why their biographies often fade into the background behind their work.

Regardless of their confessional allegiance, all have received at any rate part of their academic training in the West, in the USA or Europe.[1] Many have also written doctoral theses on the classical dogmatic themes or traditional theological schemes. Common to them all is also the experience of the much-quoted epistemological break in their theological biography. On their return home the knowledge that they obtained in the West seemed of little use for overcoming the problems of their own context. On the other hand, this did not lead to a total break with the Western theological tradition. Despite occasionally very sharp polemic, the Western heritage remains present. The break has taken place at the levels of fundamental theology and method. Theology has become far more useful in character. There is theological reflection on acute problems, not so much the formation of a system. Pamphlets, manifestos, meditations, lecture manuscripts and short articles are the dominant literary forms. The basic hermeneutical structure of the dialectical relationship between text and context is recognizable throughout. The perception of the context is itself always a hermeneutical construction. The liberation theologians create their own picture of history with partly mythological traits. The theologies of inculturation or dialogue develop a special view of cultures and religions, often in the framework of cultural renaissances.

During our way through the different sketches, the typology of theologies of liberation and inculturation or dialogue introduced at the beginning, on the basis of the thematic focal points within a particular context, has also taken on theological contours from the side of the text. When the liberation theologians were confronted with the suffering of the poor and oppressed, the theology of the cross presented itself to them as a central perspective for interpreting their experiences theologically. Jesus' concern for the ordinary people, the poor, sick and sinners, toll collectors and prostitutes, the Galilean *ochlos,* and his death on the cross, which countless of these people before him and after him suffered, also make present-day situations of suffering, poverty and oppression transparent to his presence. Christ did not suffer *for* these people, but time and again he suffers *with* them. He is the *Christus praesens*, the Son of God present in the Spirit in their suffering. This in fact replaces the traditional theology of expiation and sacrifice with a *corporate theologia crucis.*

The fabric of christological themes is here structured in quite different ways from contextual theology to contextual theology. Whereas in the African and Asian liberation theologies, which are predominantly Protestant, the crucifixion is emphasized as the central event in the life of Jesus, the Catholic liberation theology of Latin America inscribes the death on the cross in the span of the incarnation. But common to all the theologies is their *function as a basis for identity,* which they attribute to christology. Christ's presence in suffering bestows on the poor and oppressed a dignity before God contrary to the facts of the conditions in which they live, and makes them inscribe their own history in the history of Jesus Christ.

In the African and Asian theologies of inculturation or dialogue the theme *vere homo, vere deus* is unfolded again in critical discussion with the soteriological notions which are prevalent in the particular cultures and religions.[2] The Africans are fond of identifying the Christian God with their own tribal God and regard Jesus Christ as the new element in which their own religion really comes to fulfilment. By giving him an honorific African name they want to make him at home among them. Here African theology becomes a *theologia gloriae,* which praises Christ as the *Christus victor.* Among the contextual theologies it comes closest to the Orthodox option. There is also a widespread view among Asian theologians that the same God is really hidden behind the different religions. As result, the divinity and humanity of Jesus Christ part company. As the side of God turned towards human beings, Christ is absorbed into the doctrine of God, and Jesus threatens to become one holy man or prophet among others.[3]

The theologies of the cross in their different African and Asian conceptualizations are an important corrective. This function of christology or the cross as a critical authority in a multicultural religious situation can also be found in some christocentric theologies of inculturation or dialogue. However, they restrict christology to a purely formal criterion; the story of Jesus is not related further. Generally speaking, the theologies of inculturation, apart from those of C. S. Song and Kosuke Koyama, show a weakness in narrative. They operate almost exclusively on the level of the generative themes and the links between themes.

Let us once again recall the different central perspectives of christology mentioned at the beginning: the life, death and resurrection of Jesus Christ. The liberation theologians approach the themes of the life and death in a more strongly narrative way, whereas the theologies of inculturation keep to the formal level.

The perspective of the incarnation serves as a theological basis for their efforts at inculturation, with the cross as criterion. Generally speaking, the perspective of the resurrection remains implicit, but has its support in the *Christus praesens* or *Christus victor.*

The confessional boundaries between Catholic and Protestant theology have long ago become fluid. By contrast, the Orthodox hardly take any part in these discussions. The liberation theologians say that God acts in history, whereas for the theologians of inculturation and dialogue God was always already present in the cultures and religions. This God has revealed himself in Jesus Christ. The liberation theologians see here the hermeneutical key to their experiences of reality, but the theologians of inculturation and dialogue are occasionally led to doubt the uniqueness of this event. Does not salvation largely lie in God's creative action? Is it not already grounded in God's fundamental concern for his creatures?

Like the perspective of the resurrection, pneumatology too is generally weak, even if it is always included in the *praesentia Dei* and the *Christus praesens.* It is no coincidence that a conflict with the Orthodox was sparked off over contextual theologies by the question of the Holy Spirit. When the young Korean theologian Chung Hyun-Kyung at the Seventh General Assembly of the World Council of Churches in Canberra turned her main lecture on the slogan of the conference, 'Come, Holy Spirit . . . Renew the Whole Creation',[4] into a happening, and then stylized the Korean spirits of the ancestors as icons of the Holy Spirit, there was an outrage.[5] As well as the question of the saving significance of the cross, the relationship between the Godhead and the manhood in Jesus Christ, the divine Trinity also needs renewed clarification.

So it is again the great generative themes of Christian faith which the text also evokes in the new contexts. Now it cannot be a matter of translating the terminological clarifications of the early church, which are steeped in the cultural and religious world of Hellenistic ideas, one by one into the contexts of Africa, Asia and Latin America. Rather, we must keep investigating the conceptions which lie behind them. In addition, in the case of the theology of the early church we have to do with tradition long

Table 10: Models of contextual christology

	Socio-economic and political type (liberation theologies)	Cultural and religious type (inculturation and dialogue theologies)
generative themes ↓ *text / context* →	• Poverty and oppression • Reconstruction of the people's history of suffering • Human dignity	• Cultural-religious pluralism • Cultural renaissances • Cultural identity
Incarnation	The life of Jesus as an ingredient of christology	Theological foundation for the process of inculturation
vere homo – vere deus	• *theologia crucis* • *Christus patiens* (emphasis on the humanity)	• *theologia gloriae* • *Christus victor* (emphasis on the deity)
theology of the cross	Providing identity	Criterion of identity
the triune God	God acts in history	God is present in the cultures and religions
	Jesus Christ as the hermeneutical key	Christ as the side of God turned towards human beings
	(The *Holy Spirit* as the medium of communication *ad intra* and *ad extra*)	

become doctrine, which has excluded various heresies, whereas the contextual theologies are still open processes.

The Third World theologians have added meaning to the text by linking the generative themes of the text with the generative themes of their particular context; at the same time they have broken open narrownesses in the Western theological tradition. The programme of the liberation theologies is evocatively summarized in the 'option for the poor'. In many respects, their re-reading of the story of Jesus against the background of experiences of poverty and oppression coincides with the insights of the Western exegesis of the Gospels in terms of social history.

By contrast, Paul has so far been marginalized in the contextual theologies. One can only speculate about the reasons. This may be connected with the literary genre of the epistolary literature or Paul's theological conceptuality, which seem at first to be a bar to narrative reception. Anyone who investigated what the contextual theologies have to say, for example, as an explanation of the doctrine of justification would soon have to make a zero return. The term as such occurs only rarely.[6]

Whereas the liberation theologies are biblical theologies, many theologies of inculturation and dialogue operate on the level of themes. Nevertheless, in what follows I want to open up the dialogue with a reconstruction of Paul's theological biography. I link to that the thesis that just as Jesus' concern for the poor and oppressed has become a generative theme of liberation theology, so Paul and his doctrine of justification by faith alone would be especially appropriate for the problems of inculturation. At the same time, the question of the cultural and religious factors taken up in the contextual theologies may give new impetus to our understanding of Paul.

Epilogue: Paul and Culture

Paul embodies in person the basic conflict in primitive Christianity, the crossing of the boundary between Jews and Gentiles or Jewish Christians and Gentile Christians. Predestined by his origin in the Diaspora and his consequent familiarity with the Hellenized environment to a mission to the Gentiles which crossed boundaries, he never denied his Jewish origins. However, after his calling, his own denial of the efficacy of the law for salvation brought him into conflict not only with the Jews but soon also with the Jewish Christians. Nevertheless, at the cost of his life he took the side of unity in the diversity of the early church.

Like Jesus himself, his contemporary Paul[1] was also a born Jew. They never met. Paul is that figure in primitive Christianity who still emerges most clearly for us from the darkness of history. For the reconstruction of his biography I shall use primarily his own letters, all composed within a few years towards the end of his life. To this I shall add the Acts of the Apostles by way of a supplement. I adopt a centrist position over their historicity.[2] They are certainly not the first church history in the modern sense; their author writes with a theological intention for a particular clientele.[3] On the other hand, some things can also be tested by means of the letters. Of the seven letters of Paul commonly regarded as authentic today, I Thessalonians is generally regarded as the earliest and Romans as Paul's theological testament.[4] The sequence of the other letters is disputed. Like the chronology,[5] the places of composition also offer much occasion for speculation. Paul himself refers only in passing to his biography except in his account of himself in the first two chapters of Galatians. Nevertheless the author still remains recognizable for us behind his letters.

That Paul wrote letters at all is already an indication of his education. He proves to be familiar with Hellenistic popular philosophy and rhetoric.[6] He dictated his correspondence (Rom. 16.22), but occasionally also wrote in his own hand (Gal. 6.11); he probably wrote the whole of the short letter to Philemon from prison by himself (Philemon 19). It is the only letter that is addressed to an individual and his household (Philemon 1f.). The others are all addressed to communities in big cities and are to be read aloud in the assembly (I Thess. 5.27). The letters were often delivered by collaborators, who commuted between the particular place where Paul was staying and the communities. Sometimes the communities also sent envoys to him. He reacts in writing to some of the things that are reported (I Cor. 5.1; 7.1).

Paul's letters show him to us at the culmination of his career as missionary to the Gentiles. He demonstrates an amazing talent for organization. Paul had built up a staff of collaborators to look after his communities, which time and again came into conflict with the local synagogue, were attacked by Judaizing itinerant missionaries, and were oppressed by their Hellenistic environment.[7] These collaborators not only maintained communication between him and his communities but sometimes also had to represent him locally. Paul recruited them in the communities, and sometimes they were also sent out directly by these communities, to collaborate for a time in the mission. But the communities supported Paul not only personally but also spiritually (Phil. 1.19) and financially (Phil. 4.10–14,18; II Cor. 11.8f.).

By comparison, we learn little more about his origin and early days[8] than that he is of the tribe of Benjamin and counts himself among the Pharisees (Phil. 3.5). His familiarity with an urban milieu and his Hellenistic education indicate that he comes from the Jewish Diaspora in one of the large cities of the empire. Acts mentions Tarsus in Cilicia as his place of birth. He is said to have been a citizen of his home town (Acts 21.39) and to have already inherited his Roman citizenship from his father (Acts 16.37f.; 22.25–29; 23.27; indirectly 25.10f.; 21.25f.; 28.19). He received his Jewish education at the feet of Gamaliel, one of the leading Pharisaic scholars of his time (Acts 22.3). By profession he was a tentmaker (Acts 18.3).

What is most disputed is his Roman citizenship.⁹ There are several reasons against:

* In Paul's time it was still relatively rare even among provincial dignitaries.
* The rights and duties of a Roman citizen are difficult to reconcile with Paul's self-attested membership of the Pharisees, who observed the law strictly.
* The beatings by the synagogues and the state authorities which he repeatedly suffered (II Cor. 11.24f.) could not have been inflicted on a Roman citizen.

This suggests that the author of Acts inferred from Paul's transportation to Rome that he was a Roman citizen, especially as this corresponded completely with his conception that Paul was a model Jew and Christian and a loyal citizen of the Roman empire at the same time. For similar reasons, whether he was a citizen of Tarsus as well is also questionable. For example, in the long run Paul could hardly have avoided worship of the city gods.

Paul's education in Jerusalem, under Gamaliel at that, is dubious. By his own account (Gal. 1.22) he was not known personally to the communities in Judaea. However, study in Jerusalem would again fit well into the picture of Paul that Luke is concerned to draw.

The information about Tarsus as his birthplace is itself less open to suspicion. At any rate Paul reports that he carried on a mission in this region in his early days (Gal. 1.21). The information that he was a tentmaker by trade may also fit with this. The apostle was proud that he could dispense with the support from the community which was really due to him and live by the work of his own hands. Often he worked far into the night (I Thess. 2.9; cf. I Cor. 4.12).¹⁰ He will have been an itinerant craftsman, without a workshop of his own, paid by the day. In the catalogues of his vicissitudes Paul himself reports that things sometimes did not go at all well with him (I Cor. 4.10–13; II Cor. 6.4–10; 11.23–30, 32f.). Yet he knew 'being full and hungry, having a surplus and suffering from want' (Phil. 4.11f.). His communities supported him when he was in need (Phil. 4.10–20; II Cor. 11.9), and he found lodging in their houses (Philemon 22).

Like Paul himself, his communities are also to be located more in the lower class; just a few rich people will have belonged to them. But there were none of the utterly rich and powerful, just as there were none of the utterly poor.[11]

As a Pharisee who was loyal to the law, Paul had become a persecutor of the followers of Christ around the synagogues of the Diaspora (Gal. 1.13f.; Phil. 3.5f.; I Cor. 15.9); whether this was also the case in Jerusalem (Acts 8.3) is doubtful, given Gal. 1.22f. Paul depicts his calling to be apostle to the Gentiles as a revelation of the son of God 'in me' (Gal. 1.16). He sees this event as the last of a series of appearances which began with the appearance to Peter (I Cor. 15.5–8). What Paul reports briefly is elaborated at length in Acts (Acts 9; 22; 26).

Paul is concerned to appear as independent as possible. After his calling, he did not 'confer with flesh and blood, nor did he go up to Jerusalem' (Gal. 1.16f.), but on his own initiative went to Arabia. In Damascus he barely escaped persecution (II Cor. 11.32f.). During these three years he apparently attempted to carry on a mission with moderate success, for otherwise in accordance with his practice elsewhere (Phil. 2.16, etc.), he would have boasted of having founded these communities. After a first visit to Peter in Jerusalem, which lasted only fourteen days, during which he also met James, he went to Syria and Cilicia, in other words possibly to his homeland. There he came into contact with the communities in Antioch,[12] initially as the companion of Barnabas, not *vice versa*. Here he will have learned much that he handed on to his communities (I Cor. 15.3). What later came to be called the Apostolic Council in Jerusalem (Gal. 2.1–10; cf. Acts 15.1–35) and the conflict with Peter and Barnabas which is to be put soon after it (Gal. 2.11–21) mark the end of these years of learning and travelling.

Paul deliberately begins his own missionary project. He founds his communities in the big cities along the arterial routes of the Roman empire. This draws him indefatigably westwards. He writes to the community in Rome that he no longer 'has a task in these countries' (Rom. 15.23). Just as Jesus thought it sufficient to have preached his message all over Galilee, so too Paul sets out to disseminate his message. There is not enough time to do more, for Paul too is governed by a specific expectation of the end (I Thess. 4.15,17; I Cor. 15.51). He carries on an apocalyptic missionary programme of the kind that is, for example, formulated in Mark 13.10.

If we take the repeated beatings (II Cor. 11.24f.) and imprisonments (Phil. 1.7, 12–26; Philemon 1.9f., 13)[13] which Paul had to endure as an indication of the underlying conflicts, then after his conversion he will probably have worked in the environment of the synagogues of the Diaspora. He received the synagogue punishment of the 'forty stripes less one' for his teaching, which was felt to be polemic against the law and the Jewish way of life. The stoning which is mentioned (II Cor. 11.25) must also be seen in this context. His opponents must have accused him of this to the state authorities (cf. I Cor. 6.1–8). Moreover he will himself have sometimes preached the gospel in public places, in the markets and street corners, where the itinerant philosophers were also active. In this way Paul had provoked a public scandal. The houses which are occasionally mentioned (I Cor. 1.16; 16.15, 19; Philemon 2; Rom. 16.23) will have been far less dangerous places for missionary preaching.[14] Finally, his activity as a craftsman will have offered the possibility for some informal missionary conversation.

We lose trace of Paul somewhere in Rome; whether he got as far as Spain, which was his plan (Rom. 15.24), is doubtful. According to I Clem. 5, Paul suffered martyrdom in Rome.

Crossing boundaries became the theme of Paul's life. He disseminated the faith in Christ, which had its origin in the milieu of the ordinary people of Palestine, in the Hellenistic city centres of the Roman empire. Whereas Jesus avoided the cities, Paul came from the urban milieu of the Jewish Diaspora. As a member of the religious minority in the midst of Hellenism which was capable of a high degree of absorption, brought up to be particularly faithful to the law, he was at the same time nevertheless familiar with Hellenistic education and the attitudes which went with it.[15] Jesus still moved within the limits of Judaism. Paul had *de facto* gone beyond them, even if for him his Jewish descent always remained an essential ingredient of his identity.[16] For Paul, belief in Jesus Christ transcends ethnic, social and sexual differences, without doing away with them.

Here is neither Jew nor Greek, here is neither slave nor free, here is neither man nor woman, for you are all one in Christ Jesus. (Gal. 3.28)

What was later called Paul's doctrine of justification is also directly connected with conflicts of identity on the frontier between Jews or Jewish Christians and Gentiles or Gentile Christians. Galatians 2.15f. is introduced by the statement, 'We are by birth Jews and not sinners from the Gentiles.' Romans 3.28 is followed in v.29 by the assertion, 'Or is God God only of the Jews? Is he not also the God of the Gentiles? Yes indeed, of Gentiles also.'

What is Christian, indeed primarily Jewish-Christian, identity? Did not the newly gained Gentiles, or Greeks as Paul sometimes also calls them, first have to become Jews in order then to become Christians? For Paul, only faith in Jesus Christ was to count. But his Jewish-Christian opponents insisted on circumcision, the observance of feast days and the effectiveness of the law for salvation. Here cultural and religious elements are closely woven together. The fact that Paul may have already drawn on the tradition for his doctrine of justification does not make any fundamental difference to this assessment.[17] It is clear that as a Pharisee loyal to the law he had persecuted the community for its departure from the effectiveness of the law for salvation.[18] After his call he adopted its standpoint with similar zeal. The doctrine of justification, or the ideas which formed it, probably first came into being as a criterion of difference within Judaism from other emancipatory movements. It was not so much a direct reason for the mission to the Gentiles, but it smoothed the way for it. The Hellenists who were driven from Jerusalem had themselves already crossed cultural boundaries. Moreover, in the community in Antioch which they founded, the boundaries with the Gentiles were crossed for the first time.

Paul was inevitably disappointed in his hope that he had convinced everyone of his theology at the Apostolic Council in Jerusalem. The Jerusalem people interpreted the agreement 'we among the Gentiles, you among the Jews' (Gal. 2.9) in the sense of two distinct communities. Therefore they refused to share meals with the Gentile Christians in Antioch. Paul's doctrine of the end of the saving efficacy of the law, which was felt to be polemical, was not approved once and for all, but, once it reached Jerusalem, poisoned the atmosphere. To settle the matter Paul himself wanted to travel there and bring the collection (Rom. 15.25–33) which he had made in his communities for the needy in Jerusalem according to the agreement at the Apostolic Council.[19] Paul saw the unity of young Christianity endangered, and in no circumstances did he want to put it at risk. The anonymous figures addressed in Romans therefore had to be sought in Jerusalem. Here Paul corrects his polemical propositions from Galatians, in which he had to struggle with specific opponents.

Paul was no more concerned than Jesus to abolish the law. He preaches God's righteousness,[20] which has achieved its fullness in Jesus Christ. The Torah, moderated for Gentile Christians by the omission of some ritual precepts and summed up in the commandment to love (Rom. 13.8–10; Gal. 5.14), is a help to life. Its effectiveness for salvation has come to an end in Jesus Christ, but its holiness remains.[21] For both, the commandment to love is of central importance. People can know that they are safe in the love of God, in which they are to encounter God and their fellow human beings.

Jesus had proclaimed the kingdom of God to ordinary people in Palestine and thus, contrary to the facts of the circumstances in which they lived, promised them a dignity before God which at the same time bestowed on them their own identity. In the course of Paul's crossing boundaries, in his case the emphasis shifts to the question of cultural identities. But the social components continue, a fact which is often overlooked.[22] The promise of God's righteousness especially for the weak (I Cor. 1.27) stands in continuity with Jesus' proclamation of the kingdom of God.[23]

I remarked at the beginning that mission is always also cultural contact, and I characterized the contextual christologies as forms of cultural contact. Paul and the earliest Christian missionary movement set the direction here. The fact that Paul 'became a Jew to the Jews and a Greek to the Greeks' and emphasized 'righteousness by faith alone' first made room for the cultural pluralism of Christianity generally. Through the promise of God's righteousness, especially for the weak, at the same time a special dignity before God was bestowed on the poor and oppressed. Understood in this way, justification by faith alone is an event which grounds and preserves identity. In the context of the cultural and social conflicts with which the message of justification was closely connected from the very beginning, an interpretation of them which is more strongly related to the community can also be legitimated. It could prove to be a corrective to our tradition of interpretation, which is strongly orientated on the individual.

During our journey through the contextual christologies, the question of *identity* has quickly become the hidden leading theme. That was also the starting point for a re-reading of the biography of Paul and his message of justification. The theologies of inculturation and dialogue make the problem of *cultural and religious identity* their theme. The question is still, as it already was for Paul himself, how one's particular cultural and religious heritage can be reconciled with one's conversion to the Christian faith.[24] The Balinese Christian artist Nyoman Darsane,[25] himself a converted Hindu, once put this to me in the formula, 'Christ is my soul and Bali is my body'. In the liberation theologies the whole weight lies on the problem of the personal *dignity* of each individual before God,[26] even contrary to the fact of the experience of poverty and oppression which governs the whole of life. Whereas their protagonists mainly appeal to Jesus' preaching of the kingdom of God for this, we have seen that Paul's message of justification also makes this promise. In both respects Paul is waiting to be rediscovered by the contextual theologians.

The sketches of contextual christologies presented in this book are primarily a human effort to go beyond cultural and social boundaries. At the same time the gospel, Christ present in the Spirit, itself continually takes new form in the different contexts. Full of trust in this, Paul wrote to his communities in Galatia that he was to go on struggling for them until 'Christ takes form in you' (Gal. 4.19).

Notes

Introduction

1. Anton Wessels, *Images of Jesus. How Jesus is Perceived and Portrayed in Non-European Cultures*, London and Grand Rapids 1990, has succinctly summarized the ambivalence inherent in these efforts in the word-play 'portrayal or betrayal'.

2. Mercy Amba Oduyoye, 'Reflections from a Third World Woman's Perspective. Women's Experience and Liberation Theologies', in Virginia Fabella and Sergio Torres (eds), *Irruption of the Third World. Challenge to Theology. Papers from the Fifth International Conference of the Ecumenical Association of Third World Theologians, August 17–29, 1981, New Delhi, India*, Maryknoll, NY 1983, 246–55: 247. Cf. Dorothea Erbele, 'Töchter Afrikas, steh auf! Die ghanaische Theologin Mercy Amba Oduyoye', *EK* 30 (8/1997), 453f.

3. Cf. Volker Küster, 'Aufbruch der dritten Welt. Der Weg der ökumenischen Vereinigung von Dritte-Welt-Theologen (EATWOT)', *VF* 37, 1992, 45–67.

4. Virginia Fabella and Sergio Torres (eds), *Doing Theology in a Divided World. Papers from the Sixth International Conference of the Ecumenical Association of Third World Theologians, January 5–13, 1983: Geneva, Switzerland*, Maryknoll, NY 1985, 179–93, 186.

5. Doris Strahm, *Vom Rand in die Mitte. Christologie aus der Sicht von Frauen in Asien, Afrika und Lateinamerika*, Theologie in Geschichte und Gesellschaft 4, Lucerne 1997, has produced a comprehensive study on this, full of material.

6. As early as the 1950s, Alfred L. Kroeber and Clyde Kluckhohn, *Culture. A Critical Review of Concepts and Definitions*, Cambridge, Mass. 1952, collected 160 different definitions of culture.

7. Cf. Clifford Geertz, 'Thick Description: Toward an Interpretative Theory of Culture', in id., *The Interpretation of Cultures. Selected Essays*, New York 1973, 3–30.

8. Geertz, 'Thick Description' (n.7), 5; cf. id., 'Religion as a Cultural System', in id., *The Interpretation of Cultures* (n.7), 87–125, 89.

9. Geertz, 'Religion as a Cultural System' (n.8).

10. Ibid., 90.

11. Gerd Theissen, *On Having a Critical Faith*, London 1979, 41.

12. Geertz, 'Religion as a Cultural System' (n.8), 110.

13. Cf. Urs Bitterli, *Alte Welt – neue Welt. Formen des europäisch-überseeischen Kulturkontaktes vom 15. bis zum 18. Jahrhundert*, Munich 1992.

14. Cf. Volker Küster, *Theologie im Kontext. Zugleich ein Versuch über die Minjung-Theologie*, SIM 62, Nettetal 1995.

15. For the reception of Lange in the German context cf. Volker Drehsen, 'Kirche für die Welt und andere Indigenisationen', *PT* 86, 1997, 483–97.

Prologue: Jesus and Culture

1. From the wealth of literature on Jesus see Christoph Burchard, 'Jesus of Nazareth', in Jürgen Becker et al., *Christian Beginnings. Word and Community from Jesus to Post-apostolic Times,* Louisville, Kentucky 1993, 15–72; J. D. Crossan, *The Historical Jesus. The Life of a Mediterranean Jewish Peasant*, San Francisco and Edinburgh 1993; Bruce Chilton and Craig A. Evans (eds), *Studying the Historical Jesus. Evaluations of Current Research,* Leiden, etc. 1994; Gerd Theissen and Annette Merz, *The Historical Jesus*, London and Minneapolis 1998; Peter Müller, 'Trends in der Jesusforschung', *ZNT* 1, 1998, 2–16.

2. Depending on whether the chronology of the Synoptics or that of the Gospel of John is the basis.

3. Cf. Stanley E. Porter, 'Jesus and the Use of Greek in Galilee', in Chilton and Evans, *Studying the Historical Jesus* (n.1), 123–54.

4. Cf. Theissen and Merz, *Jesus* (n.1), 129f.

5. Cf. Crossan, *Jesus* (n.1), 17–19; Theissen and Merz, *Jesus* (n.1), 165; Willibald Bösen, *Galiläa als Lebensraum und Wirkungsfeld Jesu*, Freiburg im Breisgau 1988/1998, 54–74.

6. Cf. Carsten Colpe, 'Strasse 2', in *BHH*, study edition, Göttingen 1994, 1880–82: 1881: the Via Maris led 'from Egypt through the coastal plain of Palestine, past the east side of Carmel into the plain of Jezreel and from there either south or north of Lake Gennesaret . . . through Damascus to the Euphrates'.

7. Cf. Ekkehard W. Stegemann and Wolfgang Stegemann, *The Jesus Movement. A Social History of its First Century*, Minneapolis 1999, 104–125; Theissen and Merz, *Jesus* (n.1), 171f.

8. Cf. Josephus, *Antt.* 18, 116–19; Jürgen Becker, *Johannes der Täufer und Jesus von Nazareth*, BS 63, Neukirchen-Vluyn 1972.

9. Cf. Luise Schottroff and Wolfgang Stegemann, *Jesus and the Hope of the Poor*, Maryknoll, NY 1986; Wolfgang Stegemann, *The Gospel and the Poor*, Minneapolis 1984.

10. Cf. Elisabeth Schüssler Fiorenza, *In Memory of Her . . . A Feminist Theological Reconstruction of Christian Origins*, New York and London ²1995, 106–159; Luise Schottroff, *Lydia's Impatient Sisters. A Feminist Social History of Early Christianity*, Louisville and London 1994.

11. Cf. Wolfgang Stegemann, 'Lasset die Kinder zu mir kommen. Sozialgeschichtliche Aspekte des Kinderevangeliums', in Willy Schottroff and Wolfgang Stegemann (eds), *Traditionen der Befreiung. Sozialgeschichtliche Bibelauslegungen, Vol.1, Methodische Zugänge*, Munich and Berlin 1980, 114–44.

12. Cf. Theissen and Merz, *Jesus* (n.1), 281–315.

13. Cf. Martin Hengel, *Was Jesus a Revolutionist?*, Philadelphia 1971.

14. Cf. Klaus Wengst, *Pax Romana and the Peace of Jesus Christ*, London and Philadelphia 1987.

15. Cf. Gerd Theissen, 'Das "schwankende Rohr" (Mt 11,7) und die Gründungsmünzen vom Tiberias', in id., *Lokalkolorit und Zeitgeschichte in den Evangelien. Ein Beitrag zur Geschichte der synoptischen Tradition*, Göttingen ²1992, 26–44.

16. Cf. Volker Küster, *Jesus und das Volk im Markusevangelium. Ein Beitrag zum interkulturellen Gespräch in der Exegese*, BTS 28, Neukirchen-Vluyn 1996.

17. Cf. Christoph Burchard, 'Das doppelte Liebesgebot in der frühen christlichen Überlieferung', in Eduard Lohse et al. (eds), *Der Ruf Jesu und die Antwort der Gemeinde*, FS Joachim Jeremias, Göttingen 1970, 39–62.

18. Cf. Gerd Theissen, *The First Followers of Jesus* (US title *The Sociology of Earliest Christianity*), London and Philadelphia 1978.

19. Cf. Theissen and Merz, *Jesus* (n.1), 133–40.

20. Cf. Klaus Wengst, *Bedrängte Gemeinde und verherrlichter Christus. Ein Versuch über das Johannesevangelium*, Munich 1990.

21. Cf. Gerd Theissen, 'Die Geschichte von der syrophönikischen Frau und das tyrisch-galläische Grenzgebiet', in id., *Lokalkolorit* (n.15), 63–85.

22. Cf. Christoph Burchard, 'Zu Matthäus 8, 5–13', ZNW 84, 1993, 278–88.

23. Cf. Christoph Burchard, 'Jesus für die Welt. Über das Verhältnis von Reich Gottes und Mission', in Theo Sundermeier (ed.), *Fides pro mundi vita. Missionstheologie heute*, FS Hans-Werner Gensichen, MWF 14, Gütersloh 1980, 13–27.

24. Cf. Dieter Lührmann, 'Biographie des Gerechten als Evangelium. Vorstellungen zu einem Markuskommentar', *WuD* 14, 1977, 25–50; Odil Hannes Steck, *Israel und das gewaltsame Geschick der Propheten. Untersuchungen zur Überlieferung des deuteronomistischen Geschichtsbildes im Alten Testament, Spätjudentum und Urchristentum*, WMANT 23, Neukirchen-Vluyn 1967.

25. Cf. Gerd Theissen, 'Die Tempelweissagung Jesu. Prophetie im

Spannungsfeld von Stadt und Land', in id., *Studien zur Soziologie des Urchristentums*, Tübingen ²1983, 142–59: 157f.

26. Cf. Klaus Wengst, *Ostern – Ein wirkliches Gleichnis, eine wahre Geschichte. Zum neutestamentlichen Zeugnis von der Auferweckung Jesu*, Munich 1991.

27. Cf. Ferdinand Hahn, *Mission in the New Testament*, London 1965; Andreas Feldtkeller, *Identitätssuche des syrischen Urchristentums. Mission, Inkulturation und Pluralität im ältesten Heidenchristentum*, NTOA 25, Fribourg, CH and Göttingen 1993.

28. See below, 187–94.

§1. Christology and Culture

1. H. Richard Niebuhr, *Christ and Culture*, New York 1951. For the German theology of those years, which was under the strong influence of Karl Barth and his school, Niebuhr's notions were untimely.

2. Ernst Troeltsch, *The Social Teaching of the Christian Churches* (1912), London and New York 1931, II, 993f.

3. Cf. Niebuhr, *Christ and Culture* (n.1), xif.

4. Cf. John Hick, 'The Non-Absoluteness of Christianity', in John Hick and Paul F. Knitter, *The Myth of Christian Uniqueness. Toward a Pluralistic Theology of Religions*, Maryknoll, NY and London 1987, 16–36.

5. Cyprian, *Ep.*73, 21, in CSEL Vol.III, Pars II, 795: '*Salus extra ecclesiam non est.*'

6. Cf. Justin, *Apol.* I, 44, etc.; see Reinhold Bernhardt, *Der Absolutheitsanspruch des Christentums. Von der Aufklärung bis zur Pluralistischen Religionstheologie*, Gütersloh ²1990, 100–3.

7. Karl Rahner, 'Christianity and the Non-Christian Religions', *Theological Investigations* 5, New York and London 1966, 115–134.

8. For what follows see in detail Volker Küster, *Theologie im Kontext. Zugleich ein Versuch über die Minjung-Theologie*, SIM 62, Nettetal 1998. 18–52.

9. Cf. Anton Wessels, *Europe. Was It Ever Really Christian? The Interaction between Gospel and Culture*, London 1994.

10. Cf. Niebuhr, *Christ and Culture* (n.1), 116f.

11. See below on M. M. Thomas (§ 7) and Kosuke Koyama (§ 9).

12. He first went out to India with his wife Helen in 1936.

13. Cf. Lesslie Newbigin, *The Other Side of 1984. Questions for the Churches*, Risk Books 18, Geneva 1983; id., *Foolishness to the Greeks. The Gospel and Western Culture*, WCC Mission Series 6, Geneva 1986; id., *The Gospel in a Pluralist Society*, Grand Rapids and Geneva 1989; id., *Truth to Tell. The Gospel as Public Truth*, Grand Rapids and Geneva 1991. For criticism see Werner Ustorf, 'A Partisan's View. Lesslie Newbigin's Critique of Modernity', in id., *Christianized Africa – De-Christianized*

Europe? Missionary Inquiries into the Polycentric Epoch of Christian History, PWM 14, Ammersbek bei Hamburg 1992, 107–17.

14. Cf. Lesslie Newbigin, *Unfinished Agenda. An Autobiography*, Geneva 1985.

15. Newbigin, *The Other Side* (n.13, page references in the text).

16. Lesslie Newbigin, 'Das Evangelium und Wahrheit', in *Das Evangelium in unserer pluralistischen Gesellschaft*, EMW informationen 107, 1995, 55–60: 58.

17. Cf. Newbigin, *Truth to Tell* (n.13).

18. Newbigin, 'Evangelium und Wahrheit' (n.16), 55.

19. Ibid.

20. Newbigin, *Truth to Tell*, 56.

21. Michael Welker, 'Der missionarische Auftrag der Kirchen in pluralistischen und multireligiösen Kontexten', in *Missionarische Kirche im multireligiösen Kontext*, Weltmission heute 25, Hamburg 1996, 47–64: 50, defines pluralism as 'a highly developed form of social, cultural and religious communal life'. He opposes this systematic understanding to three negative definitions: pluralism is neither relativism, nor individualism, nor egotism (ibid., 50f.). Eilert Herms, 'Pluralismus aus Prinzip', in id., *Kirche für die Welt. Lage und Aufgabe der evangelischen Kirchen im vereinigten Deutschland*, Tübingen 1995, 467–85, is also opposed to a 'random pluralism'. In this context Wilfried Härle, 'Aus dem Heiligen Geist. Positioneller Pluralismus als christliche Konsequenz', in *Die Zeichen der Zeit. Lutherische Monatshefte* 1 (7/1998), 21–4 speaks of a 'positional pluralism'. Theo Sundermeier, 'Pluralismus, Fundamentalismus, Koinonia', *EvTh* 54, 1994, 239–310, opposes a '*connective pluralism*' to the 'pluralism *in principle* of postmodernity' (304). Cf. Peter Gerlitz, Christoph Schwöbel and Albrecht Grözinger, 'Pluralismus', *TRE* 26, Berlin and New York 1996, 717–42.

Pluralism is primarily a phenomenon which can be described empirically. It easily leads to an understanding that 'anything goes', but also opens up so far unknown opportunities of development to men and women of late modernity who are aware of their responsibility. There is great anxiety about this 'new complexity', which leads people to escape into fundamentalism as a supposedly simpler solution. Here the great challenge to the Christian churches is to give orientation, lay down norms and also form something of a counter-society (cf. Michael Welker, *Kirche im Pluralismus*, Gütersloh 1995). Christian faith is in many respects suitable as a model of pluralism. The canon of the biblical writings is pluralistic in itself (cf. Ernst Käsemann, 'The Canon of the New Testament and the Unity of the Church?', in id., *Essays on New Testament Themes*, London 1964, 95–107). The doctrine of God speaks of the trinity of God the Father, the Son and the Holy Spirit. Finally, the global community of narrative and interpretation in Christianity is intrinsically a plural structure of different confessions, denominations and groups, which preserve the broad current of tradition and generate it further.

22. Newbigin has found a fellow-traveller in the Gambian Lamin Sanneh (born 1942, cf. id., 'Theologische Reflexionen zu einer Missions-ehre und westlicher Kultur', in *Das Evangelium in unserer pluralistischen Gesellschaft*, 8–18). Born a Muslim, Sanneh converted to Christianity at the age of eighteen. He studied history and Islam in the USA, Great Britain and the Near East. After working as an adviser and teacher in Africa he taught first in Harvard, and since 1989 has been Professor of Mission and World Christianity in Yale. With Sanneh, the tenor of the argumentation takes on a post-colonial emphasis. Western Christianity has become decadent, whereas Christianity in the Third World is vital and growing ('Reflexionen', 17). Sanneh emphasizes custom and morality even more strongly than Newbigin: 'The perfection of technological apparatus has with unshakeable and inexorable certainty extended our control over institutions, of a personal and a public kind, and over the space, whereas our knowledge of the moral truth has become weak and uncertain . . . In the present advanced stage of the rejection of religion as unscientific, society confronts these epoch-making challenges with the disappearance of corresponding moral resources which would be necessary to oppose them' ('Reflexionen', 17f.). Otherwise the arguments are interchangeable. Cf. Lamin Sanneh, *West African Christianity. The Religious Impact*, Maryknoll, NY 1983; id., *Translating the Message. The Missionary Impact on Culture*, Maryknoll, NY 1989; id., *Encountering the West. Christianity and the Global Cultural Process: The African Dimension*, Maryknoll, NY 1993; also Martha Frederiks, 'Congruency, Conflict or Dialogue. Lamin Sanneh on the Relation between Gospel and Culture', *Exchange* 24, 1995, 123–34.

23. Cf. John C. England, *The Hidden History of Christianity in Asia. The Churches of the East before 1500*, Delhi 1996.

24. Cf. Horst Rzepkowski, 'Ritenstreit', in id., *Lexikon der Mission. Geschichte, Theologie, Ethnologie*, Graz, etc. 1992, 366–8.

25. English now Matteo Ricci, *The True Meaning of the Lord of Heaven*, St Louis 1985.

26. The four Vedas are the oldest holy scriptures of the Hindus.

27. Cf. Thomas Ohm, 'Neuer Wein in neuen Schläuchen', in id., *Ex Contemplatione Loqui. Gesammelte Aufsätze*, MWAT 25, Münster 1961, 150–72: 150: 'By *accommodation* I mean the deliberate and planned adaptation of the church and the expressions of its life to the peoples in the missionary countries; by *assimilation* the taking over into the treasury of the church what is true, valuable, noble and beautiful among these peoples; and by *transformation* a special form of what is assimilated, a transformation which makes what is assimilated suitable for use by the church and in the church.'

28. Cf. Johannes Christian Hoekendijk, *Kirche und Volk in der*

deutschen Missionswissenschaft, TB 35, Munich 1967; Hans-Werner Gensichen, 'Kirche und Volk in der Mission', in id., *Mission und Kultur. Gesammelte Aufsätze*, TB 74, Munich 1985, 71–81.

29. Cf. Shoki Coe, 'Contextualizing Theology', in Gerald H. Anderson et al. (eds), *Mission Trends 3. Third World Theologies*, Toronto and Grand Rapids 1976, 19–24.

30. Cf. Charles H. Kraft, *Christianity in Culture. A Study in Dynamic Biblical Theologizing in Cross-Cultural Perspectives*, Maryknoll, NY 1979, 261–75.

31. The Constitution on the Sacred Liturgy, *Sacrosanctum Concilium*, was the first Council text to be discussed (1962) and proclaimed (1963). Cf. Austin Flannery (ed), *Vatican Council* II, New York 1981, 1–40.

32. *Gaudium et Spes* 53, in ibid., 903–1001.

33. Cf. Ari Roest Crollius, 'Inculturation and Incarnation. On Speaking of the Christian Faith and the Cultures of Humanity', in *Bulletin Secretariatus pro non Christianis* 13 (38/1978), 134–40.

34. Cf. Theo Sundermeier, 'Inkulturation und Synkretismus. Probleme einer Verhältnisbestimmung', *EvTh* 52, 1992, 192–209: 195f.; Hans Waldenfels, 'Das "Kenotische" als Grundzug missionarischer Kommuni-kation', in id. (ed.), *'Denn ich bin bei Euch' (Matt. 28.20). Pespektiven im christlichen Missionsbewusstsein heute. FS Josef Glazik and Bernward Willeke*, Zurich, etc. 1978, 327–38.

35. Cf. the encyclical *Redemptoris Missio* of Pope John Paul II on the ongoing validity of the missionary task, 7 December 1990, 17. 52–53.

36. Whereas Theo Sundermeier, 'Inkulturation und Synkretismus' (n.34), 194, proposes inculturation as a umbrella term, Deane William Ferm, *Third World Liberation Theologies. An Introductory Survey*, Maryknoll, NY 1986, speaks throughout of liberation theologies with respect to the theologies of the Third World.

37. Cf. *Ministry in Context. The Third Mandate Programme of the Theological Education Fund (1970–1977)*, Bromley 1972; *Learning in Context. The Search for Innovative Patterns in Theological Education*, Bromley 1973.

38. Cf. Volker Küster, 'Models of Contextual Hermeneutics: Liberation and Feminist Theological Approaches Compared', *Exchange* 23, 1994, 149–62; id., *Theologie im Kontext*, 39–52; id., 'Text und Kontext. Zur Systematik kontextueller Hermeneutik', in *Der Text im Kontext. Die Bibel mit anderen Augen gelesen*, Weltmission heute 31, Hamburg 1998, 130–43.

39. See above 2f.

40. Cf. Martin Heidegger, *Being and Time*, Oxford 1978; Hans-Georg Gadamer, *Truth and Method*, London 1997; id., 'Vom Zirkel des Verstehens', in id., *Hermeneutik II. Wahrheit und Methode. Ergänzungen, Register*, GW 2, Tübingen 1986, 57–65.

41. It is here that I disagree basically with Dietrich Ristchl, as he has indicated equally clearly once again in his review of my book *Theologie im Kontext* (id., 'Der Kontext als Chance und Problem', *ÖR* 46, 1997, 247–9). I fully agree with Ritschl that contextual theologies would not be viable as the sole basis on which 'pastors could be trained and communities orientated and nourished' (ibid., 249). But without them theological education in the contexts concerned would also remain defective. To keep to the Korean example: the ignorance of many theological teachers about the social situation in which young theologians are to preach the Gospel was as constricting to see as their complete ignorance of their own cultural and religious tradition.

42. Final Statement of the Founding Assembly of EATWOT, in Sergio Torres and Virginia Fabella (eds), *The Emergent Gospel. Theology from the Developing World. Papers from the Ecumenical Dialogue of Third World Theologians, Dar es Salaam, August 5–12, 1976*, London and New York 1978, 259–271, 269.

43. See below, §2, 33–5.

44. See above, 15f.

45. Cf. Albrecht Grözinger, *Erzählen und Handeln. Studien zu einer trinitarischen Grundlegung der Praktischen Theologie*, Munich 1989; Francis Schüssler Fiorenza, 'Die Kirche als Interpretationsgemeinschaft. Politische Theologie zwischen Diskursethik und hermeneutischer Rekonstruktion', in *Habermas und die Theologie. Beiträge zur theologische Rezeption. Diskussion und Kritik der Theorie kommunikativen Handelns*, ed. Edmund Arens, Düsseldorf 1989, 115–44.

46. Cf. David Tracy, *Plurality and Ambiguity*, New York and London 1988.

47. See below, §2, 34f.

§2. Christology in Context – Intercultural Christology

1. Walter Kasper, 'Christologie von unten? Kritik und Neuansatz gegenwärtiger Christologie', in Leo Scheffczyk (ed.), *Grundfragen der Christologie heute*, QD 72, Freiburg im Breisgau, etc. 1975, 141–70: 145.

2. Cf. e.g. Luther's Christmas sermon of 1530, WA 29, 642–56.

3. WA 1, 353–74; I am quoting from Kurt Aland (ed.), *Luther Deutsch. Die Werke Martin Luthers in neuer Auswahl für die Gegenwart*, 1, Stuttgart and Göttingen 1969, 379–94 (more details in the text).

4. Cf. Max Seidel, *Der Isenheimer Altar von Mathis Grünewald*, Stuttgart and Zurich 1990; Theo Sundermeier, 'Contextualizing Luther's Theology of the Cross', in Yacob Tesfai (ed.), *The Scandal of a Crucified World. Perspectives on the Cross and Suffering*, Maryknoll, NY 1994, 99–110.

5. I am using the term neutrally and not polemically, as Luther does in his criticism of the theology of his time.

6. 'All holy', an Orthodox title of honour for Mary, the mother of God.

7. Dietrich Ritschl ventures similar notions. However, whereas he is indebted to the analytical method (id., *The Logic of Theology*, London 1986, 82–5), I am attempting to develop the hermeneutical method further. My starting point is that the texts evoke themes; Ritschl investigates the implicit axioms behind the texts which guide our thinking. For Ritschl, the story is merely the raw material of theology, whereas for me the biblical stories and the experiences of men and women with the triune God are its constitutive element. Here the differing understanding of theology already mentioned comes again into play (see above, 202 n.41). Cf. Dietrich Ritschl and Hugh O. Jones, *'Story' als Rohmaterial der Theologie*, TExh 192, Munich 1976, 7–41; id., 'Die Erfahrung der Wahrheit. Die Steuerung von Denken und Handeln durch implizite Axiome', in id., *Konzepte. Ökumene, Medizin, Ethik. Gesammelte Aufsätze*, Munich 1986, 147–66; id., 'The Regulatory Function of Implicit Axioms in Thought and Action', *ISR* 11, 1986, 136–40; id., 'The Search for Implicit Axioms behind Doctrinal Texts', *Gregorianum* 74, 1993, 207–21.

8. Cf. Wilhelm Schapp, *In Geschichten verstrickt. Zum Sein von Mensch und Ding*, Frankfurt am Main ³1985 (page references in the text); id., *Philosophie der Geschichten*, Frankfurt am Main ²1981.

9. Paulo Freire, *Pedagogy of the Oppressed*, NY 1970 (Harmondsworth 1996); cf. id., *Erziehung als Praxis der Freiheit*, Stuttgart and Berlin 1974; Freire and Frei Betto, *Schule die Leben heisst. Befreiungstheologie konkret. Ein Gespräch*, Munich 1986; Dimas Figueroa, *Paulo Freire zur Einführung*, Hamburg 1989; Werner Simpfendörfer, 'Paulo Freire, Erziehung als Praxis der Freiheit', in id., *Ökumenische Spurensuche. Porträts*, Stuttgart 1989, 143–63.

10. Freire, *Erziehung* (n.9), 58.

11. Freire, *Pedagogy* (n.9), 58.

12. Ibid., 33.

13. Cf. ibid., 92 n.19.

14. Freire, *Erziehung* (n.9), 68.

15. Ibid., 100–3. See below Kosuke Koyama, §9, 120.

16. Freire, *Pedagogy* (n.9), 114.

17. Here there is some proximity to Wilhelm Schapp, who is similarly indebted to phenomenology.

18. Cf. Heinrich Bedford-Strohm, *Vorrang für die Armen. Auf dem Weg zu einer theologischen Theorie der Gerechtigkeit*, Öffentliche Theologie 4, Gütersloh 1993.

19. The 'comparative theology' propagated by the Catholic pastoral theologian Adolf Exeler in the 1970s lacks this fundamental theological dimension of intercultural theology. Initially it has a purely empirical orien-

tation. Cf. Exeter, 'Vergleichende Theologie statt Missionswissenschaft?', in Waldenfels, '. . . *denn ich bin bei Euch*', 199–211; id., 'Wege einer vergleichenden Pastoral', in *Evangelisation in der Dritten Welt. Anstösse für Europa*, TDW 2, ed. Ludwig Bertsch and Felix Schlösser, Freiburg im Breisgau, etc. ²1987, 92–121. Considerations of method are decisive both in comparative and in intercultural theology. They are no substitute for missiology as a theological discipline. Cf. Giancarlo Collet, 'Bekehrung – Vergleich – Anerkennung: Die Stellung des Anderen im Selbstverständnis der Missionswissenschaft', *ZMR* 77, 1993, 202–15.

§3. Historical Reconstruction: Christological Discourse at the Time of the Conquista

1. Cf the German title of the book by Leonardo Boff, *Gott kam früher als der Missionar*, Düsseldorf 1991.

2. Cf. J. A. Mackay, *The Other Spanish Christ. A Study in the Spiritual History of Spain and South America*, New York 1932; Sául Trinidad, 'Christologie – Conquista – Kolonisierung', in Giancarlo Collet (ed.), *Der Christus der Armen. Das Christuszeugnis der lateinamerikanischen Befreiungstheologen*, Freiburg im Breisgau, etc. 1988, 23–36; Maximiliano Salinas, in Riolando Azzi et al., *Theologiegeschichte der Dritten Welt. Lateinamerika*, Gütersloh 1993, 65f.

3. Miguel de Unamuno, quoted in Trinidad, 'Christologie' (n.2), 24.

4. Cf. Trinidad, 'Christologie' (n.2), 29f.

5. Cf. Jon Sobrino, *Christology at the Crossroads. A Latin American View*, Maryknoll, NY and London 1978, 180; Giancarlo Collet, 'Im Armen Christus begegnen. Einleitung', in id., *Der Christus der Armen* (n.2), 7–22: 17f.; Trinidad, 'Christologie' (n.2), 33.

6. Cf. Bartolomé de Las Casas, *Werkauswahl* (3 vols), ed. Mariano Delgado, Paderborn, etc. 1994–1997; in it Mariano Delgado, 'Bartolomé de Las Casas (1485–1566), Weg, Werk und Wirkung oder Vom Nutzen mystisch-politischer Nachfolge in Krisenzeiten', Vol.1, 11–34; Martin Neumann, *Las Casas. Die unglaubliche Geschichte von der Entdeckung der Neuen Welt*, Freiburg im Breisgau, etc. 1990; Matthias Gillner, *Bartolomé de Las Casas und die Eroberung des indianischen Kontinents. Das friedensethische Profil eines weltgeschichtlichen Umbruchs aus der Perspektive eines Anwalts des Unterdrückten*, ThFr 12, Stuttgart, etc. 1997.

7. Cf. Gustavo Gutiérrez, *Las Casas. In Search of the Poor of Jesus Christ*, Maryknoll, NY 1993; id., *Gott oder das Gold. Der befreiende Weg des Bartolomé de las Casas*, Freiburg im Breisgau, etc. 1990; id., 'Auf der Suche nach den Armen Jesu Christi. Evangelisierung und Theologie im 16. Jahrhundert', in Collet, *Der Christus der Armen*, 37–56. Gutiérrez established a Bartolomé de Las Casas Centre in Rimac, the Lima slum in which

he has worked for many years as priest, with a small library and conference room; it has since moved and expanded greatly.

8. Quoted from Gutiérrez, 'Auf der Suche' (n.2), 40.

9. Quoted ibid., 53.

§4. *Christopraxis in the Discipleship of Jesus: Leonardo Boff (Brazil) and Jon Sobrino (El Salvador)*

1. It appeared in Peru as early as 1971; then in 1972 in Salamanca, Spain, and in English in Maryknoll, NY 1973 (second edition, Maryknoll, NY and London 1988, to which reference is made here).

2. Cf. Robert McAfee Brown, *Gustavo Gutiérrez. An Introduction to Liberation Theology*, Maryknoll, NY 1990.

3. Gustavo Gutiérrez, *Theology of Liberation*, Maryknoll, NY and London 1988, xiii.

4. Cf. Gutiérrez, *Theology of Liberation* (n.3), xvii; now id., 'Toward a Theology of Liberation', in Alfred T. Hennelly (ed.), *Liberation Theology. A Documentary History*, Maryknoll, NY 1990, 62–76.

5. Cf. *The Church in the Present-Day Transformation of Latin America in the Light of the Council* (two vols), Second General Conference of Latin American Bishops, Medellin, Colombia 1968, ed. Louis Michael Colonese, Washington DC 1969; John Eagleson and Philip Scharper (eds), *Puebla and Beyond*; Maryknoll, NY 1979.

6. Gutiérrez, *Theology of Liberation*. Leonardo Boff, *Jesus Christ Liberator. A Critical Christology of Our Time'*, London 1978, 134–8.

7. Initially published in article form in 1971 in ten issues of the journal *Grande Sinal*, the book was brought out in 1972 by the publishing house Vozes, with which Leonardo Boff is closely associated. I quote from the English edition.

8. Enrique Dussel, in *Theologiegeschichte der Dritten Welt. Lateinamerika*, 308, puts Boff in the second generation. However, this division seems to me to be implausible. I put the boundary between the generations substantially later.

9. Cf. Horst Goldstein, *Leonardo Boff. Zwischen Poesie und Politik*, Mainz 1994, 37.

10. Cf. Boff, *Jesus Christ* (n.6), xii.

11. Cf. ibid., 43.

12. Dussel, *Theologiegeschichte der Dritten Welt, Lateinamerika*, 315, also puts Sobrino in the second generation. He describes him as a 'new face'.

13. I quote from the English edition, Jon Sobrino, *Christology at the Crossroads*, Maryknoll, NY and London 1978.

14. In what follows I am less concerned to give an overall description of the christologies of the two authors as to indicate the christological stimuli they have provided for the liberation theologies, which here emerge in their

originality. Boff later adopted many stimuli from modern christologies which put this solemnity in the background. Cf. Antonio Carlos de Melo Magalahães, *Christologie und Nachfolge. Eine systematisch-ökumenische Untersuchung zur Befreiungschristologie bei Leonardo Boff und Jon Sobrino*, PWM 11, Ammerbek bei Hamburg 1991; also the later ambitious five-volume christology by Juan Luis Segundo (1982), *Jesus of Nazareth Yesterday and Today*, Maryknoll, NY 1984–1988.

15. Cf. Deane William Ferm, 'Leonardo Boff', in id., *Profiles in Liberation. 36 Portraits of Third World Theologians*, Mystic, CN 1988, 124–8; Joaoa Batista Libanio and Andreas Müller, 'Mysterium Liberationis: Leonardo Boff, Brasilien', in Hans Waldenfels (ed.), *Theologen der Dritten Welt. Elf biographische Skizzen aus Afrika, Asien und Latein-amerika*, Munich 1982, 30–42; Horst Goldstein, *Leonardo Boff* (n.9).

16. Cf. Clodovis Boff, *Theology and Praxis. Epistemological Foundations*, Maryknoll, NY 1987.

17. Leonardo Boff, *Die Kirche als Sakrament im Horizont der Welter-fahrung. Versuch einer strukturfunktionalistischen Grundlegung in Hinblick auf das II. Vatikanische Konzil*, Paderborn 1972.

18. Cf. Ferm, 'Leonardo Boff' (n.9), 125f.

19. Cf. *Der Fall Boff. Eine Dokumentation*, produced by the Brazilian Movement for Human Rights, Düsseldorf 1986.

20. Cf. Goldstein, *Leonardo Boff* (n.9), 57.

21. Cf. Deane William Ferm, 'Jon Sobrino', in id., *Profiles in Liberation* (n.15), 184–8.

22. Jon Sobrino, *El significado de la cruz e de la resurrection en las teolo-gias de Jürgen Moltmann y Wolfgang Pannenberg*, typescript dissertation, Frankfurt am Main 1970.

23. To distinguish them, the numbers in the text are marked B (= Boff) and S (= Sobrino). The references have been chosen for their significance; I have not aimed at completeness.

24. Leonardo Boff, *Church, Charism and Power*, London and New York 1986.

25. See § 10–12 below.

26. In the preface to the English edition, xxi; implicit in the introduction (12–14, cf. 110).

27. Cf. Hermann Brandt, *Gottes Gegenwart in Lateinamerika. Inkarnation als Leitmotiv der Befreiungstheologie*, Hamburger Theologische Studien 4, Hamburg 1992.

28. Sobrino makes this explicit in the preface to the English edition (ibid., xx, xxv).

29. I use the phrase 'contrary to the facts' here in the sense of a divine reality which transcends the reality of human life.

30. Ignacio Ellacuria, 'The Crucified People', in Ellacuria and Jon Sobrino (eds), *Mysterium Liberationis Fundamental Concepts of*

Liberation Theology, Maryknoll, NY 1993, 580–603 (page references in the text).

31. Jon Sobrino, 'The Witness of the Church in Latin America', in Sergio Torres and John Eagleson (eds), *The Challenge of Basic Christian Communities. Papers from the International Ecumenical Congress of Theology, February 20 – March 2, 1980, Sao Paulo, Brazil*, Maryknoll, NY 1981, 161–88: 176: 'Here we can talk about a "material" martyrdom, since in many cases the victims die without consciously realizing why they are dying or to what they are bearing witness by their death.'

32. Luther, Heidelberg Disputation, supporting argument for Thesis XXI (WA 1, 362).

33. Cf. Luther, Heidelberg Disputation, Thesis XXI.

§5. Models of African Christology

1. In distinguishing this from the South African variant of liberation theology, 'Black Theology' (see §10 below), I am using the self-chosen epithet 'African' theology as a two-part technical term.

2. John S. Mbiti, 'Afrikanische Beiträge zur Christologie', in *Theologische Stimmen aus Asien, Afrika und Lateinamerika* III, ed. Georg F. Vicedom, Munich 1968, 72–85 (page references in the text).

3. Charles Nyamiti, 'African Christologies Today', in Robert J. Schreiter (ed.), *Faces of Jesus in Africa*, London 1992, 3–23 (first published in J. N. K. Mugambi and Laurenti Magesa [eds], *Jesus in African Christianity. Experimentation and Diversity in African Christology*, Nairobi 1989, 17–39).

4. Nyamiti, 'African Christologies' (n.3), 3.

5. Harold W. Turner, *Profile through Preaching*, London 1965; cf. Kofi Appiah-Kubi, 'Christology', in John Parratt (ed.), *A Reader in African Christian Theology*, London 1987, 69–79 (Geneva 1976).

6. The African independent churches arose out of an encounter with or a split from the missionary churches. They were founded by African prophets. Cf. Hans-Jürgen Becken, *Wo der Glaube noch jung ist. Afrikanische Unabhängige Kirchen im Südlichen Afrika*, Erlangen 1985, 11: 'The African independent churches want to give an African answer to the Christian message and themselves shape their church life in accordance with African forms and patterns of thought under African leadership.'

7. Cf. Werner A. Wienecke, *Die Bedeutung der Zeit in Afrika in den traditionellen Religionen und in der missionarischen Verkündigung*, SIGC 81, Frankfurt am Main, etc. 1992; Bénézet Bujo, 'Der Afrikanische Ahnenkult und die christliche Verkündigung', ZMR 64, 1980, 293–306: 296: id., *African Theology in Its Social Context*, Maryknoll, NY 1992, 27–32.

8. Cf. John Mbiti, 'as an African experience', in Barnabas Lindars and Stephen S. Smalley (eds), *Christ and Spirit in the New Testament*, ὁ σωτὴρ ἡμῶν Cambridge 1973, 397–414; id., 'Some Reflections on African Experience of Salvation Today', in Stanley J. Samartha (ed.), *Living Faiths and Ultimate Goals. A Continuing Dialogue*, Geneva 1975, 108–19.

9. Nyamiti's further attempts at sub-division seem to me less plausible. The distinction between those inculturation theologies which look 'From the Bible to African Reality' and those who take the opposite approach 'From African Reality to Christology', is highly arbitrary. Here we should rather reckon with a dialectical process. Nyamiti's prognosis that alongside South African Black Theology, an African liberation theology will become established which 'because of its broader perspective . . . has a more promising future' (13, cf. Bénézet Bujo, *African Theology* [n.7], 15), has not been fulfilled. For example, the African feminist theology which he brings under this heading draws on both currents of tradition and goes its own ways (cf. Doris Strahm, *Vom Rand in die Mitte. Christologie aus der Sicht von Frauen in Asien, Afrika und Lateinamerika*, Theologie in Geschichte und Gesellschaft 4, Lucerne 1997, 151–269).

10. I base my account of the models of African christology on the documentation of a symposium with contributions from Francophone Africa which took place in Paris at the beginning of the 1980s. The Frenchmen Joseph Doré and René Luneau had initially consulted some African doctoral students in Paris, and among them, with François Kabasélé from Zaire, was already one of those who were later to be the main speakers at the conference. This group brought together a series of themes and deliberately involved a number of hitherto unknown African theologians as speakers. The volume, which appeared in the series 'Jesus und Jesus Christus', was circulated widely. Cf. *Chemins de la Christologie Africaine*, ed. François Kabasélé, Joseph Dore and René Luneau, Paris 1986; in Germany the volume was brought out, with three contributions omitted, by the missiological institute Missio in Aachen, *Der schwarze Christus. Wege afrikanischer Christologie*, TDW 12, Freiburg im Breisgau, etc. 1989; for English speakers, in *Faces of Jesus in Africa*, Maryknoll, NY 1981, Robert Schreiter presented an anthology which alongside the central texts of the French volume also takes up a collection that appeared in Africa (Mugambi and Magesa, *Jesus in African Christianity* [n.3]). In addition, I also introduce the authors reported on by Nyamiti.

11. François Kabasélé, 'Christ as Chief', in *Faces of Jesus* (n.3), 103–15 (page references in the text).

12. The Luba from southern Zaire are counted among the Bantu peoples (see n.14 below).

13. See above, §1, 23.

14. Bantu (English 'human beings') is a collective designation for a large group of peoples and tribes in central and southern Africa with related

languages. The around 100 million people do not form an ethnic or cultural unity.

15. The Anglican theologian from Ghana, John S. Pobee, *Toward an African Theology*, Nashville 1979, 94, gives Jesus the title Nana, in the language of his Akan tribe the designation for the ancestors and the supreme being. The supreme being is at the same time thought of as the senior chieftain, to whom all chieftains are subordinate as his representatives. 'In our Akan Christology we propose to think of Jesus as the *okyeame*, or linguist, who in all public matters was as the Chief, God, and is the first officer of the state, in this case, the world' (95).

16. The Xhosa Ntsikana from South Africa (died 1821) already praises God as a chieftain in his great hymn. He addresses God directly. In the brief christological verses, which manage not to mention the name of Jesus Christ, Ntsikana takes over the traditional sacrificial theology. Cf. Theo Sundermeier, 'Erstgestalten afrikanischer Theologie', in id., *Konvivenz und Differenz. Studien zu einer verstehenden Missionswissenschaft*, MF.NF 3, Erlangen 1995, 126–51: 126–34.

17. Cf. Anselme Titianma Sanon, 'Jesus, Master of Initation', in *Faces of Jesus*, 85–102; id., *Das Evangelium verwurzeln. Glaubenserschliessung im Raum afrikanischer Stammesinitiationen*, TDW 7, Freiburg im Breisgau 1985, esp. 106–48.

18. Cf. Sanon, *Evangelium* (n.17), 85.

19. Ibid., 125.

20. Cf. ibid., 108f.

21. Cf. Engelbert Mveng, 'Christus der Initiationsmeister', in Theo Sundermeier (ed.), *Zwischen Kultur und Politik. Texte zur afrikanischen und zur Schwarzen Theologie*, Zur Sache 15, Hamburg 1978, 78–81: 79: 'If the African encounters Jesus Christ, he sees in him the Son of God, the Lord over life and death, the one who through his life, his teaching, his miracles, his suffering, his death and his resurrection is the supreme master of initiation for people. For Africans he is the one who knows the ultimate truth of the meaning of life and death, the one who brings the final victory of life over death.'

22. Sanon, *Evangelium* (n.17), 117.

23. Ibid., 111f.

24. Sanon, 'Jesus' (n.17), 94.

25. See below 63; Harry Sawyerr, *Creative Evangelism. Towards a New Christian Encounter with Africa*, London 1968, 72f., has proposed addressing Christ as the elder brother.

26. Cf. Sanon, *Evangelium* (n.17), 125: 'To be initiated then means to enter into Christ's own initiation and to take part in his trials.'

27. Cf. Bujo, *African Theology* (n.7), 92.

28. Cf. Mercy Amba Oduyoye, *Hearing and Knowing. Theological Reflections on Christianity in Africa*, Maryknoll, NY 1986, 54.

29. Sanon, *Evangelium* (n.17), 118.

30. Sanon, 'Jesus' (n.17), 90.

31. Cf. François Kabasélé, 'Christ as Ancestor and Elder Brother', in *Faces of Jesus* (n.3), 116–27 (page references in the text).

32. Cf. Pobee, *Toward an African Theology* (n.15), 94.

33. See above, 62.

34. Cf. Fritz Kollbrunner, 'Auf dem Weg zu einer christlichen Ahnenverehrung? Die Diskussion um den Heimholungsritus der Shona', *NZM* 31, 1975, 19–29, 110–23; Jean-Marc Ela, 'Die Ahnen und der christliche Glaube. Eine Afrikanische Frage', *Concilium* 13, 1977, 84–94 (at this time *Concilium* was not appearing in English).

35. See above, 62.

36. Charles Nyamiti, *Christ as our Ancestor. Christology from an African Perspective*, Gweru 1984, 96–151, differs.

37. Cécé Kolié, 'Jesus as Healer?', in *Faces of Jesus* (n.3), 128–50 (page references in the text). Cf. Aylward Shorter, *Jesus and the Witchdoctor. An Approach to Healing and Wholeness*, Maryknoll, NY 1985.

38. Kolié explains the success of the independent churches in terms of this 'cult of life' (132). Cf. Appiah-Kubi, 'Christology' (n.5), 78.

39. John S. Mbiti, *African Religions and Philosophy*, Oxford, second enlarged edition 1990 (1969), 81–9.

40. See above, n.38.

41. Cf. Ferdinand Hahn, *The Titles of God in Christology*, London and New York 1969.

42. Cf. François Kabasélé, 'Jenseits der Modelle', in *Der schwarze Christus* (n.10), 138–61; Bénézet Bujo, 'Auf der Suche nach einer afrikanischen Christologie', in Hermann Dembowski and Wolfgang Greive (eds), *Der andere Christus. Christologie in Zeugnissen aus aller Welt*, Erlangen 1991, 87–99.

43. Cf. Sawyerr, *Creative Evangelism* (n.25), 72f.; Pobee, *Toward an African Theology* (n.15), 97; Kabasélé, 'Jenseits' (n.42), 141–7; Bujo, 'Auf der Suche' (n.42), 88f.

44. Pobee, *Toward an African Theology* (n.15), 97.

45. Kabasélé, 'Christ as Chief' (n.11), 111f.

46. Cf. Kabasélé, 'Jenseits' (n.42), 158f.; Bujo, 'Auf der Suche' (n.42), 89f.

47. Cf. Kabasélé, 'Jenseits' (n.42), 153f.; Bujo, 'Auf der Suche' (n.42), 93.

48. Cf. the christology of black theology, which similarly emphasizes the presence of Jesus Christ in suffering. It also has in common with African christology a centredness on life and community (see §10).

49. Baëta quoted in Bengt Sundkler, *The Christian Ministry in Africa*, SMU 11, Uppsala 1960, 289; cf. Theo Sundermeier, 'Auf dem Weg zu einer afrikanischen Kirche'; Christian G. Baëta, 'Ghana', in Hans Waldenfels

(ed.), *Theologen der Dritten Welt. Elf biographische Skizzen aus Afrika, Asien und Lateinamerika*, Munich 1982, 71–81: 76; id., *The Individual and Community in African Traditional Religions*, Beiträge zur Missionswissenschaft und Interkulturellen Theologie 6, Hamburg 1998, 121.

50. Bujo, 'Auf der Suche' (n.42), 92.

51. Cf. Sundermeier, *Individual and Community* (n.48), 120–36.

§6. *Christology in the Context of African Ancestor Worship: Charles Nyamiti (Tanzania) and Bénézet Bujo (Zaire)*

1. Cf. Charles Nyamiti, *African Theology: Its Nature, Problems and Methods*, Kampala 1971; id., *The Scope of African Theology*, Kampala 1973.

2. Nyamiti, *African Theology*, (n.1) 33, cited in Heribert Rücker, 'Afrikanische Theologie': Charles Nyamiti, Tansania', in Hans Waldenfels (ed.), *Theologen der Dritten Welt. Elf biographische Skizzen aus Afrika, Asien und Lateinamerika*, Munich 1982, 54–70: 56.

3. Charles Nyamiti, *Christ as our Ancestor. Christology from an African Perspective*, Gweru 1984 (page references in the text); cf. Rücker, 'Afrikanische Theologie: Charles Nyamiti' (n.2); id., *'Afrikanische Theologie'. Darstellung und Dialog*, ITS 14, Innsbruck and Vienna 1985, 80f.; Ulrike Linke-Wieczorek, *Reden von Gott in Afrika und Asien. Darstellung und Interpretation afrikanischer Theologie im Vergleich mit der koreanischen Minjung-Theologie*, FSÖTh 60, Göttingen 1991, 156–84.

4. Cf. Kabasélé (see above, §5, 63).

5. The survey follows Nyamiti's diagrammatic comparison, using key words, between the African brother-ancestor and Christ's relationship to human beings (Nyamiti, *Christ* [n.3], 19–24).

6. Charles Nyamiti, 'Approaches to African Theology', in Sergio Torres and Virginia Fabella (eds), *The Emergent Gospel. Theology from the Developing World. Papers from the Ecumenical Dialogue of Third World Theologians, Dar es Salaam, August 5–12, 1976*, London and NY 1978, 31–45: 41.

7. Theo Sundermeier, 'Fremde Theologien', *EvTh* 50, 1990, 524–34: 529–33, comes to another conclusion.

8. Bénézet Bujo, 'Der afrikanische Ahnenkult' (page references in the text); id., *African Theology in Its Social Context*, Maryknoll, NY 1992, 75–92; id., 'Auf der Suche nach einer afrikanischen Christologie', in *Der andere Christus. Christologie in Zeugnissen aus aller Welt*, ed. Hermann Dembowski and Wolfgang Greive, Erlangen 1991.

9. Cf. Nyamiti, 'Approaches' (n.6), 37.

10. Bujo refers to Dietmar Mieth (cf. Günther Stachel and Dietmar Mieth, *Ethisch handeln lernen. Zu Konzeption und Inhalt ethischer Erziehung*, Zurich 1978, 106–16): 'Where there is an invitation to imitation

and following we speak of examples; where there is a stimulus to our own initiative we speak of models' (110).

11. Cf. Johann Baptist Metz, *Faith in History and Society. Toward a Practical Fundamental Theology*, London 1980.

12. Bujo, *African Theology* (n.8), 87.

13. Ibid., 80.

14. Cf. Wilhelm Maas, '"Abgestiegen zur Hölle": Aspekte eines vergessenen Glaubensartikels', *IKaZ* 10, 1981, 1–18; Herbert Vorgrimler, 'Christ's Descent to Hell. Is it Important?', *Concilium* 1.2, 1966, 75–81; Metz, *Faith* (n.11), 129.

15. Sundkler, *Christian Ministry* (n.8), 290–4: 290.

16. Bujo, 'Der afrikanische Ahnenkult' (n.8), 302.

17. In this connection Nyamiti emphasizes that Jesus' descent from Adam makes him 'the natural Brother-Ancestor only of those who lived on earth after His death' (Nyamiti, 'Christ', 28). It is his God-manhood which first transcends this status: 'Christ is the Brother-Ancestor of all men not on account of His Adamite origin but merely because of His divine-human structure' (ibid.).

18. Cf. Bujo, *African Theology* (n.8), 77.

19. Cf. Bujo, 'Auf der Suche' (n.8), 97f.

20. Cf. e.g. Nyamiti, 'Approaches' (n.6), 42–4. On the other hand there is a critical reaction to an *ethnographic* approach from the South African side in Manas Buthelezi, 'Toward Indigenous Theology in South Africa', in Torres and Fabella, *The Emergent Gospel* (n.6), 56–75: 59. Buthelezi himself favours an *anthropological* approach (ibid., 65). The concept of *anthropological poverty* put forward by Engelbert Mveng, 'Third World Theology – What Theology? What Third World? Evaluations by an African Delegate', in Virginia Fabella and Sergio Torres (eds), *Irruption of the Third World. Challenge to Theology. Papers from the Fifth International Conference of the Ecumenical Association of Third World Theologians, August 17–29, 1981, New Delhi, India*, Maryknoll, NY 1983, 217–21: 220, offers a certain balance between the two schools.

21. Bujo, *African Theology* (n.8), 16.

22. John S. Mbiti, 'Afrikanische Beiträge zur Christologie', in *Theologische Stimmen aus Asien, Afrika und Lateinamerika* III, ed. Georg F. Vicedom, Munich 1968, 78. Cf. Kwesi A. Dickson, *Theology in Africa*, Maryknoll, NY 1984, 185–99; Theo Sundermeier, *Das Kreuz als Befreiung. Kreuzesinterpretationen in Asien und Afrika*, Munich 1985, 45–72; Yacob Tesfai, 'Afrikanische Reflexionen zum Kreuz', *ZMiss* 18, 1992, 6–15.

§7. Christology in the Context of Hinduism: M. M. Thomas and Stanley Samartha (India)

1. Cf. M. M. Thomas, 'My Pilgrimage in Mission', *IBMR* 13, 1989, 28–31; id., *My Ecumenical Journey*, Trivandrum 1990; Hielke T. Wolters, *Theology of Prophetic Participation. M. M. Thomas' Concept of Salvation and the Collective Struggle for Fuller Humanity in India*, Delhi 1996 (with bibliography).

2. The Thomas Christians derive their origins from the missionary activity of the apostle Thomas in India. However, the first communities can be demonstrated only for the third century. Because of a history full of vicicissitudes, today, as well as the originally Orthodox church, which has meanwhile similarly split, there are various groupings within the Roman Catholic Church. The Syrian Mar Thoma Church in Malabar is a church which is oriented more towards the Reformation, which in the middle of the nineteenth century split under the influence of the Anglican Church Missionary Society.

3. Cf. Joachim Wietzke, *Theologie im modernen Indien – Paul David Devanandan*, SIGC 4, Frankfurt am Main and Bern 1975.

4. Cf. *Religion and Society*, Bangalore, 1958ff.

5. Cf. M. M. Thomas, *The Acknowledged Christ of the Indian Renaissance*, London 1969. With this title Thomas dissociates himself from Raimundo Panikkar, *The Unknown Christ of Hinduism*, London 1964, revised edition 1981. For Panikkar, Christ is a cipher for the mystical primal ground, the unity of reality which is also hidden in Hinduism and which he clearly dissociates from the person of Jesus. By contrast, Thomas wants simply to describe the reception of Jesus Christ in the Hindu Renaissance. Cf. Robin Boyd, *An Introduction to Indian Christian Theology*, New Delhi 1969, reprint of the revised edition of 1975, 312.

6. The German edition of Stanley J. Samartha, *Hindus vor dem universalen Christus. Beiträge zu eine Christologie in Indien*, Stuttgart 1970, appeared four years before the English (id., *The Hindu Response to the Unbound Christ*, Madras 1974). The book is based on a series of lectures which Samartha already gave in 1963 at UTC in Bangalore. Thomas, too, could refer back to lectures from his time as visiting professor at Union Theological Seminary, New York (1966/67). Like Thomas, Samartha offers variations on the theme once proposed by Panikkar, but not without then critically dissociating himself from it (cf. Samartha, *The Hindu Response*, 139–42). Whereas Thomas gave a broad selection and with Keshab Chandra Sen and P. C. Mozoomdar presents two further representatives of the Brahmo Samaj ('Society of God') founded by Rammohan Roy (1772–1833), Samartha concentrates wholly on the representatives of Neo Advaita, who link up with Shankara's Advaita philosophy; here their accounts largely run parallel. The following table sets side by side by way of

comparison the exponents of the Hindu Renaissance discussed by Thomas and Samartha.

Table 5: Account of the Hindu Renaissance in M. M. Thomas and
S. J. Samartha

M. M. Thomas	S. J. Samartha
Raja Rammohan Roy	Raja Rammohan Roy
Keshab Chandra Sen	
P. C. Mozoomdar	
Ramakrishna	Ramakrishna
Vivekananda	Vivekananda
	Akhilananda
Radhakrishnan	Gandhi
Gandhi	Radhakrishnan

7. Cf. Stanley J. Samartha, *Between Two Cultures. Ecumenical Ministry in a Pluralist World*, Geneva 1996; Jan A. B. Jongeneel, 'Kraemer und Samartha, zwei "feindliche Brüder"', *ZMiss* 14, 1988, 197–205; Eeuwout Klootwijk, *Commitment and Openness. The Interreligious Dialogue and Theology of Religions in the Work of Stanley J. Samartha*, Zoetermeer 1992 (with bibliography).

8. Samartha, *Between Two Cultures* (n.7), 9.

9. Stanley J. Samartha, *The Hindu View of History according to Dr S. Radhakrishnan*, typescript, New York 1950.

10. Stanley J. Samartha, *The Modern Hindu View of History. According to Representative Thinkers*, typescript dissertation, Hartford 1958.

11. The study on *The Word of God and the Living Faiths of Men*, resolved on by the Central Committee in 1955, was to work out the problems which had been accumulating since Tambaram (1938). Cf. Carl F. Hallencreutz, 'Dialogue in Ecumenical History: 1910–1971', in *Living Faiths and the Ecumenical Movement* ed. Stanley J. Samartha, Geneva 1971, 57–71.

12. Sub-unit of Dialogue with People of Living Faiths and Ideologies.

13. Cf. Joachim Zehner, *Der notwendige Dialog. Die Weltreligionen in katholischer und evangelischer Sicht*, Studien zum Verstehen fremder Religionen 3, Gütersloh 1992, 65–106.

14. Cf. Stanley J. Samartha, '. . . and Ideologies', *ER* 24, 1972, 479–86.

15. Thomas: Serampore (1970), Leiden (1975); Samartha: Serampore (1986) and Utrecht (1986).

16. Cf. M. M. Thomas, *Men and the Universe of Faiths*, Madras 1975.

17. Cf. M. M. Thomas, *The Secular Ideologies of India and the Secular Meaning of Christ*, Madras 1976.

18. Cf. M. M. Thomas, *Risking Christ for Christ's Sake. Towards an Ecumenical Theology of Pluralism*, Geneva 1987.

19. Cf. the collection of meditations and prayers composed as early as 1937, in M. M. Thomas, *The Realization of the Cross. Fifty Thoughts and Prayers Centred on the Cross*, Madras 1972.

20. See below, § 10, 142.

21. Thomas, *Universe of Faiths* (n.16), 137; cf. 135: 'The affirmation Jesus is Messiah means that the life, death and resurrection of Jesus is the centre of the historical movement of fulfilment of the divine purpose of the whole world; and that the history of the people acknowledging it and awaiting the promise inherent in it, signifies the power and the presence in the world of the divine goal, namely the transformation of the Kingdoms of this world into the Kingdom of God and His Christ.'

22. M. M. Thomas, 'Die Herausforderung an die Kirchen in den jungen afrikanischen und asiatischen Nationen', in Focko Lüpsen (ed.), *Neu Delhi Dokumente. Berichte und Reden auf der Weltkirchenkonferenz 1961*, Witten 1962, 437–54: 442. Cf. Thomas, *Universe of Faiths*, 138: 'But the historical Cross remains the clue, the criterion of discernment of the stirrings and positive responses of faith to the Universal Cross.'

23. Thomas, *Universe of Faiths* (n.16), 129.

24. See n.22.

25. Thomas, 'Herausforderung an die Kirchen' (n.22), 440.

26. Cf. ibid., 448.

27. Hans Heinrich Wolf, 'Christus am Werk in der Geschichte. Im Licht der "Barmer Theologischen Erklärung" der Bekennenden Kirche von 1934', *ÖR* 15, 1966, 28–47; M. M. Thomas, 'Einige Bemerkungen zu dem Artikel von H. H. Wolf', ibid., 47–53.

28. Thomas, *Risking Christ* (n.18), 112.

29. Thomas, *Universe of Faiths* (n.16), 147.

30. Ibid., 151; cf. id., *Risking Christ* (n.18), 119.

31. Cf. M. M. Thomas, 'The Absoluteness of Jesus Christ and Christ-centred Syncretism', *ER* 37, 1985, 387–97 [revised version, expanded in the third part of 'Chist-Centred Syncretism', *RelSoc* 26, 1979, 26–35] (page references to *ER* in the text).

32. Cf. Thomas, 'Secular Meaning of Christ'; also the discussion on the question of so-called '*secular ecumenism*' between M. M. Thomas and Wolfhart Pannenberg: Wolfhart Pannenberg, 'Die Hoffnung der Christen und die Einheit der Kirche', report on the session of the Faith and Order Commision in Bangalore, India, 15–30 August 1978, in *ÖR* 27, 1978, 473–84; M. M. Thomas, 'Christlicher Ökumenismus und Sakulärökumenismus', *ÖR* 28, 1979, 172–8; Wolfhart Pannenberg, Die "westliche" Christenheit in der Ökumene. Eine Antwort an M. M. Thomas', *ÖR* 28, 1979, 306–16.

33. Cf. Thomas, *Universe of Faiths* (n.16); id., 'Christology and Pluralistic Consciousness', *IBMR* 10, 1986, 106–8.

34. Hendrik Kraemer, *The Christian Message in the Non-Christian World*, Grand Rapids, Michigan 1938.

35. Cf. Volker Küster, *Theologie im Kontext. Zugleich ein Versuch über die Minjung-Theologie*, SIM 62, Nettetal 1995, 25–9.

36. Cf. Volker Küster, 'Dialog VII. Dialog und Mission', *RGG*⁴, vol. 2, 821.

37. Cf. Karl Rahner, 'Christianity and the Non-Christian Religions', in id., *Theological Investigations 5*, New York and London 1966, 115–134; Thomas, *Universe*, 138, refers directly to Rahner.

38. Moreover the two stand on different sides in the controversy over the pluralistic theology of religion. Whereas Samartha gave a paper at the Claremont conference of 1986 the documentation of which was vigorously discussed, Thomas made a contribution to a counter-project published in the same series. Cf. Stanley Samartha, 'The Cross and the Rainbow. Christ in a Multireligious Culture', in John Hick and Paul F. Knitter (eds), *The Myth of Christian Uniqueness. Toward a Pluralistic Theology of Religions*, Maryknoll, NY and London 1987, 69–88; M. M. Thomas, 'A Christ-Centred Humanistic Approach to Other Religions in the Indian Pluralistic Context', in Gavin D'Costa (ed.), *Christian Uniqueness Reconsidered. The Myth of a Pluralistic Theology of Religions*, Maryknoll, NY 1990, 49–62.

39. Klootwijk, *Commitment* (n.7), 267.

40. Stanley J. Samartha, *One Christ – Many Religions. Toward a Revised Christology*, Maryknoll, NY 1991, 82.

41. Ibid., *One Christ*, 77.

42. Samartha, *The Hindu Response* (n.6, page references in text).

43. Cf. Samartha, *One Christ* (n.40), 107f.

44. Holy scriptures of Hinduism, added to the four Vedas as Vedanta ('End of the Vedas').

45. Samartha, *One Christ* (n.40, page references in the text).

46. Samartha, *The Hindu Response* (n.6), 188f. 190f, differs.

47. Cf. ibid., 191–200.

48. Cf. ibid., 198.

49. Ibid., 162–164.

50. Incarnation of a deity.

§8. Christology in the Context of Buddhism: Katsumi Takizawa and Seiichi Yagi (Japan)

1. A Buddhist sect founded by Nichiren (1222–82).

2. Uchimura, a lay preacher and founder of the No-Church Movement (Mukyokai), rejected the denominationalism of Western missionaries and fixed church structures. Cf. Hannelore Kimura-Andres, *Mukyokai. Fortsetzung der Evangeliumsgeschichte*, EMMÖ 1, Erlangen 1984.

3. Katsumi Takizawa, 'Zen-Buddhismus und Christentum im gegenwärtigen Japan', in Seiichi Yagi and Ulrich Luz (eds), *Gott in Japan, Anstösse zum Gesprach mit japanischen Philosophen, Theologen,*

Schriftstellern, Munich 1973, 139–59: 141; id., *Was und wie ich bei Karl Barth gelernt habe*, typescript, 21pp., 2.

4. Cf. Takizawa, 'Zen-Buddhismus und Christentum' (n.3), 141f.

5. Cf. Takizawa, 'Zen-Buddhismus und Christentum' (n.3), 142–4; cf. id., *Was und wie ich bei Karl Barth gelernt habe* (n.3), 5.

6. Takizawa, 'Zen-Buddhismus und Christentum' (n.3), 144.

7. From an autobiographical sketch by Yagi, quoted in Ulrich Luz, 'Zwischen Christentum und Buddhismus: Seiichi Yagi, Japan', in Hans Waldenfels (ed.), *Theologen der Dritten Welt. Elf biographische Skizzen aus Afrika, Asien und Lateinamerika*, Munich 1982, 161–78: 162f.

8. Takizawa, *Was ich bei Karl Barth gelernt habe* (n.3), 6f.

9. Cf. Markus Himmelmann, 'Im Dialog mit Japan, Wilhelm Gundert und Werner Kohler', *ZMiss* 22, 1996, 169–88.

10. *Bi-Yän-Lu. Meister Yüan-wu's Niederschrift von der Smaragdenen Fels-wand* (composed at the Djia-shan near Li in Hunan between 1111 and 1115, printed in Szechuan around 1300, translated into German with a commentary by Wilhelm Gundert), 3 vols, Munich 1960, 1967, 1973.

11. Cf. the First Example in *Bi-Yän-Lu*, 37–59. In Zen Buddhism, sayings like this are called *koan*. With them the Master responds to questions from the pupil who is seeking the way to awakening. The Rinzai school developed a *koan* system. However, 'awakening' (*satori*) is not causally linked with this system but is more an interruption, a sudden enlightenment of knowledge (cf. Daisetz Suzuki, *Leben aus Zen*, Frankfurt am Main 1982).

12. Yagi quoted in Luz, 'Zwischen Christentum und Buddhismus' (n.7), 164.

13. Cf. Katsumi Takizawa, 'Die Lage der Kirche und der Universität in Japan', in Ferdinand Hahn (ed.), *Probleme japanischer und deutscher Missionstheologie,* Heidelberg 1972, 8f.

14. Luz, 'Zwischen Christentum und Buddhismus' (n.7), 178; cf. John O. Barksdale, 'Seiichi Yagi's Typology of New Testament Thought', *NEAJT* 17, 1978, 36–52: 49.

15. Katsumi Takizawa, *Reflexionen über die universale Grundlage von Buddhismus und Christentum*, SIGC 24, Frankfurt am Main et al. 1980, 53, 135.

16. Ryôsuke Ohashi, 'Einführung', in id. (ed.), *Die Philosophie der Kyoto-Schule. Texte und Einführung*, Freiburg im Breisgau and Munich 1990, 11–45: 14.

17. Nishida, quoted in Fritz Buri, *Der Buddha-Christus als der Herr des wahren Selbst. Die Religionsphilosophie der Kyoto–Schule und das Christentum*, Bern and Stuttgart 1982, 54.

18. Sometimes called the 'self-identity of the absolute contradicting', this variant appears in the German translation of the article by Kitaro Nishida, 'Was liegt dem Selbstsein zugrunde?', in Yagi and Luz, *Gott in Japan* (n.3),

94–112, and in some unpublished manuscripts of Takizawa.

19. Takizawa, *Reflexionen* (n.15), 53, 144, etc. (cf. index).

20. Takizawa, *Reflexionen* (n.15), 10f. Takizawa quoted a poem by the Zen master Daito Kokushi in this connection:

Separated for ever,
but not for a moment parted,
together the whole day,
but at no moment one.
This Logos dwells in every man.

Takizawa, *Reflexionen*, 160; cf. Heyo E. Hamer, Preface, in Takizawa, *Reflexionen*, I-VIII, II.

21. Cf. Katsumi Takizawa, 'Die Überwindung des Modernismus – Kitaro Nishidas Philosophie und die Theologie Karl Barths', in id., *Reflexionen* (n.15), 127–71: 157: 'In reality there is no independent philosophy of Nishida until the discovery of the primal point mentioned several times above.'

22. Cf. Karl Barth, *CD* I/1, 107f. This word does not appear in the index.

23. Cf. Takizawa, 'Überwindung des Modernismus' (n.21), 162f.

24. Cf. Katsumi Takizawa, postscript to Walter Böttcher, *Rückenansicht. Perspektiven japanischen Christentums*, Stuttgart and Berlin 1973, 154–73: 171f.

25. Takizawa, *Reflexionen* (n.15), 122; cf. 161.

26. Takizawa, *Reflexionen* (n.15), 9.

27. Cf. Takizawa, *Reflexionen* (n.15), 86, 124; later he abbreviates the prefix to *the*-anthropology.

28. Takizawa, *Reflexionen* (n.15), 19f.

29. Katsumi Takizawa, '"Rechtfertigung" im Buddhismus und im Christentum', in id., Theo Sundermeier (ed.), *Das Heil im Heute. Texte einer japanischen Theologie*, ThÖ 21, Göttingen 1987, 181–96: 181.

30. Quoted in Takizawa, '"Rechtfertigung"' (n.29), 182.

31. See above, 217 n.11.

32. Katsumi Takizawa, 'Die Kraft des Anderen und die Kraft des Selbst im Buddhismus verglichen mit dem Christentum', in id., *Reflexionen* (n.15), 46–65: 49f.

33. Takizawa, 'Die Kraft des Anderen' (n.32), 54.

34. Cf. Takizawa, '"Rechtfertigung"' (n.29), 181: 'i.e. the seeker who contains in himself the Buddha-Dharma, the enlightening-redeeming truth'.

35. Cf. Takizawa, '"Rechtfertigung"' (n.29), 189 n.1.

36. Katsumi Takizawa, 'Das Grundproblem der Christologie', *Jahrbuch der Literarischen Fakultät der Kyushu Universität*, 4/1956, 1–51: 3.

37. Takizawa, '"Rechtfertigung"' (n.29), 194.

38. Cf. Katsumi Takizawa, 'Theologie und Anthropologie – ein Widerspruch? Entwurf einer reinen The-anthropologie', in Jochanan Hesse

(ed.), '*Mitten im Tod – vom Leben umfangen.*' *Gedenkschrift für Werner Kohler*, SIGC 48, Frankfurt am Main, etc. 1988, 59–68: 65: 'But that does not mean that in Jesus of Nazareth the difference which cannot be confused and the order which cannot be reversed between God and man has been obliterated in the primal fact (primal relationship) Immanuel.'

39. Cf. Karl Barth, *CD* I/1, 131.

40. Cf. Katsumi Takizawa, 'Eine Frage an die Theologie Karl Barths und das Problem des historischen Jesus', in *Philosophisches Jahrbuch der Kyushu Universität* 26, 1967, 1–34: 23; Takizawa, *Reflexionen* (n.15), 122. For this Takizawa refers to Barth.

41. Takizawa, 'Grundproblem der Christologie' (n.36), 29.

42. Cf. Takizawa, 'Nachwort' (n.24), 159.

43. Takizawa, 'Theologie und Anthropologie' (n.38), 61.

44. Cf. his last article, published posthumously, which he wanted to give as a speech of thanks for the bestowal of an honorary doctorate in theology in Heidelberg: id., 'Theologie und Anthropologie' (n.38); also Theo Sundermeier's Laudatio on Takizawa: id., 'Präsentische Theologie. Der Beitrag K. Takizawas im interkulturellen Gespräch', in Takizawa, *Das Heil im Heute*, 11–24.

45. This book was never translated. I have reconstructed the argument reported in what follows from Yagi's remarks in early articles and from the secondary literature. Cf. Seiichi Yagi, 'Was hindert uns, das Neue Testament zu verstehen?', in Ferdinand Hahn (ed.), *Probleme japanischer und deutscher Missionstheologie*, 63–93 (page references in the text); Barksdale, 'Yagi's Typology' (n.14).

46. Seiichi Yagi, 'Geschichte und Gegenwart der neutestamentlichen Forschung in Japan', in Gerhard Rosenkranz (ed.), *Theologische Stimmen aus Asien, Afrika und Lateinamerika* II, Munich 1967, 29–39: 37. Yagi himself on his book 'which is based on his encounter with Buddhism' (ibid.).

47. Barksdale, 'Yagi's Typology' (n.14), 36.

48. Yagi refers to Max Weber's concept of 'types'. However, because of criticism of his acceptance of the term 'types' he then also uses the term 'structure'; cf. id., 'Was hindert uns?' (n.45), 80 n.17.

49. Seiichi Yagi, 'Paul and Shinran; Jesus and Zen: What lies at the Ground of Human Existence?', in P. O. Ingram and F. J. Streng (eds), *Buddhist-Christian Dialogue. Mutual Renewal and Transformation*, Honolulu 1986, 197–215: 199.

50. Cf. Martin Buber, *I and Thou*, Edinburgh 1937.

51. Yagi, 'Paul and Shinran' (n.49), 199.

52. Yagi here is explicitly opposing Cullmann and the salvation-history school.

53. Seiichi Yagi, 'Der Weg zum Heil: Christus und Buddha – Ein Vergleich aus christlicher Sicht', in *Der Buddha-Christus. Zum christlich-*

buddhistischen Dialog (Tagungsprotokoll 18/1992), ed. Evangelische Akademie Iserlohn 1992, 54–72: 63.

54. Cf. Seiichi Yagi, '"I" in the Words of Jesus', in John Hick and Paul F. Knitter, *The Myth of Christian Uniqueness. Toward a Pluralistic Theology of Religions*, Maryknoll, NY and London 1987, 117–34: 124–6; id., 'Das Ich bei Paulus und Jesus – zum neutestamentlichen Denken', *AJBI* 5, 1979, 133–53: 148–51; id., 'Paul and Shinran' (n.49), 208f.

55. Rudolf Bultmann, *Theology of the New Testament* I, New York 1951 and London 1952, 30.

56. Yagi, '"I" in the Words of Jesus' (n.54, page references in the text).

57. The term 'change of subject' (118) also used by Yagi in this connection is open to misunderstanding and would be better avoided.

58. Occasionally Yagi also speaks of the self as the seat of the 'vow of life' (id., 'A Bridge from Buddhist to Christian Thinking: The "Front-Structure"', in Seiichi Yagi and Leonard Swidler, *A Bridge to Buddhist Christian Dialogue*, Mahwah, New York 1990, 75–152: 114–118), an allusion to the vow of the Amida Buddha (see above, 101f.).

59. Yagi, 'Paul and Shinran' (n.49), 208.

60. Illustrations 5–10 are taken from Yagi, '"Front-Structure"' (n.58). Reproduced by kind consent of the author.

61. Cf. Seiichi Yagi, 'Weder persönlich noch generell – Zum neutestamentlichen Denken anhand Röm VII', *AJBI* 2, 1976, 159–73.

62. Cf. Seiichi Yagi, 'Christ and Buddha', in R. S. Sugirtharajah (ed.), *Asian Faces of Jesus*, Maryknoll, NY and London 1993, 25–45 (page references in the text).

63. 'Menschwerdung Gottes im Buddhismus und im Christentum' (ZRP interview with Prof. Seiichi Yagi), *ZRelPäd* 35, 1980, 55–7: 57.

64. Cf. Theo Sundermeier, 'Gott im Buddhismus?', *EvTh* 48, 1988, 29–35: 24.

65. Yagi, 'Was hindert uns?' (n.45), 86.

66. Seiichi Yagi, 'Buddhistischer Atheismus und christlicher Gott', in *Gott in Japan*, 160–91: 181.

67. Cf. Yagi, '"Front-Structure"' (n.58, page references in the text).

68. Takizawa too occasionally uses the term 'field' (cf. index in id., *Reflexionen* [n.15], 190), which goes back to Nishida himself (Takizawa, *Reflexione*n, 148f.), but in him the emphasis is clearly on the punctual contact: 'The field in which the person is put in his place and in his time is the ground of the origin and existence of the I-self, which preceded all works of his own, and time and again is absolutely and unconditionally one with the true subject which is not this self' (ibid., 16).

69. Cf. Barksdale, 'Yagi's Typology' (n.14), 52.

70. Cf. Kenzo Tagawa, 'The Yagi-Takizawa Debate', *NEAJT*, March 1969, 41–59: 49; Barksdale, 'Yagi's Typology' (n.14), 37; Yagi, in *Theologiegeschichte der Dritten Welt: Japan*, Munich 1991, 148f.

71. Yagi, *Theologiegeschichte der Dritten Welt. Japan* (n.70), 148f. The three points of criticism of Takizawa cited here all centre on the question of truth.

72. Tagawa, 'Yagi-Takizawa Debate' (n.70), 57f.: 'Influenced by Takizawa, he [Yagi] now develops a theory about the essential structure of human existence.'

73. Yagi, '"I" in the Words of Jesus' (n.54), 128.

74. Yagi himself on the Takizawa-Yagi debate in *Theologiegeschichte der Dritten Welt. Japan* (n.70), 150.

75. Yagi also speaks of *integration* in this connection, cf. id., '"Front-Structure"' (n.58), 125–38.

76. Cf. Kohler's talk of the 'basic identity' behind the 'secondary identities' (id., *Umkehr und Umdenken. Grundzüge einer Theologie der Mission*, SIGC 56, Frankfurt am Main 1988, 189–220).

77. Werner Kohler, 'Japanische Christologische Versuche', in Heribert Bettscheider (ed.), *Das asiatische Gesicht Christi*, VMStA 25, St Augustin 1976, 49–67: 62.

78. Ulrich Schoen, *Das Ereignis und die Antworten. Auf der Suche nach einer Theologie der Religionen heute*, Göttingen 1984, 142; for the problem cf. now also id., *Bi-Identität. Zweisprachigkeit, Bi-Religiosität, doppelte Staatsbürgerschaft*, Zurich and Düsseldorf 1996.

79. Cf. Takizawa, *Reflexionen* (n.15), 105.

80. Karl Barth, *CD* I, 2, 326.

81. Takizawa, *Reflexionen* (n.15), 28.

82. 'Finally I want to add a word about the so-called "philosophy of religion". What I have presented to you this evening has nothing to do with the "philosophy of religion" which is customarily so called both in the modern West and also among us in Japan. For in this philosophy, at the beginning the person or the human I-self is presupposed, and fundamentally it is not at all clear what this is. Religion is postulated as a special act which in contrast to all other acts relates to the absolutely all-embracing All-being, the First and the Last of human life. But as philosophy it does not want to go into the affair of religion itself. It remains always conscious in the far removed external circle which never touches on the core problem, the question of the truth of religion. In withdrawing from the real difficulty of the problem and choosing to remain in the antechamber, it imagines that it is proceeding in a strictly scientific way. And it unashamedly fills this fatal gap with the concept of "special revelation", indeed with the name of Jesus Christ. In so doing it does not think once of the seriousness with which Hegel himself still dealt with this real, difficult problem. The pseudo-scientific nature and pseudo-piety of this approach must be radically rooted out today, especially as here we have great predecessors like Karl Barth in the West and Kitaro Nishida in the East' (Katsumi Takizawa, *Philosophie und Theologie in meinem Denken*, typescript, 14pp., 14).

83. Yagi, in *Theologiegeschichte des Dritten Welt. Japan* (n.70), 150.

84. Cf. Theo Sundermeier, 'Das Kreuz in japanischer Interpretation', *EvTh* 44, 1984, 417–40.

§9. *Christology in the Overall Asian Context: Kosuke Koyama and Choan-Seng Song*

1. Cf. Merrill Morse, *Kosuke Koyama. A Model for Intercultural Theology*, SIGC 71, Frankfurt am Main, etc. 1991 (with bibliography), 15–19; Deane William Ferm, 'Kosuke Koyama', in id., *Profiles in Liberation. 36 Portraits of Third World Theologians*, Mystic, CN 1988, 87–90; Kosuke Koyama, *Mount Fuji and Mount Sinai, A Critique of Idols*, London and Maryknoll, NY 1985, 15f.

2. See n.1.

3. Cf. Koyama, *Mount Fuji* (n.1), 5; id., 'Vergebung und Politik. Eine japanische Sicht', in Wolfgang Huber (ed.), *Schuld und Versöhnung in politischer Perspektive. Dietrich Bonhoeffer-Vorlesungen in Berlin*, IBF 10, Gütersloh 1996, 42–54: 45.

4. Kosuke Koyama, *Three Mile an Hour God. Biblical Reflections*, London and Maryknoll, NY 1980, 108.

5. Koyama, *Mount Fuji* (n.1), 22.

6. Koyama, *Three Mile* (n.4), 108. Cf. also 'Vergebung und Politik'.

7. The topic raises the question how far his choice was not governed by biography. Morse is silent about it, and in any case devotes only a few pages to Koyama's biography. In the case of a man like Koyama, whose theology is so closely bound up with his personal experiences, this is a decision which is hard for me to comprehend.

8. During the Second World War, under massive repression from the government, there was an alliance of thirty-four Protestant denominations (1941). After the end of the war the Lutherans, Anglicans and some smaller groups left. The Methodists, Congregationalists and part of the Presbyterians form the nucleus of the present-day Kyodan.

9. Kosuke Koyama, *Waterbuffalo Theology*, London and Maryknoll, NY 1974.

10. Koyama, *Waterbuffalo Theology* (n.9), viif. Cf. Paulo Freire's scheme of generative words and themes. See above, §2, 33–5

11. The *South East Asia Journal of Theology* (*SEAJT*, Singapore 1, 1959/60 – 23, 1982) fused with the *North East Asia Journal of Theology* (*NEAJT*, Toyko 1, 1968–28/29, 1982) to become the *East Asia Journal of Theology* (*EAJT* 1, 1983–4, 1986), which later was once again renamed the *Asia Journal of Theology* (*AJTh* 1, 1987ff.).

12. Cf. Justus Freytag, 'Theologie mit einem Dritten Auge: Choang-Seng Song, China', in Hans Waldenfels (ed.), *Theologen der Dritten Welt. Elf biographische Skizzen aus Afrika, Asien und Lateinamerika*, Munich 1982,

141–60; Deane William Ferm, 'Choan-Seng Song', in id., *Profiles in Liberation* (n.1), 107–11; Karl H. Federschmidt, *Theologie aus asiatischen Quellen. Der theologische Weg Choan-Seng Songs vor dem Hintergrund der asiatischen ökumenischen Diskussion*, Beiträge zur Missionswissenschaft und interkulturellen Theologie 7, Münster and Hamburg 1994.

13. Cf. C. S. Song, *The Relation of Divine Revelation and Man's Religion in the Theologies of Karl Barth and Paul Tillich*, typescript dissertation, New York 1965.

14. Cf. C. S. Song, 'Die zeitgenössische chinesische Kultur und ihre Bedeutung für die Aufgabe der Theologie', in Hans-Werner Gensichen (ed.), *Theologische Stimmen aus Asien, Afrika und Lateinamerika* I, Munich 1965, 52–72; id., 'Die Bedeutung der Christologie in der christlichen Begegnung mit den östlichen Religionen', in Georg F. Vicedom (ed.), *Theologische Stimmen aus Asien, Afrika und Lateinamerika III*, Munich 1968, 86–111.

15. Cf. C. S. Song, *Third-Eye Theology*, Revised Edition, Maryknoll, NY 1991, 237–40; id., *Theology from the Womb of Asia*, Maryknoll, NY and London 1986, 101f.; also John Jyigiokk Tin, 'Christianity in Taiwan', in T. K. Thomas (ed.), *Christianity in Asia. North-East Asia*, Singapore 1979, 89–112.

16. Song, *Third-Eye Theology* (n.15), 239.

17. Cf. Odagaki Masaya, in *Theologiegeschichte der Dritten Welt: Japan*, Munich 1991, 207f.

18. Cf. Koyama, *Waterbuffalo Theology* (n.9, page references in the text).

19. Cf. Kazo Kitamori, *Theology of the Pain of God*, Richmond, Virginia and London 1965.

20. Song, *Third-Eye Theology* (n.15), 98.

21. Ibid., 97f.

22. Cf. Song, 'Die zeitgenössische chinesische Kultur' (n.14), 70.

23. Cf. C. S. Song, *Jesus in the Power of the Spirit*, Minneapolis 1994, 159.

24. Song dedicated *Theology from the Womb of Asia* to the directors of TEF, Shoki Coe, Aharon Sapsezian and Samuel Amirtham. Already in the foreword to C. S. Song, *The Compassionate God*, Maryknoll, NY 1982, he thanks Shoki Coe for his commitment to the contextualization of theology (xiii).

25. Song, *Third-Eye Theology* (n.15), 26. With '*köyi*' Song later takes up a further Buddhist term which describes the 'method of extension' of Buddhism in an alien culture (cf. Song, *Compassionate God* [n.24], 178f.). '*Köyi*' is comparable to the anthropological term 'acculturation'.

26. Daisetz Suzuki, quoted in Song, *Third-Eye Theology* (n.15), 26f.

27. Cf. Song, *Third-Eye Theology* (n.15), 26f.

28. C. S. Song, 'Von Israel nach Asien. Ein theologischer Sprung', in *Europäische Theologie herausgefordert durch die Weltökumene*, KEK Studienheft 8, Geneva 1976, 10–29.

29. Cf. Song, 'Introduction', in id., The *Compassionate God* (n.24), 1–17: 5–12.

30. Koyama, *Mount Fuji* (n.1), x.

31. Ibid., 243.

32. Kosuke Koyama, *No Handle on the Cross. An Asian Meditation on the Crucified Mind*, Maryknoll, NY 1977, 86.

33. Koyama, *No Handle* (n.32), 3, etc.

34. Ibid., 10.

35. Cf. the book of the same title, Koyama, *Three Mile an Hour God* (n.4).

36. Kosuke Koyama, *Fifty Meditations*, Maryknoll, NY ²1983, 9.

37. Koyama, *Waterbuffalo Theology* (n.9), 24.

38. Koyama, *Fifty Meditations* (n.36), 124; cf. Song, *Compassionate God* (n.24), 64: 'This long established use of the word "non-Christian" in our Christian vocabulary makes us Christians the centre of all people and all things. It is an expression of Christian centrism.'

39. Koyama, *Waterbuffalo Theology* (n.9), 89–94.

40. Ibid., 91. Cf. Song, *Third-Eye Theology* (n.15), 111: 'The correlation between questions about God and questions about our neighbor cannot be disputed.'

41. Koyama, *Waterbuffalo Theology* (n.9), 91f.

42. Cf. ibid., 129–32.

43. Cf. Koyama, *Mount Fuji* (n.1), 178.

44. Ibid., 187.

45. Koyama, *Three Mile an Hour God* (n.4), 67f.

46. Koyama, *Waterbuffalo Theology* (n.9), 93.

47. Koyama, *Three Mile an Hour God* (n.4), 54.

48. Koyama, *Mount Fuji* (n.1), 8f.

49. Ibid., 8.

50. Kosuke Koyama, '"Extended Hospitality to Strangers" – A Missiology of *Theologia Crucis*', IRM 82, 1993, 283–95: 292.

51. Cf. Koyama, *Mount Fuji* (n.1), 56.

52. Cf. Ernst Troeltsch, *The Absoluteness of Christianity and the History of Religions*, Richmond, Va and London 1972, 91–3.

53. Koyama, *Three Mile an Hour God* (n.4), 48.

54. Cf. Koyama, *Mount Fuji* (n.1), 118–20.

55. Ibid,. 116; cf. 115: 'Ignorance causes greed and greed causes suffering.'

56. Kosuke Koyama, 'The Asian Approach to Christ', *Missiology* 12, 1984, 435–47: 436.

57. Koyama, 'Asian Approach' (n.56), 437.

58. Ibid., 436.
59. Koyama, *Fifty Meditations* (n.36), 72.
60. Koyama, 'Asian Approach' (n.56), 435.
61. Koyama,*Three Mile an Hour God* (n.4), 24f.
62. Song, *Third-Eye Theology* (n.15), 74.
63. Ibid., 56.
64. Cf. ibid., 112.
65. Ibid., 97.
66. Ibid., 74.
67. Choan-Seng Song, 'The Decisiveness of Christ', in *What Asian Christians are thinking. A Theological Source Book*, (ed.), Douglas J. Elwood, Quezon City 1976, 240–264:24.
68. Song, *Jesus in the Power of the Spirit* (n.23, page references in the text).
69. Choan-Seng Song, *Jesus, the Crucified People*, New York 1990, 215f.
70. Song, *Third-Eye Theology* (n.15), 184. Cf. Song, *Crucified People* (n.69), 215f.
71. Song, *Crucified People* (n.69), 19; cf. 114.
72. Ibid., 98.
73. Ibid, 116.
74. Song, *Third-Eye Theology* (n.15), 78; cf. id., *Crucified People* (n.69), 98.
75. Cf. Song, *Jesus and the Reign of God*, Minneapolis 1993, 17 (page references in the text).
76. Song, *Compassionate God* (n.24) 38; cf. 180f.
77. Cf. Song, *Jesus in the Power of the Spirit* (n.23), 243.
78. Cf. ibid., 179.
79. Cf. Song, *Third-Eye Theology* (n.15); id., *Reign of God* (n.75), 243.
80. Cf. Song, Jesus in te Power of the Spirit (n.23), 281.
81. Cf. 'Choan -Seng Song Replies', *OBMR* 1:3, 1977, 13–15, quoted in Federschmidt, *Theologie aus asiatischen Quellen*, 149.
82. Song, *Third-Eye Theology* (n.15), 70.
83. Ibid., 119.

§10. The Black Messiah – Christology in the Context of Racism: James H. Cone (USA) and Allan Boesak (South Africa)

1. Cf. James H. Cone, *Martin & Malcolm & America. A Dream or a Nightmare*, Maryknoll, NY 1991.
2. James H. Cone, *Black Theology and Black Power*, New York 1969.
3. James H. Cone, *A Black Theology of Liberation. Twentieth Anniversary Edition*, Maryknoll, NY 1990.

4. Allan A. Boesak, *Farewell to Innocence. A Socio-Ethical Study on Black Theology and Black Power*, Maryknoll, NY 1977.

5. On the other hand Boesak, *Farewell* (n.4), 79, explicitly opposes a division between American and South African Black Theology.

6. For biography cf. James H. Cone, *God of the Oppressed*, Maryknoll, NY Revised Edition 1997, 1–14; id., *My Soul Looks Back*, Maryknoll, NY ²1991.

7. Cf. Cone, *God of the Oppressed* (n.6), 1–14; id., *My Soul* (n.6), 17–24.

8. Cf. Cone, *My Soul* (n.6), 17–40.

9. Cf. Gayraud S. Wilmore and James H. Cone, *Black Theology. A Documentary History, 1966–1979*, Maryknoll, NY 1979, 23–30.

10. Cone, *My Soul*, (n.6), 38f.

11. Cf. Volker Küster, *Theologie im Kontext. Zugleich ein Versuch über die Minjung-Theologie*, SIM 62, Nettetal 1995, 106–9.

12. Cf. James H. Cone, 'Christianity and Black Power', in *Is Anybody Listening to Black America?*, (ed.) C. Eric Lincoln, NY 1968, 3–9.

13. Cone, *My Soul* (n.6), 44f.

14. Ibid., 45.

15. Cf. similar notions in the Minjung theologian Hyun Young-Hak, 'A Theological Look at the Mask Dance in Korea', in *Minjung Theology. People as the Subjects of History*, ed. Commission on Theological Concerns of the Christian Conference of Asia (CTC-CCA), 47–54: 53: 'As Christians we have to start with the premise that God, as the Lord of History, has worked in and through our history and that God, as revealed in the life, death, and resurrection of Jesus Christ, has a special concern for the underdogs, namely, the minjung. Otherwise, the Christian God would have no place in our history, in the events of our time, or for that matter in the future.'

16. See above, §3.

17. Cone, *God of the Oppressed* (n.6), 12.

18. Cone, *Black Theology of Liberation* (n.3), xi.

19. Cf. ibid., 23–35.

20. Cone, *God of the Oppressed* (n.6), 103f.

21. Cf. Cone, *Black Theology* (n.2), 34. id., *Black Theology of Liberation* (n.3), 110; id., *God of the Oppressed* (n.6), 9, 101; id., *My Soul* (n.6), 97; id., *For My People. Black Theology and the Black Church*, Maryknoll, NY 1984, 34.

22. Cone, *Black Theology of Liberation* (n.3), 38, cf. 5, 114; id., *Black Theology* (n.2), 117; id., *God of the Oppressed* (n.6), 71,122,125f.

23. Cf. Gustavo Gutiérrez, *Theology of Liberation*, Maryknoll, NY and London 1988 (= G); for Cone I refer mainly to his first book, *Black Theology and Black Power* (n.2, = C). Page references with letters in the text.

24. Cf. Cone, *God of the Oppressed* (n.6), 120.

25. Cf. Cone, *Black Theology of Liberation* (n.2), 2–4.

26. Cf. ibid., 51.

27. Raymund Fung, 'Good News to the Poor – A Case for a Missionary Movement', in *Your Kingdom Come. Mission Perspectives. Report on the World Conference on Mission and Evangelism, Melbourne, Australia 12–25 May 1980*, Geneva 1980, 83–92.

28. Cf. Allan Boesak, *The Finger of God. Sermons on Faith and Responsibility*, Maryknoll, NY 1982; id., *Gerechtigkeit erhöht ein Volk. Texte aus dem Widerstand*, Neukirchen-Vluyn 1995 (English cf. id., *Walking on Thorns. The Call to Christian Obedience*, Geneva 1984); id., *Black and Reformed. Apartheid, Liberation and the Calvinist Tradition*, Maryknoll, NY 1984. In what follows I discuss his dissertation *Farewell to Innocence* (n.4, page references in the text).

29. Cf. Erhard Kamphausen, 'Schwarze Theologie: Allan Aubrey Boesak, Südafrika', in Hans Waldenfels (ed.), *Theologen der Dritten Welt. Elf biographische Skizzen aus Afrika, Asien und Lateinamerika*, Munich 1982, 96–114; Deane William Ferm, 'Allan Boesak', in id., *Profiles in Liberation. 36 Portraits of Third World Theologians*, Mystic, CN 1988, 14–18.

30. Boesak, quoted in Kamphausen, 'Schwarze Theologie' (n.29), 100.

31. Cf. Boesak's original preface to his Kampen dissertation translated in the German edition id., *Unschuld die schuldig macht. Eine sozialethische Studie über Schwarze Theologie und Schwarze Macht*, Hamburg 1977, XI-XIII.

32. Basil Moore, 'What is Black Theology?', in *The Challenge of Black Theology in South Africa*, (ed.) Basil Moore, Atlanta 1974, 1–10: 1.

33. Moore, 'What is Black Theology?' (n.32), 1.

34. Cf. Boesak, *Farewell* (n.4), 13–16.

35. Cf. Boesak's introduction, 'Relevant Preaching in a Black Context', to his volume of sermons, Boesak, *The Finger of God* (n.28), 1–17. This is a text which throughout is strongly reminiscent of Ernst Lange's theory of preaching. Cf. E. Lange, *Predigen als Beruf. Aufsätze zu Homiletik, Liturgie und Pfarramt*, Munich ²1987 (1982).

36. Page references with letters in the text: Boesak, *Farewell* (n.4 = B) and Cone, *Black Theology* (n.2 =C).

37. Cf. the SASO manifesto in Theo Sundermeier (ed.), *Christus – der Schwarzer Befreier*, Erlangen ³1981, 82–4.

38. In this sensitive question it probably also counts that Bonhoeffer was white.

39. Cf. Cone *God of the Oppressed* (n.6), 199–206.

40. Cf. Cone, *Black Theology of Liberation* (n.3), 31; id., *God of the Oppressed* (n.6), 103–5.

41. Cf. Cone, *My Soul* (n.6), 123–38, esp. 131.

42. Cf. Cone, *God of the Oppressed* (n.6), 122–5.

43. Cf. Theo Sundermeier, 'Schwarzes Bewusstsein – Schwarze Theologie', in id., *Christus, der schwarze Befreier* (n.37), 9–36.

44. Cf. Cone, *God of the Oppressed* (n.6), 207–25.

45. Ibid., 126.

46. Cf. ibid., 71: 'This is what the Incarnation means. God in Christ comes to the weak and the helpless, and becomes one with them, taking their condition of oppression as his own and thus transforming their slave-existence as slaves into a liberated existence.'

47. The concept of 'anthropological poverty' coined by Engelbert Mveng (see above 212), is an attempt at mediation.

§11. Encountering Jesus Christ in the Minjung – Christology in the Context of a Development Dictatorship

1. Cf. Volker Küster, *Theologie im Kontext. Zugleich ein Versuch über die Minjung-Theologie*, SIM 62, Nettetal 1995, 116–32; there is also a detailed account of Minjung theology generally. I had the interviews with Ahn which are quoted here during a study visit to South Korea in 1987/88.

2. After its victory in the Russo-Japanese war (1904–5), Japan had first made the Korean peninsula its protectorate and then annexed it in 1910. This occupation only ended with the Japanese defeat in the Second World War.

3. Manchuria was first occupied by the Japanese in 1931.

4. Interview of 20 July 1988.

5. Interview of 14 May 1988.

6. Cf. especially Ahn Byung-Mu, 'Das leidende Minjung. Koreanische Herausforderung an die europäische Theologie', *EK* 20, 1987, 12–16.

7. Interview of 14 May 1988.

8. See above, §10, 141.

9. Quoted from Hyun, Young-Hak, 'Minjung: The Suffering Servant and Hope', *Inter-Religio* 7, 1985, 2–14:4.

10. Cf. 'Widerstand in Korea: Erklärung zur demokratischen Rettung der Nation', *epd-Dokumentation* 43/77, 11–15. This manifesto centres on the great themes of political resistance: democratization, social justice and reunification. The marked anti-Communism which is expressed in it is significant.

11. In Kwangju, the capital of Cholla province, the region of South Korea with the weakest structure, the population had proclaimed a kind of city state governed by commisars. The government sent in troops who acted against their own population with the utmost brutality. This trauma has overshadowed Korean politics to most recent times.

12. Cf. *Minjung Theology. People as the Subjects of History*, Maryknoll, NY, second revised edition 1983 (first published Singapore 1981); the

German volume, Jürgen Moltmann (ed.), *Minjung. Theologie des Volkes Gottes in Südkorea*, Neukirchen-Vluyn 1984, is a combination of the English-language conference volume and a more extensive Korean collection.

13. Cf. Ahn Byung-Mu, 'Jesus and the Minjung in the Gospel of Mark', in *Minjung Theology*, 138–52; id., 'The Transmitters of the Jesus-event', *CTC Bulletin* 5 no.3, Vol. 6, No 1 (December 1984–April 1985), 26–39; id., *Draussen vor dem Tor. Kirche und Minjung in Korea. Theologische Beiträge und Reflexionen*, ThÖ 20, Göttingen 1986; Volker Küster, *Jesus und das Volk im Markusevangelium. Ein Beitrag zum interkulturellen Gespräch in der Exegese*, BTS 28, Neukirchen-Vluyn 1996.

14. Ahn, 'The Transmitters' (n.13), 27.

15. Cf. Ahn, 'Minjung-Bewegung und Minjung-Theologie', *ZMR* 73, 1989, 126–33 (= *ZMiss* 15, 1989, 18–26).

16. Cf. Kim Yong-Bok, 'Theology and the Social Biography of the Minjung', *CTC Bulletin* 5 no.3, Vol. 6, No 1 (December 1984–April 1985), 66–78: 'At present, the only way to understand the social biography of the minjung is to approach it through dialogue and involvement with the minjung and through the minjung's telling of their own story' (70). 'Social biography encompasses the minjung's subjective experiences as well as objective conditions and structures and societal power relations' (71).

17. Cf. e.g. Peter Beyerhaus, 'Theologie als Instrument der Befreiung. Die Rolle der neuen "Volkstheologien" in der ökumenischen Diskussion', *Theologie und Dienst* 49, Giessen 1986; cf. Küster, *Theologie im Kontext*, 53–67.

18. Ahn Byung-Mu, 'Der Befreier Jesus (Lk 4, 18–19)', in id., *Draussen vor dem Tor* (n.13), 60–5: 65.

19. Ahn Byung Mu, 'Was ist die Minjung Theologie? Zur "Theologie des Volkes" in Südkorea', *JK* 43, 1982, 290–6: 295.

20. Suh Nam-Dong, 'Towards a Theology of Han', in *Minjung Theology* (n.12), 55–69; 58.

21. Suh Nam-Dong, 'Han: Darstellungen und theologische Reflexionen', in Moltmann, *Minjung* (n.12), 27–46, 43 (the English and German version differ considerably!).

22. Interview of 20 July 1988.

23. Suh Nam-Dong, 'Historical References for a Theology of Minjung', in *Minjung Theology*, 155–82: 177.

24. Chung Hyun-Kyung, *Struggle to be the Sun Again. Introducing Asian Women's Theology*, Maryknoll, NY and London 1990, 111.

25. Hyun Young-Hak, 'A Theological Look at the Mask Dance in Korea', in *Minjung Theology* (n.12), 47–54: 54.

26. Cf. Volker Küster, 'The Priesthood of Han. Reflections on a woodcut by Hong Song-Dam', *Exchange* 26, 1997, 159–171.

27. Hyun, 'A Theological Look' (n.25), 50.

28. Cf. Hyun, 'Suffering Servant' (n.9), 7.
29. Cf. ibid., 9.

§12. *Jesus with Us – Christology in the Context of New
Departures in Liberation Theology in the 1980s*

1. Cf. *God, Christ & God's People in Asia*, ed. Dhyanchand Carr, Hong Kong 1995.
2. The Rig Veda, a collection of hymns, is the oldest holy scripture of the Hindus among the four Vedas.
3. Rig Veda, X, 90, 11–12, quoted in Arvind P. Nirmal, 'Towards a Christian Dalit Theology', in James Massey (ed.), *Indigenous People: Dalits. Dalit Issues in Today's Theological Debate*, ISPCK Contextual Theological Education Series 5, Delhi 1994, 214–30: 214. *Purusa* means 'primal man'.
4. In the literature Mahatma Jyotirao Phule (1827–1890) is always also mentioned as a forerunner, cf. James Massey, 'Historical Roots', in id., *Indigenous People* (n.3), 3–55; John C. B. Webster, *The Dalit Christians. A History*, ISPCK Contextual Education Series 4, Delhi 1994, 32, 72; M. E. Prabhakar, 'The Search for a Dalit Theology', in Massey, *Indigenous People* (n.3), 201–13: 204.
5. Nirmal, 'Towards a Christian Dalit Theology' (n.3), 214. Without giving any references, Nirmal is reporting the entry in a Sanskrit-English Dictionary; he has merely put the definite article in front of the individual meanings (cf. *The Practical Sanskrit-English Dictionary*, Vol.2, Poona 1958, 804).
6. Cf. Webster, *The Dalit Christians* (n.4), 1–5.
7. Cf. Massey, 'Historical Roots' (n.4), 7–31. For the problem see Hermann Kulke and Dietmar Rothermund, *Geschichte Indiens*, Stuttgart, etc. 1982.
8. Massey, 'Historical Roots' (n.4), 55.
9. Cf. Nirmal Minz, 'Dalit-Tribal: A Search for a Common Ideology', in Massey, *Indigenous People* (n.3), 134–42; id., 'Dalits and Tribals: A Search for Solidarity', in V. Devasahayam (ed.), *Frontiers of Dalit Theology*, Madras 1997, 130–58.
10. See above, §11, 155.
11. Webster, *The Dalit Christians* (n.4), 5.
12. Cf. Klaus Schäfer, introduction to *Gerechtigkeit für die Unberührbaren*, Beiträge zur indischen Dalit-Theologie *Weltmission heute* 15, 5–16: 11.
13. Cf. Nirmal, 'Towards a Christian Dalit Theology' (n.3), 223.
14. Cf. M. Azarijah, 'The Church's Healing Ministry to the Dalits', in Massey, *Indigenous People* (n.3), 316–23: 318.

15. Nirmal, 'Towards a Christian Dalit Theology' (n.3), 215.

16. Quoted ibid., 214.

17. Quoted ibid., 221.

18. *Towards a Dalit Theology*, ed. M. E. Prabhakar, Delhi 1989.

19. Cf. e.g. *A Reader in Dalit Theology*, ed. Arvind P. Nirmal, Madras 1991; Massey, *Indigenous People* (n.3).

20. Cf. the Kairos Document *Challenge to the Church. A Theological Comment on the Political Crisis in South Africa*, PCR Information: Reports and Background Papers, Special Issue, Geneva 1985, which in this connection speaks of a state theology (13–16).

21. Cf. Gustavo Gutiérrez, 'Two Theological Perspectives: Liberation Theology and Progressivist Theology', in Sergio Torres and Virginia Fabella (eds), *The Emergent Gospel, Theology from the Developing World*, Maryknoll, NY 1978, 227–55: 242. What the Kairos Document calls 'Church Theology' (ibid., 17–22) is also to be put here.

22. Cf. Klaus Zöller, 'Arvind P. Nirmal – Porträt eines indischen Befreiungstheologen', in *ems Informationsbrief* 3/1994, 2f.

23. Nirmal was appointed dean of the theological college in Pune.

24. Arvind P. Nirmal, 'A Dialogue with Dalit Literature', in *Towards a Dalit Theology*, 64–82: 65f.

25. Arvind P. Nirmal, 'Dalittheologie. Vom "Nicht-Volk" zum "Gottes-Volk" – ein neues theologisches Paradigma', in *Befreiender Dialog – Befreite Gesellschaft. Politische Theologie und Begegnung der Religionen in Indien und Europa*, Loccumer Protokolle 55/93, Loccum 1994, 41–52: 47.

26. See above. n.3.

27. The farewell lecture of 1981 is not included in the anthology: Arvind P. Nirmal, *Heuristic Explorations*, Madras 1991. In his 1986 contribution to the Madras Conference, Nirmal had put Dalit theology in the context of Dalit literature as an expression of the secular emancipation movement (id., 'A Dialogue'); he includes the theological part, sometimes word for word, in his inaugural lecture (id., 'Towards a Christian Dalit Theology' [n.3]). In a third lecture for a conference at the Evangelical Academy at Loccum (id., 'Vom "Nicht-Volk"' [n.25]), too, he is still working with passages from the two previous texts. In addition there are also two shorter texts, but they contain nothing new (id., 'Developing a Common Ideology: Some Theological Considerations', in id. [ed.], *Towards a Common Dalit Ideology*, Madras nd [1989], 121–6; id., 'Doing Theology from a Daliy Perspective', in id., *A Reader*, 139–44).

28. Quoted in Zöller, 'Nirmal' (n.22), 3.

29. Ibid., 2, wrongly mentions Cambridge.

30. See n.27.

31. Nirmal, *Heuristic Explorations* (n.27), 106.

32. Nirmal, 'Hermeneutics, Some Issues', in ibid., 28–38.

33. Cf. Arvind P. Nirmal, 'Theological Research: Its Implications for the Nature and Scope of the Theological Task in India', in ibid., 18–27: 27 (originally in Gnana Robinson (ed.), *For the Sake of the Gospel*, Mandurai 1978). Nirmal refers to this in id., 'A Dialogue' (n.24), 65; id. 'Towards a Christian Dalit Theology' (n.3), 214f.; id., 'Vom "Nicht-Volk"' (n.25), 44f.

34. Cf. Arvind P. Nirmal, 'Some Theological Issues Connected with Inter-Faith Dialogue and their Implications for Theological Education in India', in id., *Heuristic Explorations*,(n.27), 61–81.

35. Nirmal, 'Towards a Christian Dalit Theology' (n.3, page references in the text).

36. Cf. Nirmal, 'A Dialogue' (n.24), 64f.

37. Cf. J. Severino Croatto, *Biblical Hermeneutics. Towards a Theory of Reading as the Production of Meaning*, Maryknoll, NY 1987, 6f.

38. Cf. the chapter on the rights and freedom of disadvantaged groups in Terazono Yoshiki and Heyo E. Hamer (eds), *Brennpunkte in Kirche und Theologie Japans. Beiträge und Dokumente*, Neukirchen-Vluyn 1988, 44–67.

39. Cf. Teruo Kuribayashi, *A Theology of the Crown of Thorns: Towards the Liberation of the Asian Outcasts*, New York 1987, UMI Dissertation Services 1996. Excerpts from this first appeared in the *Japanese Christian Review* 58, 1992, 19–32, and in the meantime have been reprinted in various collections: R. S. Sugirtharajah (ed.), *Frontiers in Asian Christian Theology. Emerging Trends*, Maryknoll, NY 1994, 11–26; *God, Christ & God's People in Asia* (n.1), 93–114. I quote from the version entitled *Theology of Crowned with Thorns* in *God's People in Asia*.

40. The Shogun dynasty was founded by Tokugawa Ieyasu (1543–1616). The Shogun (Japanese originally general) carried on government business in the name of the emperor. *De facto* he held power in the state.

41. Kuribayashi, *Theology of the Crown of Thorns* (n.39), 93. In *Brennpunkte* (n.38), 44, it is said succinctly: *buraku* = community; *min* = inhabitant'.

42. *God's People in Asia* (n.1), 90.

43. *Brennpunkte* (n.38), 44.

44. Kuribayashi, *Theology of the Crown of Thorns* (n.39), 25. According to *Brennpunkte* (n.38), 44, '*Hinin* (non-person) in the Japanese Middle Ages was used as a further synonym for Burakumin.'

45. *Brennpunkt*, (n.38), 44.

46. *God's People in Asia* (n.1), 90.

47. Cf. ibid., 91.

48. In 1867, the fifteenth Tokugawa Shogun Yoshinobu gave the power of government back to the emperor Mutsuhito. The emperor, who went down in history under the honorific name Meiji ('Enlightened Rule'), developed further the rapprochement to the West which had already begun under Yoshinobu and fundamentally reformed the country. He decreed a

new constitution, which made Japan a constitutional monarchy. At the same time, however, the divine descent of the emperor was also established in this constitution. Shinto became the state religion.

49. Statement of the Inaugural Convention of the Outcast in Japan, in Kuribayashi, *Theology of Crowned with Thorns* (n.39), 98 (my italics); cf. *Brennpunkte* (n.38), 61.

50. Cf. Kuribayashi, *Theology of Crowned with Thorns* (n.39), 94.

51. Quoted ibid., 100.

52. Cf. page references in the text.

53. The summary article, Kuribayashi, *Theology of Crowned with Thorns* (n.39), brings this even more clearly into the foreground.

54. Kuribayashi, *Theology of Crowned with Thorns* (n.39), 93f.

55. Ibid., 94.

56. Ibid., 98–101: 100.

57. Ibid., 106–110.

58. Cf. the appeal to Christians on the problem of the discrimination against the Burakumin (outcasts), in *Brennpunkte* (n.38), 62–4.

59. Cf. James H. Cone, 'A Black American Perspective on the Asian Search for a Full Humanity', in Virginia Fabella (ed.), *Asia's Struggle for Full Humanity: Toward a Relevant Theology. Papers from the Asian Theological Conference, January 7–20, 1979, Wennappuwa, Sri Lanka,* Maryknoll, NY 1980, 178–82: 187f.

§13. *Models of Contextual Christology – Commonalities, Divergences and Opportunities for Ecumenical Learning*

1. A special position is occupied by the US minorities, who are often stylized by their exponents as the Diaspora of the Third World. James Cone has repeatedly written on the problem of their *double identity.* Cf. id., 'A Black American Perspective on the Future of African Theology', in Kofi Appiah-Kubi and Sergio Torres (eds), *African Theology en Route. Papers from the Pan-African Conference of Third World Theologians,* Maryknoll, NY 1979, 176–86: 177.

2. Karl-Heinz Ohlig, *Fundamentalchristologie im Spannungsfeld von Christentum und Kultur,* Munich 1986, 16, puts forward the theory that christology is *a function of soteriology*: 'But the soteriological *question* is what Christian preaching already *finds*; it is not first produced by it, at any rate it can take it up and modify it or correct it and guide it along the "right" lines. People of all times and cultures have this religious question about salvation, and they have it *in their own way.*' Cf. id., 'Gibt es eine Einheit der multikulturellen Christologien? Transkulturelle Christologie als Herausforderung', in Hermann Dembowski and Wolfgang Greive (eds), *Der andere Christus. Christologie in Zeugnissen aus aller Welt,* Erlangen 1991, 186–205.

3. The criterion of identity mentioned by Herman Dembowski, that in Jesus Christ *God, human being and salvation* must be spoken of together, applies here only in an indirect way. Cf. id., *Einführung in die Christologie*, Darmstadt 1976; id., 'Christologie weltweit – Einleitung', in id. and Greive, *Der andere Christus*, 9–24; id., 'Christologie im Kontext Europas', ibid., 30–52; id., 'Unsere Christus? Der einzige Weg?' *JM* 24, 1992, 190–219.

4. Cf. Chung Hyun-Kyung, 'Come, Holy Spirit – Renew the Whole Creation', in Michael Kinnamon (ed.), *Signs of the Spirit. World Council of Churches Official Report Seventh Assembly, Canberra, Australia, 7–20 February 1991*, Geneva and Grand Rapids 1991, 37–47.

5. Cf. the reflections of Orthodox participants addressed to the Seventh General Assembly in *Signs of the Spirit* (n.4), 279–82; Athanasios Basdekis, 'Canberra und die Orthodoxen. Anfragen und Forderungen an den ÖRK im Anschluss an die 7. Vollversammlung', *ÖR* 40, 1991, 356–74.

6. An exception here is the theologian Elsa Tamez, who teaches in Costa Rica. Cf. ead., *The Amnesty of Grace. Justification by Faith from a Latin American Perspective*, Nashville, Tennesee 1993; ead., Recht-fertigung als Bejahung des Lebens', *ZMiss* 16, 1990, 107–10; ead., 'Die Option für die Ausgeschlossenen in einer ausschliessenden Welt, Zu Römer 9–11', *ZMiss* 21, 1995, 24–34, also Dorothea Erbele, 'Der Blick von unten. Die Theologin Elsa Tamez liest die Bibel anders', *EK* 31 (1/1998), 16–18.

Epilogue: Paul and Culture

1. Cf. Günther Bornkamm, *Paul*, London and New York 1971; E. P. Sanders, *Paul*, Oxford 1991; Jürgen Becker, Paul and his Churches, in id., *Christian Beginnings: Word and Community from Jesus to Post-Apostolic Times*, Louisville, Kentucky 1993, 132–210; id., Paul: Apostle to the Gentiles, Louisville, Kentucky 1993; Hans Hübner, 'Paulus', *TRE* 26, Berlin and New York 1996, 133–53.

2. Cf. Claus-Jürgen Thornton, *Der Zeuge des Zeugen. Lukas als Historiker der Paulusreisen*, WUNT 56, Tübingen 1991; Rainer Riesner, *Die Frühzeit des Apostel Paulus. Studien zur Chronologie, Missions-strategie und Theologie*, WUNT 71, Tübingen 1994, both of whom rate Acts highly as a source for the biography of Paul; but see Philipp Vielhauer, *Geschichte der urchristlichen Literatur*, Berlin and New York 1975, 393–9; Gerd Lüdemann, *Paul. Apostle to the Gentiles I. Studies on Chronology*, Minneapolis and London 1984; François Vouga, *Geschichte des frühen Christentums*, Tübingen 1994, 85.

3. Cf. Christoph Burchard, *Der dreizehnte Zeuge. Traditions- und kompositionsgeschichtliche Untersuchungen zu Lukas' Darstellung der Frühzeit des Paulus*, FRLANT 103, Göttingen 1970, 169–85.

4. Cf. Günther Bornkamm, 'Der Römerbrief als Testament des Paulus',

in id., *Geschichte und Glaube* II, BEvTh 53, Munich 1971, 120–39.

5. Robert Jewett, *Dating Paul's Life*, Philadelphia and London 1979; Niels Hyldahl, *Die paulinische Chronologie*, ATD 19, Leiden 1986; Alfred Suhl, 'Paulinische Chronologie im Streit der Methoden', *ANRW* II 26.2, 1995, 940–1188.

6. Cf. Rudolf Bultmann, *Der Stil der paulinischen Predigt und die kynisch-stoische Diatribe*, FRLANT 13, Göttingen 1910; Carl Joachim Classen, 'Paulus und die antike Rhetorik', *ZNW* 82, 1991, 1–33.

7. Cf. Wolf-Hennig Ollrog, *Paulus und seine Mitarbeiter. Untersuchungen zu Theorie und Praxis der paulinischen Mission*, WMANT 50, Neukirchen-Vluyn 1979.

8. Cf. Martin Hengel, *The Pre-Christian Paul*, London 1991.

9. Cf. Wolfgang Stegemann, 'War der Apostel Paulus ein römischer Bürger?', *ZNW* 78, 1987, 200–29; Ekkehard W. Stegemann and Wolfgang Stegemann, *The Jesus Movement: A Social History of its First Century*, Minneapolis, 1999, 297–303; Klaus Wengst, *Pax Romana and the Peace of Jesus Christ*, London 1987, 72–88: 74f. Gerd Lüdemann, *Early Christianity according to the Traditions of the Acts of the Apostles*, London 1989, 240f., differs.

10. Cf. Gerd Theissen, 'Legitimation und Lebensunterhalt. Ein Beitrag zur Soziologie urchristlicher Missionare', in id., *Studien zur Soziologie des Urchristentums*, Tübingen, second enlarged edition 1983, 201–30; Gerhard Dautzenberg, 'Der Verzicht auf das apostolische Unterhaltsrecht. Eine exegetische Untersuchung zu 1 Kor.9', *Bib* 50, 1969, 212–32.

11. Stegemann and Stegemann, *The Jesus Movement* (n.9), 72, 135, 301, base themselves on a clearly two-part pyramidal model of Roman society which distinguishes between elite (upper-class groups) and non-elite (lower-class groups). The lower-class groups are further divided into the relatively prosperous or poor and the absolute poor, who live below a minimal level of existence, there is also a difference between the city and the country. Cf. Gerd Theissen, 'Soziale Schichtung in der korinthischen Gemeinde. Ein Beitrag zur Soziologie des hellenistischen Urchristentums', in id., *Studien zur Soziologie*, 231–71; Wayne A. Meeks, *The First Urban Christians. The Social World of the Apostle Paul*, New Haven and London 1983.

12. Cf. *Jews and Christians in Antioch in the First Four Centuries of the Common Era*, SBL Sources for Biblical Study 13, ed. Wayne A. Meeks and Robert L. Wilken, Ann Arbor, Michigan 1978, 13–24.

13. Cf. also the catalogue of his vicissitudes in I Cor. 4.10–13; II Cor. 6.4–10; 11.23–30, 32f.; also Stegemann, 'War der Apostel?' (n.9), 223f.; Stegemann and Stegemann, *The Jesus Movement* (n.9), 299.

14. Cf. Becker, *Paul and his Churches* (n.1), 163–167.

15. Cf. Christoph Burchard, 'Erfahrungen multikulturellen Zusammenlebens im Neuen Testament', in *Multikulturelles Zusammenleben.*

Theologische Erfahrungen, Beiträge zur Ausländerarbeit 3, ed. Jürgen Micksch, Frankfurt am Main 1983, 24–41.

16. Cf. Gerd Theissen, 'Judentum und Christentum bei Paulus. Sozialgeschichtliche Überlegungen zu einen beginnenden Schisma', in *Paulus und das antike Judentum*, WUNT 58, ed. Martin Hengel and Ulrich Heckel, Tübingen 1991, 331–56.

17. Cf. Christoph Burchard, 'Nicht am Werken des Gesetzes gerecht, sondern aus Glauben an Jesus Christus – seit wann?', in Hubert Cancik et al. (eds), *Geschichte – Tradition – Reflexion, FS Martin Hengel*, Vol.3, Tübingen 1997, 405–15.

18. Dieter Zeller, 'Zur neueren Diskussion über das Gesetz bei Paulus', *ThPh* 62, 1987, 481–9; Hermann Lichtenberger, 'Paulus und das Gesetz', in Hengel and Heckel, *Paulus und das antike Judentum*, 361–78.

19. Cf. Dieter Georgi, *Der Armen zu Gedenken. Die Geschichte der Kollekte des Paulus für Jerusalem*, Neukirchen-Vluyn, second revised and expanded edition 1994; Klaus Berger, 'Almosen für Israel. Zum historischen Kontext der paulinischen Kollekte', *NTS* 23, 1977, 180–204.

20. Cf. Ernst Käsemann, '"The Righteousness of God" in Paul', in *New Testament Questions of Today*, London and Philadelphia 1969, 168–82; Eduard Lohse, 'Die Gerechtigkeit Gottes in der paulinischen Theologie', in id., *Die Einheit des Neuen Testaments, Exegetische Studien zur Theologie des Neuen Testaments*, Göttingen 1973, 209–27.

21. Cf. Peter von der Osten-Sacken, *Die Heiligkeit der Tora. Studien zum Gesetz bei Paulus*, Munich 1989; id., *Evangelium und Tora, Aufsätze zu Paulus*, TB 77, Munich 1987.

22. But cf. the works of Elsa Tamez mentioned (see above 234 n.6).

23. Cf. Eberhard Jüngel, *Paulus und Jesus. Eine Untersuchung zur Präzisierung der Frage nach dem Ursprung der Christologie*, Tübingen [6]1986, 267: 'Rather, Rom. 14.17 gives us the right to assert that Paul replaced the concept of the *basileia* with that of *dikaosyne*.'

24. Christian faith has always also had the function of preserving culture. The much-criticized missionaries of the nineteenth century did basic research into the cultures and religions, their languages and symbol systems and documented them, in order to be able to hand on the gospel. The post-colonial elite was educated at the mission schools. These aspects of the missionary project tend to fade into the background in the face of the necessary and unfortunately all too often justified criticism of the link between mission and colonialism. At a very early stage there were already indigenous collaborators, above all translators, who to some degree served the missionaries as guides (cf. Theo Sundermeier, *Den Fremden verstehen. Eine praktische Hermeneutik*, Göttingen 1996, 33), but at the same time also themselves became messengers of the gospel. Here early forms of indigenous theology developed which still have not sufficiently been investigated.

25. Cf. *Das schöne Evangelium. Christliche Kunst in balinesischen Kontext*, SIM 51, ed. Theo Sundermeier and Volker Küster, Nettetal 1979; Volker Küster, 'Accommodation or Contextualization? Ketut Lasia and Nyoman Darsane – Two Balinese Christian Artists', *Mission Studies* 16, 1999, 157–72.

26. Cf. Wilfried Härle and Eilert Herms, *Rechtfertigung, Das Wirklichkeitsverständnis des christlichen Glaubens. Ein Arbeitsbuch*, Göttingen 1979, 78–99: 99: 'And as such a definition it [the message of the resurrection] is not only a *limitation* of humanity but at the same time an *honour*; in the light of Jesus Christ it shows justified humanity as humanity raised up and exalted by God and to this degree as the irrevocable appointment of human beings to the dignity of being in the image of God.'

Index of Authors